W9-BTN-576

THE CHESAPEAKE BAY OF YORE

Mainly about the ROWING and SAILING CRAFT

by
FREDERICK TILP

Foreword by
LOUIS L. GOLDSTEIN

International Standard Book Number 0-9601786-2-7
Library of Congress Catalog Number 82-80682
Printed in the United States of America

First edition.

Chesapeake Bay Foundation, Inc.
Annapolis and Richmond
Distributors . . .

To
Howard Irving Chapelle

CONTENTS

FOREWORD

A labor of love is sometimes best described by the one who performs it. For Frederick Tilp, *The Chesapeake Bay of Yore* was a labor of love and his description cannot be improved upon.

"I sailed (no engine) into every estuary on the Bay from Port Deposit, Md to Portsmouth, Va; from Snow Hill, Md to Richmond, Va . . . . my new book is enclosed for your perusal. It is the result of 52 years of spare time," he wrote to Dr. Edward C. Papenfuse, Maryland State Archivist.

Mr. Tilp is a native of the Chesapeake Bay region who has spent a lifetime exploring and enjoying the Chesapeake Bay and its tributaries, large and small.

In addition to numerous articles and works which he has authored or coauthored, Mr. Tilp produced *This Was Potomac River,* chronicling the history of that mighty waterway.

The Chesapeake Bay of Yore is a charming collection of lore gathered over a half century, the result of expeditions through various nooks and crannies of the Bay, its tributaries and archives and museums throughout the region.

The maritime heritage of the Chesapeake Bay in Maryland and Virginia is a nearly unique part of Americana that should not be lost, and it is the dedication of Mr. Tilp and those like him that will preserve that heritage for the future.

Perhaps the most valuable contribution of this work is that it provides both a narrative and visual experience for the reader; a reference of immense enjoyment thanks to the pen and ink drawings that accompany the text.

Here, we can actually see what a gunning skiff looked like, the shape of the native doryboat and the immensity of the Susquehanna arks.

Here too, are pictured and described the canoes, the skipjack and the bugeye; names familiar to most residents of the region but sometimes never seen in a lifetime along the Bay.

In special sections, Mr. Tilp relates subjects as much a part of the Chesapeake Bay lore and history as the variety of vessels he describes. The importance of the area's forest land to its maritime heritage, the shipbuilding industry that grew up along its shores and the crafts of the various maritime artisans are detailed. Sections on the oyster, the canning industry, marine police, and folklife and folklore all bring together the flavor of life in the Chesapeake Bay region.

The vignettes presented in *The Chesapeake Bay of Yore* make clear the interrelationship between the water, the other natural resources and the people and industries of the area.

For those whose interest in the subject runs especially deep, Mr. Tilp has added several extras, including a listing of maritime museums and exhibits in the region, additional period information on shipbuilding and shipyard sites in the area and even a treatise on shipbuilding woods.

A glossary, toponomy, bibliography and index make this entire collection valuable to the maritime scholar as well as the casual reader.

For those whose roots go deep into the Chesapeake Bay country and for those who have merely enjoyed cruising the region's pleasant waterways occasionally, *The Chesapeake Bay of Yore* is a treasure not to be missed. Whether your family tree contains generations of watermen or you are just mastering the arts of shucking oysters and picking crabs, Fred Tilp has presented the region you enjoy in a loveable way.

This unique contribution to a unique subject is brimming with educational and entertaining tales of the Bay, its people as well as its maritime heritage.

Diligent searches of materials published about the Chesapeake Bay convinced Fred Tilp that his was previously unbroken ground.

For the author, it was a labor of love. For the reader who loves the Chesapeake Bay it is pure enjoyment.

Louis L. Goldstein
Comptroller of the Treasury
Annapolis, Maryland

PREFACE

This book is written with the hope that it may inspire younger generations to preserve for posterity something of the history and development of traditional Chesapeake Bay rowing and sailing craft. My first awareness of these vessels, 1920, came during my grammar school days, while researching the history of my birthplace, Bladensburg, the first sizeable tobacco seaport in Maryland.

I recall finding in the *Maryland Gazette* of 4 December 1751: "Stolen about a month ago, by two Sailors, out of the North West Branch of *Patapsco* River (the inner harbor of Baltimore), a Flat that will carry about 3 Hogsheads of Tobacco, mark'd in the Stern with a Pair of Marking Irons, B.P, 1750 (the B.P. in a Diamond). Whoever takes up said Flat, and gives Notice to the Printer hereof, shall have Twenty Shillings Reward: and if brought to the Subscriber in the North West Branch of the *Patapsco* River, shall have Thirty Shillings Reward, paid by BRIAN PHILPOT, Junior." Though I knew about "hogsheads," I wondered about a "flat" and other workboats.

In 1924, as a high school student, I first sailed out of Washington on downriver trips to various Potomac ports, and saw strange types of vessels undersail called "schooner, skipjack, pungy, bugeye and ram." I even saw a "scow" carrying stone for riprap at a lighthouse. I gradually became interested in all kinds of workboats frequenting the Potomac,and later the Chesapeake Bay. During the Depression of the Thirties, my parents encouraged me to work and live downriver; it was cheaper and I could get-to-know the watermen and their families in whom I was so interested. Thus I became involved in workboats, and it was here that I learned of the differences between local traditions of the Eastern and Western shores; between Maryland and Virginia.

During the years 1930-1970 I sailed as the leader of a sea scout "ship" based at the Corinthian Yacht Club located at the mouth of the James Creek Canal, 300 W Street, SW in Washington. Our two sailing vessels *Bobcat* and *Wildcat* were centerboard catboats, former training craft of the US Naval Academy, built in 1919. They were 23′ long, with a 10′6″ beam, a 2′6″ draft (5′6″ with the board down) with one gaff-rigged sail of 345 square feet of 10 ounce raven's duck (hempen sailcloth). The only power other than wind was two 12′ white ash sweeps (oars).

We sailed the Bay as far north as Spesutie Island and camped ashore; to the south, as far as Nassawadox Creek on Virginia's Eastern Shore where mosquitoes prevented us from going further; up the James River to Petersburg; up the York River to the Mattaponi Indian Reservation; and up the Rappahannock to Port Royal. Of all the Eastern Shore Rivers, the Pocomoke was the most attractive; we drifted with tidal currents, sailed and rowed to Snow Hill, then hiked eastward 6 miles to Snow Hill Public Landing to view the Atlantic Ocean via Chincoteague Bay.

I became conscious of the greatness of the Chesapeake, a vast inland sea thrusting its deep estuaries and long tidal reaches far into the wooded coastal plain up to the Piedmont regions of Maryland and Virginia. I learned that its waterways were used originally as main arterial highways to world markets. William Robertson's book *History of America* (1799) describes the Bay: "that grand reservoir, into which are poured all the vast rivers, which...open the interior parts of the country to navigation,and render a commercial intercourse more extensive and commodious than in any other region of the globe." I discovered the length of the Bay to be an awesome 195 miles. The width varies from about 22 miles at its widest part to between 3 and 10 at the upper part. The distance between the Capes, its only natural connection with the sea, is about 12 miles. Its depths vary considerably; the deepest is 174 feet off Bloody Point Light House; the shallowest part of the natural undredged main channel near the head of the Bay, is about 17 feet.

Impressive though it is, the Bay is enhanced in scope by its many deepwater estuaries and their rivers and creeks. The Chesapeake has 48 principal tributaries,some of them navigable for upwards of a 100 miles. These in turn have 102 branches,some navigable for more than 50 miles. In all, the 150 rivers, creeks,and branches in this region provide a navigable distance within the Virginia Capes of some 1750 miles. This figure is an inadequate reflection of the length of the shore line, which is extremely indented, especially on the Eastern Shore. The total shore line of the Bay and the tidewater portions of its tributaries has been estimated at 4612 miles. The surface area of the Chesapeake is about 3237 square miles and the drainage area 64,900 square miles, approximately the combined area of the six New England states.

Because of these geographical facts, boats have always been a necessity. At first, canoes, shallops, pinnaces, skiffs, and wherries were in constant use for transportation such as ferrying, visiting friends,and going to church. Flats, sloops, tobacco boats, and small schooners served to lighter tobacco and other produce to ships anchored in deeper water. Various kinds of boats were developed as fly-boats or dispatch-boats for communication; as fishing vessels for seining, crabbing and oystering; and as traders up-and-down the Bay, from shore-to-shore, and river-to-river.

Little was known with certainty about the construction of these boats except in the case of the canoe, skipjack, sloop, bugeye, and schooner. Several superior books have been written of Chesapeake Bay craft by Marion V. Brewington and Robert H. Burgess, both formerly with the Mariners Museum at Newport News.

In 1944, a gratifying friendship was formed with the nation's leading maritime historian Howard I. Chapelle when he designed a 30′ skipjack replacing our two catboats of 1919 vintage; and two 18′ sailing skiffs for my sea scouts. From that time on, I took every opportunity to visit Mr. Chapelle at his offices and homes near Washington, Cambridge, and Rehoboth Beach where he died on 30 June 1975 at the age of 74. His ashes were spread over Town Point near his former residence on the Little Choptank, Md.

It was his suggestion that I research and write a book on rowing and sailing craft of the Chesapeake Bay; one to describe all boats from the very earliest dugout to the latest ram; the state of progress in boat construction and design, and the many types employed. This book is as complete as my spare time would allow; as I practiced architecture for 50 years in my "tidewater office" in order to survive.

The material was gained by a search of tax assessments, wills, and inventories of estates, by reading microfilm of old newspapers for advertisements describing vessels offered for "sale, lost or stolen;" and by investigation of records, photographs, and books at 64 marine and maritime museums on the East Coast.Hundreds of hours were spent at the Library of Congress, Smithsonian Institution, National Archives,and State and County Historical Societies.

Along with this documentary evidence I collected as much oral information as possible. Ship's carpenters, ships' captains and owners, sailmakers, and watermen were coaxed to talk about the vessels they had built, rigged, outfitted, sailed, or known which was immediately committed to writing; then analyzed and compared with the few existing formal records and with similar stories from other narrators. The account set forth here represents a welding of a time-consuming study of records, compared to oral traditions.

Thousands of words and numerous illustrations describing individual boats are available, but not affordable for reproduction in this book. Footnotes would have tripled the number of pages.

Every acknowledged type of Chesapeake Bay working watercraft is recorded by a one page text with one illustration, each is complete in itself; followed by related subjects of historical value. Seagoing ships such as the Virginia Pilot boat, the Baltimore Clipper, naval and military craft (except *Gunboat*) are not included.

It is my sincere hope that the reader may absorb some of the lost atmosphere and flavor of bygone days; and revive in both Virginians and Marylanders a love of our Bay and a just pride in their own maritime traditions.

Frederick Tilp
1 October 1981
Alexandria, Va

ACKNOWLEDGMENTS

The author wishes to acknowledge his recognition to the many persons living in tidewater lands along the shores of Chesapeake Bay with whom he has made friends, and for the valuable information and suggestions they have so freely given in the past 52 years.

Foremost is Howard I. Chapelle whose friendship with the author is described in the previous chapter.

Special thanks is awarded to Ralph E. Eshelman, director of the Calvert Marine Museum at Solomons, who researched all-over-the-Bay, and chased-down historical clues.

Praise is given to my associates: George Dankers of Valley Lee Md; Joseph Krafft of Alexandria Va; Peter Egeli of Drayden Md; Frederick Davis of Onancock Va; and Walter Lawson of Plum Point Md, whose maritime enthusiasm added many facts to the text, which I did not have the time to explore.

Many happy hours were spent listening to Marion V. Brewington at the Mystic Seaport Museum who enjoyed relating his historical research of many years on the Bay. On 8 December 1974, he died. His widow "cast his ashes" on the waters of his beloved Chesapeake. Nearby in Parson's Cemetery at Salisbury, his marker notes, "Buried at Sea."

Thanks is given to: William A. Baker, the well-known naval architect of Hingham Ma; Benjamin A.G. Fuller, curator at Mystic Seaport Museum; James J. Holt, director of Chesapeake Bay Maritime Museum; Dorothy Brewington, historian at Mystic Seaport; and Donald G. Shomette of Nautical Archaeological Associates.

Grateful acknowledgments are also expressed to:

DISTRICT OF COLUMBIA: Roxanna Dean and Robert Truax of MLK Library, John Vajda of Navy Department Library, Harry Patton and James Knowles of the Smithsonian Institution.

MARYLAND: Oliver Reeder, Roger Mangels, George Krantz, Merle and Laurence Monroe, Charles Lancaster, John Graham, James Richardson, Betty Rigoli, Fred Cheseldine, James Windsor, Roy Rafter, Stark McLaughlin, Elgin Dunnington, Edwin Beitzell, William Kirschenhofer, Burt Kummerow, Graham Wood, Hugh Benet, and Edward C. Papenfuse, Maryland State Archivist.

VIRGINIA: Robert Norris, Robert Burgess, Dean Allard, Donald Orth, Herman Krentz, A.R.D. Perrins, Theodore Haxall, Sam Headley, Lake Cowart, William DuPaul, John Frye, Allen Haynie, Beale DeLano, William Lee, Daniel Koski-Karell, John Refo, and Louis H. Manarin, Virginia State Archivist.

MUSEUM LIBRARIES AND ARCHIVES: Ships of the Sea Maritime Museum, Savannah; US Naval Academy Museum; Maryland Historical Society; Virginia Historical Society; Bath Marine Museum Me; Mariners Museum Va; Maine Historical Society; Chesapeake Bay Maritime Museum; Calvert Marine Museum; US Frigate Constellation; Mariners Museum; Oxford Museum; Penebscot Marine Museum; US Naval Museum, DC; Radcliffe Maritime Museum, Md; and every County library, museum and historical society in the tidewater areas of the Chesapeake Bay.

PRIVATE LIBRARIES. Association of Maryland Pilots. Cordage Institute. Distilled Spirits Council. American Forestry Association. Forest History Association. Mount Vernon Ladies Association of the Union. Alice Ferguson Association. National Colonial Farm. American Institute of Architects. National Forest Products. National Geographic Society. American Geological Institute. Oyster Growers & Shellfish Institute. Association of American Geographers. Peabody Library Association of Georgetown. Building Stone Institute. Model Shipcraft Guild. Enoch Pratt Free Library. American Ass'n for State and Local History. Nautical Research Institute.

MARYLAND STATE LIBRARIES: State Library. Maryland Historical Trust. Potomac River Fisheries. Saint Mary's City Commission. Department of Natural Resources. Hall of Records.

VIRGINIA STATE LIBRARIES: State Library. Institute of Marine Science. Fish Hatchery Board. Marine Resources Commission.

ART CONSULTANT: The superb presentation of art work in this book is credited to John M. Barber of Richmond.

And as a final favor, all typing was done by June Douglas of Falls Church Va, and Vivienne Mitchell of Alexandria Va . . . and most of all, a thanks to Fay, my wife who tolerated me for thousands of "historical hours."

A WAY OF LIFE

At "Slack water; ebb begins," during the morning of 23 June 1930, fifteen sea scouts and their skipper (the author) of Ship #322 left the Corinthian Yacht Club in Washington, DC, bound for Solomons Island on the Patuxent River. This was to be a 125 mile race between their two 23′ catboats *Wildcat* and *Bobcat.*

For weeks, the youthful crew and skipper had carefully studied Manfred Curry's new (1928) book, *Aerodynamics of Sails and Racing Tactics;* and the records of the America's Cup racers in preparation for the next five days of head-winds, fair-winds, and no-winds; ebb-currents and flood-currents, and short-choppy seas and long-rolling swells. The sea scouts soon discovered that what they learned in Curry's book was of no practical value and above all, that a short and beamy catboat was not sea-kindly on the Chesapeake Bay.

During the afternoon of 28 June, they entered the inner harbor of Solomons Island, and anchored near shipyards belonging to M.M. Davis, James Osborn Lore and Frank DeBoy. The two catboats were in the midst of an anchored fleet of sailing workboats numbering about twenty strange looking craft. Ashore the boys were informed these boats were schooners, pungies, bugeyes, and skipjacks, none of which were listed in Curry's racing manual. The crew was surprised when talking to the keeper of Webster's Store that he never heard of a catboat, but he did comment favorably upon our handling of the two small craft.

The hot summer air was laden with odors of tar and copper paint, and the metallic click-click sound of the wooden caulking mallets on caulking irons that echoed over the entire harbor. The boys were impressed to watch two black men (captain and cook) back a large bugeye under sail alone for several hundred yards out of the thicket of anchored boats in the crowded harbor. This simple and amazing feat excited no surprise among the floating neighbors. And again it was noted by the scouts that nothing like this was mentioned in Curry's book on aerodynamics.

Both crews were weary and looked haggard after 130 hours of hard day-and-night racing on wide open waters (from Point Lookout it is 11 miles west to the Virginia shore, and 24 additional miles east to the main Maryland shore.) Subsequently, a quiet 5 day exploration trip was planned. They rowed and sailed 38 miles up the narrow Patuxent River to the Chesapeake Beach Railway bridge and tied close to the swinging draw to stay in the deeper water. Some of the crew went ashore to find the Mount Calvert passenger station, while a few of them rowed upstream to Pig Point, made fast to Bristol Landing wharf, and bought Eskimo Pies at James Greenwell's store (Leon Post Office)—site of the river's first public ferry (1696).

Upon their return they found the boats covered with cinders from the passing locomotives—it looked as though the firemen had purposely heaved a shovelful of burnt coal into the two cockpits. During the return trip to Solomons, they counted at least twenty steamboat wharves, all in a sad state of repair. However, business must have been good as the Baltimore steamboat *Calvert* at Lower Marlboro wharf appeared to be fully packed with freight; the hull was down to the load water plane, and the bellowing of cattle on board was heard until the steamer was out of sight.

During the following four weeks, the sea scouts cruised along the Western Shore of the Bay, spending the night in a protected anchorage with a fleet of ten to twenty working sailboats which arrived at various hours of the night. To the youthful crew, this was a new experience with a different way of life.

During early morning hours, the clanking of anchor chains and slatting of sails woke the city-born sailors, while the Bay boats slipped out into open waters when the "rosy-fingered dawn was just appearing in the east." As the workboats squared off with the fresh morning wind, guided by the captain at the wheel, a sleepy faced, barefooted fellow sloshed down the decks; meanwhile a black fussed about an old dry goods box containing a stove which could at best be called the "galley" from which belched forth clouds of rosin-laden pine-wood smoke. The vessels were 2- and 3-masted schooners loaded with grain, watermelon, canned goods, lumber, cordwood, and boxes of shooks (barrel staves.); skipjacks were reserved for oystering; rams sailed all night long. The schooners carrying cordwood were the most dilapidated; they never attempted to go to windward in deference to their high deck load. The pungies went out in any kind of wind or weather.

If the wind was fair, the two catboats immediately joined the maritime parade, and slipped out with the fleet. As many as twenty sailing vessels may weigh anchor within a half hour; sailing down wind close-together and wing-and-wing; their crew members shouting from one boat-to-the-other until the slower ones gradually fell behind. The faster sailing vessels passed long lines of timber rafts (composed of wooden piles lashed together) being towed by ever-puffing coal-burning tugs.

Their biggest single thrill was sailing up the Patapsco into Baltimore's crowded harbor, to discover a 4-masted schooner on the marine railway at Johnson & Vane yard. At a nearby dock they watched the unloading of puncheons (84 gallon wooden casks) off schooners from Barbados and Antigua. These huge casks were filled with molasses to be taken to Mangels, Herold Company's warehouse on Boyle Street, where the sea-scouts were given free samples of King syrup and Po-T-Rik molasses.

During the following fifteen years, the two catboats followed the sailing freighters on the Bay, anchoring at night in harbors protected from northwest winds: Back River near Langley Field, Va; off Stingray Point on the Piankatank River, Va; at the mouth of Cockrell's Creek, Va; Cornfield Harbor at Point Lookout, Md; off Drum Point on the Patuxent River, Md; the inner harbors of Annapolis and Baltimore; and behind Blackwalnut Cove, Md.

It almost seemed mythical to the sea scouts that within those few years, a traditional and centurial way of life on the waters of the Chesapeake Bay completely vanished. Like the era of the clipper ships with callous captains and mates in the Cape Horn and Liverpool trade, it passed into history.

Life on sailing vessels freighting up-and-down the Bay was not as dramatic as it was in the big square-rigged ships crossing one or more oceans. The little sloops and schooners were no more than inland-sea tipcarts, hauling their matter-of-fact cargoes from one tidewater landing to another landing; sometimes from a modern wharf in Baltimore to headwaters of a creek so small that the vessel was rowed to a stone quay at the waterfalls, such as in Occoquan, Va.

Railroads did not come to many of the sparsely populated tidewater lands, and the roads were almost nonexistent. Rivers and their creeks provided outlets on which the cheapest means of transportation was by sail or rowboat. Hardly could the Chesapeake Bay have been settled without them. Yet, the rowing and sailing craft and the men and women who guided them have passed unnoticed, and are all but forgotten.

Theirs was a dangerous and wholesome life; they seemed to thrive on hard manual labor and personal consideration of other watermen as they were notoriously "bad-swimmers." The men and women who settled the tidewater land were practical, tough-minded, honest and God-fearing. The entire Bay was one vast neighborhood in which every vessel was as familiar as the house next door, and the men and their wives who sailed were as much neighbors as were city-dwellers.

Except for large vessels owned by firms in Baltimore or Norfolk, most freighters ended the day by anchoring in company at a favorite and convenient harbor. As the day waned and if the wind was "hard," vessels would come scudding-in under double reef; or if the wind was dying, they would drift-in or be pushed-in by their yawl boat; worn-out and aging vessels just remained at anchor until the wind was "just right."

As supper was prepared, smoke curled from the Charlie Nobles (stove pipes) and before long, skippers and crews appeared on deck for a breath of air and a look-at-the-weather. Rowing skiffs were slid overboard and pretty soon masters and "hands" would congregate aboard the vessel tended by the senior master in the group to talk about weather, freights and mutual acquaintances.

Skippers took seats of honor on deck in the middle of the group, while the hands lounged around wherever they found room. After the gossip-of-the-day was disposed of and a few downings of locally distilled rye whiskey (rum only in winter), the conversation was then confined solely to their ships and affairs in tidewater Maryland, Virginia, and Delaware, as though the rest of the world did not exist. To the sea scouts, this way of life was like hearing the original version of a maritime *Arabian Nights*.

A favorite anchorage was in the swash channel near to and directly west from Drum Point Lighthouse. During one of these skipper's meetings; one captain might say, "Wonder what happened to Capt' Gus Rice (master of the 67′pungy *Amanda F. Lewis* out of Coan, Va.) I see'd him comin' down tha Bay loaded heavy-down wit' 'matoe cans, I guess from Continentals Can Wharf in Balmer (Baltimore) 'bout tha same time I was raisin' anchor at Annapolis...he sure is a hard-driver, 'taint many like him no more; he musta got movin' way before dawn so he'd get to Fallin's Wharf (in Coan) by nightfall. I come down the Bay under the Calvert Cliffs cal'latin' to stay in quieter waters 'cause my hull is pretty soft, but Capt' Gus stayed out in the middle of the Bay to get stronger wind and ebb (tidal) current. I looked for him jest before I ducked in behind Drum P'int tonight. Yes sir, he musta' jes' kept on going."

"Yup," another might say, "he prob'ly did. Running cans for all those 'matoe (tomato) canneries out of Coan keeps Capt' Gus right busy freightin'...jest like a worm eatin' soft pine. Didcha' hear that Capt' Matt Bailey almost got caught inta his schooner the *Mattie Dean* runnin' whiskey from his home at River Springs (Md) to Crisfield. Well sir, last Tuesday at about midnight he had a single-reef nor'wester and out-ran the feds; unloaded all th' booze inta trucks from New York which was waitin' for him at the oyster wharf. And later when the Treasury agent-men showed-up, Capt' Matt was sittin' in his cabin eatin' breakfast wid his wife"...and so it would go one and one.

Politics, family affairs and inevitably, women received a measure of attention along with President Herbert Hoover, or whoever was "prez-e-dent" at the time. Sooner or later, the talk gradually came-around to other vessels, crews, shipyards, and ports on the Bay; sailing qualities of different ships and rigs. Their prime interest, however, was *their* vessel and the types of cargo they carried. It was the only way-of-life they knew, and they carried it on, conforming as their fathers had done, and learning as they had learned. It was an entirely different form of life from that experienced by those who went offshore; as it was carried on entirely within sight of land, it was never free of landsmen's ways.

The men depended on the land which was so near and they thought of the land as the ultimate objective of their passages, along with pride in their ships. The ports were important and the passages regarded as simply the process of getting from one place to another. Of course, there were times that produced a delightful experience and memorable to look back upon, usually because of the wind and weather. Sometimes it might be only a short haul of a few miles from Annapolis to St. Michaels. Again, it might be a long yet fast passage from Norfolk to Chesapeake City with a 25 knot southerly wind all the way; or a slow one week trip up the Potomac, moving only on the flood tidal currents without any wind night-or-day.

The author and his sea scouts frequently tied their catboats to trap stakes in a protected cove located in Coan River, Va for a week or so, and served as unpaid crew aboard the many schooners freighting out of this cosmopolitan harbor...an experience never to be available again.

The sailing captains known to the author were the most self confident, conservative, and independent group of men ever encountered. They may very well have been the last living examples of an almost extinct species, in their independence, individuality, and love of life and laughter.

Addendum. During the 1930s, the author sailed with *Capt'n Gus* (Gustavius Rice, 1862-1942) on his pungy out of ports in Virginia's Northern Neck; and with *Capt'n Matt* (Matthew Bailey, 1875-1959) on his schooner out of Southern Maryland ports; mainly to Baltimore, Norfolk, Washington and Alexandria.

ROWING and SAILING CRAFT

During the 19th-century there were over 400 distinct archetypes and subtypes of sailing and rowing boats used for work and pleasure on the East Coast of North America. Over 60 of these claim Chesapeake Bay as their birthplace, including the fast seagoing Baltimore Clipper and the Virginia Pilot-boat. Each model was developed by trial and error over a long period of time to perform its job in home waters and weather conditions within limitations of cost and available materials.

Most of these craft are now gone. Not because they were impractical, slow, leewardly, nor because they were not strong, lasting or seaworthy. The rowing pleasure boats are gone because we no longer have slave power to man the oars. The workboats have disappeared because their earning power was destroyed when sail was replaced by low cost internal combustion engines, depletion of local fishing grounds, changes in fishing gear, and competition by trucks using public roads.

Owing to the space available in this book, all Chesapeake Bay workboat types of the sail and row epoch cannot be shown and described. However, every model the author has seen, has heard of, or has read of in newspapers, wills, and archives during the spare time of his past 50 years of research is noted in the following chapters...listed in the chronological order of their appearance on the Bay. (Author's note: Each type had a specific name and an orthographic adaption from a foreign maritime nation...however, older natives living along the Bay shores may call anything that floated a *bateau.)*

The following 35 illustrations generally show the archetypes (the original form or prototype). The appendix shows 25 successive subtypes. Each tidewater community had its own specialty of craft which was named after the builder or the geographical area such as: the Jenkins Creek boat, Coan River lighter, Patuxent River rail skiff, James River bateau, Headley barge, etc.

DRAWING WITH PEN and INK

Pen drawing, as a separate and complete form of pictorial representation, is a thing of comparatively recent date; its greatest development having taken place since the beginning of the 19th-century. During the Middle Ages, pen work was usually in the form of preliminary studies for paintings, and no attempt was made to develop pen drawing as an art in itself. Today, pen drawings are made not simply as adjuncts of another art or as means to certain ends, but as finished and complete things in themselves.

In their simple black against white, pen drawings have a crispness and directness that are appealing; they are full of life and light. Many of them are only suggestive, leaving much to the imagination, and we take pleasure in this. A few lines here and a few touches there, and sometimes that is all, yet there is a power to this suggestion which often makes photographs, telling everything, boring by comparison. The following examples of art work are of practical utility and also of a fine inspirational value.

The chosen artists for pen work in this book were inspired by scholars of long ago, such as Joseph Pennell, Willy Pogany, Richard Powers and Bertram Grosvenor Goodhue; artists George C. Wales and Henry Rusk for Howard I Chapelle's books; artist Charles G. Davis of the Marine Research Society at Salem Ma; maritime illustrator H.W. Elliott for the tome *Fishery Industries of the US* (1880) written by George Brown Goode; and the late John F. Leavitt, author of *Wake of the Coasters*.

- John M. Barber AMSA, Richmond. Chesapeake marine artist.
- John E. Dundin AIA, Kensington Md. Architect and renderer.
- John C. de Grasse AFA, Quantico Va. Art director *Leatherneck*.
- Dhiru A. Thadani RA, Bombay India. Architect and renderer.
- Richards T. Miller FSNAME, Annapolis. Naval Architect.
- Charles W. Wittholz NA, Silver Spring Md. Naval architect.
- Patricia Cutts, Alexandria Va. Artist.
- Sharon H. Kirkpatrick, Oxon Hill Md. Artist.

BARK CANOE

It was from the Indians that the colonists learned of the usefulness of a bark canoe for transportation in the fresh water rivers and the upper part of the Bay. On his voyage up the Bay during the summer of 1608 Captain John Smith observed many Indians in canoes, especially those living on the Susquehanna River, with its swiftly flowing current and many rapids. Smith said: "...there are two types, one made of 'the barkes of trees, sewed with barke, and well luted with gumme': the other was the log canoe." During the early spring of 1628, the Nanticoke Indians trekked north to the vicinity of the Susquehanna River, where they would remain "till the Barque will peel soe they can make Canooes."

To Europeans, the bark canoe was a curiosity; early travelers gave much attention to these craft. A few drawings were even made, one about 1715 by Admiralty draftsmen from a canoe brought to England on a Royal Navy ship. Shaped much like the present-day canoe, although having straight blunt ends and sized 18′ long, 2′9″ wide, and a depth (height of sides) of 1′6″; this class of canoe was used for hunting and scouting parties on quiet waters.

The individual settler had to obtain a canoe from the nearby Indians by barter. With practice, he acquired sufficient skill to use the bark canoe alongshore and for travel on small open waterways. Until skilled boatbuilders and shipwrights were brought from England to build craft to meet demands of the colonists, the bark canoe was their best temporary means of transportation while the log canoe provided a more permanent type of craft. With a weight of only 50 pounds, the carrying capacity was almost 20 times as much.

The largest source of bark and building acccessories was from forests along the Susquehanna River which is the longest river on the country's Eastern seaboard; rising in New York's Lake Otsego, and flowing 520 miles to the Bay. Two additional sources were the forests along the James River, rising in the Allegheny Mountains and flowing 370 miles to the fall line at Richmond; the other being the Potomac River, rising in the mountains of West Virginia and flowing 280 miles to the fall line at Georgetown.

The various forms of the canoes were not standardized. The model was a matter of the individual builder in accord with his own needs and the material available. The winter bark of paper birch (*Betula papyrifera*) was preferred because it could be obtained in large sheets, clear of serious blemishes. Because its grain ran around the tree rather than along the line of vertical tree growth, the sheets could be sewn together to obtain length in a canoe. Moreover, because the bark was resinous and did not stretch and shrink as did other barks, it also had some elasticity when green, or when kept damp. Other barks for temporary use to be discarded after a short time were American elm, American chestnut, black spruce, bitternut hickory, and American basswood.

Stone tools used by Indians were the axe, hatchet and adze; combined with careful handling of fire for the felling of trees; knives and wooden mauls were for wood working; bone augers for drilling, and bending was accomplished by soaking with hot water. White pioneers brought metal into use: the bucksaw for felling, froe for splitting, steel awls for drilling, and axes and knives for shaping. Even a comfortable wooden sit-down bench and vise called "a shaving-horse" was built to aid in shaping.

The material used for sewing (lacing) together pieces of bark was the root of black spruce, which grew in lengths up to 20′, yet with a maximum diameter no larger than that of a lead pencil. Canoes built of nonresinous barks were lashed, instead of sewn, by thongs of the inner bark of northern whitecedar, elm or hickory.

To make a bark cover watertight, all seams were coated, and the sewing was covered with gum, the resin obtained from black spruce. Gum was accumulated by stripping a narrow length of bark from trees early in the spring and then, during warm weather, gathering the resin that appeared at the bottoms of the scars thus made; then melted to make it workable. Framing members were usually of northern whitecedar. Sugar maple, white ash, or sassafras was used for cross pieces, thwarts, and paddles. Colonists gradually discarded the bark canoe for the log canoe and boats built with pit sawn lumber. Spanish: *canoa*.

Dhiru Thadani '81

LOG CANOE

Columbus, on his second voyage discovered Carib Indians using a dugout "canoa" in the Leeward Islands. Explorers in the lower Chesapeake Bay found a similar type of boat, the Indian's spoon-ended dugouts. John Smith in 1608 stated: "These (dugouts) they make of one tree, by burning and scratching away the coles (coals) with stone and shell till they have made it in forme of a Trough... some were fortie or fiftie foot in length and some will bear 40 men... and will row (paddle) faster than our (white man's) barges."

With depletion of large trees, settlers with metal tools made watertight joints and found it easier to handle and work two small logs than one large one. Joining the two halves was accomplished by cutting mortice holes into the face of one log and corresponding mortices in the face of the other. Oak tennon pieces were fitted and the two halves drawn together by a twisted rope tourniquet. Locust treenails (trunnels) were put through the bottom and the tennons bound together. The hull form was altered to have sharp double-ends, sails added; thus the log canoe became the most popular of all Bay boats.

Three distinct models evolved: *Poquoson,* developed at a hamlet of the same name on the York River, Va; *Pocomoke,* built on Virginia's Eastern Shore and northward to Maryland's Choptank River; *Tilghman Island,* built from the Choptank northward to the Sassafras River. These models were not confined, but sailed all over the Bay.

The *Poquoson* type had a double-ended hull, straight stem and stern posts, and up through the Civil War was 2-masted (vertical) leg-of-mutton rig without bowsprit or jib. In the late 1890s this design was converted to a sloop rig with a "swan's-bow," and later to the "chicken-beak" clipper bow with a raked mast unsupported by shrouds. Centerboards replaced the false keel; washboards and a coaming were added. Except for this Virginia model, no other type was produced on the Western Shore or the extreme upper part of the Bay.

The two other types had different hull forms and sail rigs: one or two pivoted masts, (a 40×8 canoe built in 1891 had 3 masts); triangular (sharp) or square sails; loose-footed sails or laced-on sails; booms with jaws or sprits with snotters (a strap supporting the heel of a sprit to the mast); stick-up jibs or swinging-boom jibs; clubs, barndoor rudder, etc. The sail shape originated from Arabian designs and was first mentioned by John Smith in 1616 as a "sprit saile." The better-built Maryland canoes were made from a half-model, showing each log in full development as it would appear in the finished product. In poorer-built canoes, the builder's eye (known as "winchum-squinchen") was used in attaining the form. The shoveling of oysters and fish was easier (crabs went directly into barrels) because of the smooth hull interior without frames for interference: this made log canoes the preferred workboats.

The original *Pocomoke* canoe was described by Brewington as a 2-sail leg-of-mutton rig; a "stick-up" jib was added later. The *Tilghman Island* leg-of-mutton rig was altered around 1870 by addition of sprits and "clubs." In 1880, racing craft added a swinging jib; and to increase the sail area without heightening the mast, odd-shaped sails were invented such as the square sail, ringtail, watersail, balloner, staysail, and spinnaker with longer bowsprits; plus sandbag ballast. The working canoe remained unchanged. In a calm, a sculling oar was used; or a plank 8′ to 10′ long by 7″ wide, ¾″ thick at one end tapering to 1½″ at the other. To scull, the canoeman faced aft with the flat of the loom against the top of the rudder post with the blade about 2′ or 3′ in the water . . . no thole pin, oarlock or rowlock (notch).

Paint colors reflected Elizabethan traditions. Originally, log canoes were garishly colored having a "white bottom, black gunnel, and red inside;" another "paid all over within and without by using a mixture of Tar and Red Paint." Others were treated with tar alone or left "raw." Later, hulls were painted red or green up to a little above the waterline while topsides were white with decorations in red and yellow. Painted interiors reflected the owner's wealth.

Their popularity was legion, as 1880 US Census noted: "6300 canoes in use on the Bay with 175 being built yearly." Robert Lambdin of Saint Michaels built 68 canoes between the years 1865 and 1894. The working canoe has disappeared; however, in 1885 the Chesapeake Bay Yacht Club of Easton sponsored interest, specifications, and development of racing canoes, which continues in this day (1981). See appendix # 132, 133.

Dhiru Thadani '81

SHALLOP

It was common practice for 16th-century explorers to carry on their ships a shallop or some type of small craft in pieces ready to be assembled upon arrival at their base of operations. The name is derived from the French *chaloupe en fagot* meaning "a ship's boat in the form of a bundle of sticks." At the first permanent settlement in Virginia, the colonists had such a "chaloupe." John Smith recorded the arrival on 26 April 1607 of the Virginia Company colonists at Cape Henry and continued, "so next day we began to build our shallop, which had been shipped in portions, easy to be fitted together." This shallop was launched the following day, and immediately several "Gentlemen went exploring" up the James River.

The first American shallop was built of "yeiwe pyne" at James City, Va in 1621 for ferrying to the Eastern Shore. Boat building as a business was established by William Claiborne in 1631 at his fur trading post at Kent Island. That same year the shallop *Firefly* was built there, to be followed by the shallop *Star,* which was manned by a crew of five; then the shallop *Cockatrice* for a crew of fourteen. Another enterprising Virginian, Henry Fleet who traded extensively with Potomac Indians before the arrival of Maryland colonists, used a shallop which he said he had "built among the Indians... The little boat was manned with ten men carrying all manner of ammunition." Smith's 1612 map of the Chesapeake Bay shows a single-masted double-ended boat (a shallop) in one of the upper reaches of the Bay.

The first shallop used by Maryland colonists was brought aboard *Ark* from England. After they anchored in March 1634 off Saint Clements Island, Md, women servants went ashore in a shallop to wash the sea wearied voyagers' dirty clothes. No sooner than the cleaning process had started than the shallop capsized and much of the linen was lost. In spite of the bad luck which attended the first use of a shallop in Maryland waters, this type of river craft was soon in general use among colonists on both sides of the Bay. It was employed for carrying tobacco from plantation landings to seagoing vessels anchored in deeper water; for trading voyages around the Chesapeake Bay; for collecting corn from Indians, or for military expeditions against the Indians; and in actions between the settlers at Saint Marys (the seat of Lord Baltimore's government) and the Virginia traders on Kent Island. A shallop served as the first recorded pilot boat on the Chesapeake Bay. There are few references to shallops used for offshore fishing.

The smallest passenger shallop on Virginia's record of about 1630 had a keel length of 18′ with a beam of 6′6″; and for equipment she had "masts, oars, a yard and a rudder." A typical 12-ton shallop, a burdensome yet popular carrier of tobacco hogsheads or molasses puncheons (an 84 gallon cask) built at Maryland yards during the 17th-century was 34′9″ on the keel, 10′ wide, and 3′6″deep with an overall length of nearly 42′.

The two sails were generally loose-footed, lug-rigged and might be called the "shallop rig" with origin from Dutch and French fishermen. No evidence was found of the use of a ketch variation of this rig, with the main mast taller than the mizzen. Designed as open boats, a few had a cuddy or small cabin, some even with a fireplace. They were clinker built with round bottom and extreme sheer. They were fitted with leeboards.

Some of the Elizabethan character was painted into these colorful craft, as noted in a 17th-century advertisement: "A lap strake two-masted shallopp, painted black and yellow, the lower strake Chocolate color, the masts Yellow, the top of the foremast Black, the top of the Mainmast not Black; a graplin on board instead of an anchor."

For two centuries, the shallop was a favorite type of vessel for freighting on the lower Bay, because of its economical hull construction and sailing rig. Newspapers of Norfolk and Alexandria advertised more "Shallops, for sale" than any other craft.

The newspaper *Illustrated London News* of May 1861 shows four illustrations of the Potomac River between Washington and Mount Vernon. Three drawings show 28 sailing craft (2 square-riggers and 26 shallops). The fourth picture shows 12 shallops moored alongside the shores of Tiber Creek at the base of the 150′ high unfinished Washington Monument.

The shallop was the most long-lived of all the Bay sailing types, surviving through the early 1900s. Indeed, a 30′ shallop, named *Aviza,* sailed out of Neabsco Creek, Va in the 1970s.

Dhiru Thadani '81

PINNACE

The term "pinnace" has been applied recklessly to many types of vessels—from small lightly-built rowboats used as tenders on merchant and naval ships; and upward-in-size to large double-decked men-of-war "having a burden of 650 tons, keel length of 105 feet, breadth of 34 feet and propelled by sails and oars." Early dictionaries state, "a light vessel of pine suitable for privateering and exploring, of many types of rigs and sails." The term disappeared by 1981 except as the type of a captain's personal boat.

The first pinnace to enter the Bay was *Discovery* in 1607 anchoring at Jamestown, Va; the first pinnace in Maryland was *Dove,* in 1634. The first pinnace built on the Bay was named *Long Tayle* in 1631 under orders of William Claiborne at Kent Island (then claimed by Virginia); another pinnace, *Elizabeth* began trading that same year from Kent Island up into the Potomac River. The settlers' depot at Hampton, Va furnished spikes, nails, tools, metalwares, anchors, cordage, watercasks, tar, pitch: and brimstone (sulfur) to prevent teredo worms. Sails were "poldabis," a coarse canvas then used by the Royal Navy.

The pinnace became the original sailing workboat for the early settlers similar to the Bay schooner and Potomac longboat of later years. They also played an important part in local warfare, especially in the struggle between Claiborne and Calvert for possession of Kent Island. Calvert's pinnaces *Saint Helen* and *Saint Margaret* repulsed Claiborne's vessels at the mouth of Pocomoke River in 1635, the first naval action in inland waters of North America.

Pinnaces were not used for trans-Atlantic convoy-system tobacco trade, but chiefly in coastal and West Indian waters. Usually traveling alone, fending for themselves, thus demanding a design for fast sailing rather than great cargo capacity; disappearing from the Bay by the early 1800s.

As part of Virginia's 350th Anniversary Celebration in 1957, the architect Robert G.C. Fee designed replicas of two English galleons; the 100-ton *Susan Constant* and the 40-ton *Godspeed;* and the 20-ton pinnace *Discovery.* The three original vessels entered the Chesapeake Bay on 26 April 1607 with colonists sent by the Virginia Company of London. Replicas were built by Dunn's Marine Railway at West Norfolk and are now (1981) owned by the Jamestown Foundation. The pinnace *Discovery* (39×11×5) was launched on 20 December 1956 at a cost of about $40,000. It carries 392 square feet in two linen sails, one each on two masts. Built with longleaf yellow pine keel, white oak frames, Douglasfir planks and quarter-sawn white oak decks; secured with galvanized iron and trunnel fastenings.

As part of Maryland's Bicentennial Celebration in 1976, a second replica of the Pinnace *Dove* was planned (the first being in 1934). This was one of the two ships (the other being the 300-ton *Ark*) in which 140 settlers crossed the North Atlantic and entered Chesapeake Bay on 27 February 1634; and continued freighting to New England carrying grain; lost on a trip to England loaded with beaver pelts and lumber. The architect for the replica was William A. Baker of Hingham, Ma; builder James B. Richardson of Lecompte Creek, Lloyds, Md; the present (1981) owner is Saint Mary's City Commission. With keel laid on 6 June 1977, the new *Dove* was launched 14 August 1978, and commissioned on 8 October 1978 at St. Mary's City. The length (between perpendiculars) is 61′; stern to bowsprit end is 72′; beam 15′6″, and the draft 6′. The *Dove* carries 2034 square feet of canvas in mainsail, maintopsail, mizzen, spritsail, foresail, and foretopsail. All wooden members are white oak, except the mast, decking, and spars which are loblolly pine; secured with galvanized iron and locust trunnels.

Authentic methods of construction, craftsmanship, and fastenings were not always used in these reproductions, such as circular sawn lumber instead of pit sawn; galvanized hardware instead of English wrought iron; spars finished with a petroleum grease instead of boiled animal fat; and copper bottom paint instead of ox-blood, buttermilk and lime. For ballast; casks of Maryland rye were probably used instead of Sack wine from the Canary Isles, and Virginia bourbon instead of Sercial or Malvasia wine from the Madeiras. French: *pinasse.*

BARBER

SLOOP

The sloop rig, supposed to have originated in the Netherlands and adopted in England, proved peculiarly well adapted to the Chesapeake Bay. It became a popular colonial rig, especially employed in coasting and West Indian trade. The vessels were usually round-bottomed, chunky hulled, keel craft up to 60′ in length, having one mast, a huge gaff mainsail, two or more headsails, and one or two square topsails for ocean work. They first appeared shortly after 1630 on Virginia's Eastern Shore, being built by John Toulson on Nassawadox Creek. Maryland's first sloop, *Reformation,* was built in 1643 by Richard Trewe of Kent Island for Richard Ingle (a lieutenant of William Claiborne, the proprietor of that island) who sailed her for invasion of the Western Shore in an effort to oust the Catholic powers of Maryland.

The first record of seagoing sloops on the Bay was noted in Maryland archives of 1690 which says "a sloop *Amy* in the tobacco trade sailed between Saint Mary's and London." By the end of the 17th-century, sloops had become very popular; over half of all vessels built on the Bay were sloops.

In the course of the first half of the 18th-century, "Bermuda sloops," famous for their speed and weatherliness, enjoyed great vogue among traders, privateersmen, pirates and the British Navy. Several maritime historians imply the Bermuda sloop as being the inspiration for design of the famed Baltimore Clipper. By the 1730s the Chesapeake Bay trade to the West Indies became paramount, even though it was an unconvoyed route, and exposed to attack from piratical ships, both public and private. Sailing south from the Bay, cargoes consisted largely of salt fish, flour, building and cooperage materials, farm produce, tools, stoves, textiles and hardware; in returning with cargoes of dyewoods, mahogany, sugar, molasses, and rum.

In 1745, tobacco plantation owners decided to hire a vessel to serve as a "Guard la Coast," they chose a sloop, described as "Bermuda-built and a good sailer," to protect their shipping at the Virginia Capes.

Some of the colonists did not consider the sloop a satisfactory type of vessel: in 1750, Edward Brisley on the Patuxent River refused to go to sea after one voyage and so noted "she was an ugly bitch" and was very happy to sell her to his friendly neighbor, the Quaker Richard Preston.

The large mainsail, long gaff, one or two square sails, two headsails and a dangerous overhanging main boom proved especially discouraging when a skipper scrounged for a crew. . . as crew's wages and hazards were determined "by the size of the main boom when she swings." *Mediator,* a Virginia sloop of circa 1741 swung a boom 60′ long with a diameter of nearly 20″ and 20′ overhanging the stern.

By the beginning of the 19th-century, the schooner rig had displaced the sloop as the principal vessel for long voyages. The remaining sloops, confined to the Bay were between 20- and 50-tons, carrying a shorter gaff, smaller mainsail and boom, and one headsail, but retaining the gaff-topsail and omitting the square sails entirely. Still foot-for-foot, sloops were faster than schooners, because of the greater sail area in relation to displacement.

Even with this, the remaining sloops were slowly displaced in popularity by bugeyes, and later by skipjacks. In fact, they dwindled in number so badly, that many unemployed seagoing sloops from Northern waters were encouraged to emigrate to the Bay. The black-hull *Flora Elsie* (65×20×6) built at Islip, NY in 1880 sailed out of Washington for 31 years; the author served as a crew member in 1930; abandoned at James Creek, DC.

The last great surge of Bay sloop building (centerboarders) was during the 1880s at Taylor Island on the Little Choptank on Maryland's Eastern Shore. Remnants of that fleet remained active over nearby oyster grounds into the 1970s. A few gave up their traditional gaff rig to adapt the easier handled skipjack triangular mainsail. The largest sloop on the Bay was the 74′ *Charles M. Kelley* out of Severn River, Va. The 47′ *Rebecca T. Ruark,* built 1886 at Taylor Island, is sailing (1981) out of Cambridge, though with a skipjack rig. The 50 page book *Bahamian Sailing Craft* by William R. Johnson, Jr 1973, Nassau; describes native 40′ (plus) sloops which still (1981) work profitably. German: *schlup*. See appendix # 134.

BARBER

FERRY

The waters of the Chesapeake Bay were naturally the first roadway known to a settler. To cross the streams that separated him from his neighbor or for transacting business—any type of craft was pressed into service—canoes, punts, flatboats, scows, even rafts. These he propelled himself until a slave or two was acquired.

The steady increase in the number of settlers created a demand for public transportation across the water at the most traveled points. The first public ferry on record was started as a private enterprise in 1636 by Adam Thoroughgood with service across estuaries flowing into Lynnhaven Bay and Elizabeth River, near the site of Norfolk. Maryland's first was in 1638, between West Saint Mary's and Saint Mary's City.

Later, all tidewater counties were urged by their provincial (and state) governments to provide public water-taxis: "...to encourage the establishment by men (and their families)...that all persons attending ferryboats shall be free from public and county levies and from such public services as musters, constables, clearing highways, impressment, etc., and shall have their licenses without fee." And as a sop tossed in, "the ferrymen may (and they all did) maintain an ordinary (public inn and tavern) without fee for license." Ferrymen were dispensers of local news, daily current events, travel bureau data, directions for confused strangers, a feeder and stabler of horses, but above all he was approved "Keeper of the Tippling House" whose accommodations near his ferry dock normally included *filles de joie*.

The earliest ferry boats were dugout canoes which were poled or paddled across a stream. Wind gusts and rain squalls, so characteristic of the Bay region, made ferrying dangerous even where creeks were narrow. Newspapers reported many drownings when ferryboats were struck by violent squalls which caused the horses to lose their footing and overturn the craft. When carts and wagons were to be ferried, two canoes were lashed together with the right wheels of the vehicle resting in one canoe, the left wheels in the other canoe and the horses swimming alongside. This system lasted through the Civil War.

Keen rivalry between operators frequently occurred as in the case on the Potomac where six ferries were located within ten miles, (between Persimmon Point and Maryland Point, where the tidal ebb current is 1.4 knots—the strongest on that estuary) resulting in a verbal battle with advertisements in the *Maryland* and *Virginia Gazette* newspapers: 1745-47.

Chesapeake travel required two kinds of ferries: one that crossed a wide expanse of water like the Bay itself or lower courses of the large rivers, where a sudden squall may raise a rough sea. For this purpose sailing sloops or schooners were employed. For narrow rivers or creeks in protected waters, there was a "kind of flat-bottomed lighter or scow" with "upright sides of about 2′ to 3′ and sloped at each end so as to ride over the waves." Drawing little water, they could land directly on a gradual sloping sand beach and the lowering of a gangplank or apron allowed the horses, wagon, and passengers to pass directly to the dry public roadway. Lengths varied up to 30′ with a 10′ beam, carrying three to six horses besides passengers; oar propelled.

The larger "scow-ferries" were pulled across the river by means of a rope with pulleys secured to the hull; the ferry boat was slid along a fixed line, at waist height, the propulsion being accomplished by means of a wooden, notched "heaver" handled by a strong man "puller" equipped with padded gloves. When not in use, the cable sunk. During the canning seasons for fruits, vegetables, fish and oysters, these ferries operated 24 hours a day, six days a week; crossing estuaries all-over-the-Bay until World War II.

One of the first on the Bay crossed the Patapsco in 1729, having a "hemp rope of four and a half inches in diameter." The author rode on the last hand-pulled ferry, which ran between Bundicks and Coan wharves on Coan River, Va using a one inch steel wire rope cable stretched between a *fixed end* and a *tightened end* secured to a capstan;...phased out in 1938.

Between 1638-1815, there were 48 sail or hand operated ferries on the Potomac; in 1748, 52 on the James, 37 on the York and 29 on the Rappahannock. By 1870, it is estimated that there were over 1000 public and private rowing and sailing ferries in the tidewaters of the Bay...ranging from a 2-passenger punt to a 40-passenger schooner. German: *fabre*. See appendix # 135.

Dhiru Thadani '81

XEBEC

The xebec, pronounced "zeebeck" was used extensively by pirates of the Barbary States (Morocco, Algiers, Tunis, Tripoli) during 17th- and 18th-centuries. It influenced the design of the Baltimore Clipper and succeeding types such as the pungy and bugeye. Maritime records indicate numerous xebecs were built on the Bay. Maryland Archives mention frequent visits of Royal African Company xebecs at Bladensburg and Annapolis with a "hold packed with fine black-slaves." French, Spanish, West Indian slavers and pirates, and later American privateers, found the xebec a remarkably fast vessel which carried an enormous spread of sail; handy for chasing and escaping with an ability to carry guns—necessary requirements for their trades.

The favorite length for 3-masted slavers was between 75′ and 100′ between perpendiculars and a beam in proportion of sixteen (16) to four (4) and depth ranging around one (1): designed expressly for high speed. The decks were built clear, houses and hatches were smaller and fewer. Crew and officers lived largely on deck, as their payload was confined below. A 100′ xebec usually carried about 450 slaves.

The hull was round-bellied, low-waisted, shallow-draft with concave waterlines in the bow and convex sides which rounded outwards. A "grating deck" projected far out beyond the round stern as an extension of the quarter-deck like a bugeye's "patent stern." They had pronounced turtle (rounded) decks to allow seas shipped (when sailing) to run down to and through the scuppers; a feature of their construction being the provision of gratings from the centerline of the ship to the sides, thus the crew moved easily and dry-shod while water on the turtle deck ran down beneath the gratings. Resembling Mediterranean and Arabian vessels, they had a ram-like "beak-head." Steering was managed by a large tiller.

Basically the xebec was wind-propelled, but at night when becalmed, they would drop sails and use large muffled sweeps (oars wrapped with chafing gear to kill noise in the rowlocks) to steal away from an enemy, or to surprise a merchantman. Oar-ports were located between gun-ports. Rowing was especially popular with smugglers who used muscular slaves as oarsmen. A dark green or black was the traditional hull color.

The fore and main masts were called "block masts," being short and formed square at the head to receive sheaves, to reeve the "jeers" (halyards). To improve downwind performance, 18th-century English slavers fitted a topmast and a square sail on the mizzenmast.

The xebec had no bowsprit, but had a sort of bumpkin, "woolded" or lashed, and confined to the bow in an almost horizontal position to which led the bowlines. The foremast raked forward considerably and had no fore-and-aft stays. Its shrouds set up to toggles fixed in the sides, similar to runners on English cutters or the present day preventer backstays. These shrouds were easily shifted when the vessel went about. The mainmast was nearly upright, with a slight rake forward, and rigged in the same manner as the foremast. Each mast carried a large lateen sail for close-hauled work, the longer side of which was bent to a yard that hoisted by a parral around the mast at about one-third the length of the yard from its lower end. The yards were worked at the lower ends by bowlines and the sail was spread by a sheet at the clew. The upper lee yardarm was worked by a brace and the strain supported by vangs nearer the mast. The mizzenmast carried a similar lateen sail, a bit smaller in size. Square sails were carried when the wind was quartering such as in the ocean trade winds, and during head winds or heavy weather they carried smaller or reefed lateen sails, dispensing with all square canvas. The ease of changing rigs proved advantageous when sailing in the Bay and its long and narrow estuaries.

Xebec shaped hulls and lateen rigs were used for many vessels of the Chesapeake Bay Flotilla during both wars with England, and for commercial vessels prior to the Civil War.

The 154-ton privateer *Ultor,* one of several Baltimore xebecs, built near Federal Hill by Andrew Descandes in 1813 and registered as a "Schebeck," became nationally famous during the second war with England. Lateen-rigged ketches were in great favor with Eastern Shoremen through the Federal Period (c1790-c1830). As slavery was associated with xebecs, they disappeared rapidly after the Civil War. Turkish: *sumbeki.*

SNK '82

YAWL BOAT

The yawl boat seems to have been merely a small open boat for shipboard use, appearing first in 1706 and built in yards of the West Indies and Delaware Bay. It soon became popular with all Chesapeake Bay vessels that needed a burdensome workboat to moil off beaches (to work off unkindly shores) and in shoal waters; a boat to be carried from their stern davits.

During calm weather, a large sailing vessel (without engine) was moved by securing a line to the yawl boat and the crew rowed with sweeps, or by heaving-in on a kedge rope made fast to an anchor that had been carried out ahead in the yawl boat.

Around the turn of the 19th-century, the yawl boat on the Bay was transformed from a rowing tender into a working "push-boat," having an engine installed. Typically one-cylinder, two-cycle, 8HP, 5½ inch bore × 6″ stroke, 550 RPM, gasoline fueled, and weighing about 400 pounds, no reverse gear; manufactured by Mianus, Eagle, Lathrop or Palmer; or by Acadia of Nova Scotia. A 20″ propeller with the shaft through the heavy keel would push a large schooner at about 4 knots in a "slate cam," or "deesh cam," as watermen express no wind. With the muffler removed, the exhaust pipe belched a uniformly timed, slow, violent "pop-pop" noise. When the bow was hoisted up by block and tackle and padded with a fender (a bundle of rope made of hemp), placed against the large vessel's transom, the yawl boat became a required *push-boat* for every sailing vessel of any size on the Bay. Many captains were very fussy about keeping the counter name plates and carvings undamaged; thus the yawl boat was secured with a line to the end of the bowsprit, becoming a *pull-boat*.

Sizes were in proportion to the length of vessel class to which she belonged: ranging from 26′ in length, 6′ beam, and 30″ draft to lengths of 12′ for small skipjacks. It had a straight keel with a heavy skeg, a curved raking stem, a raking flat and heart shaped transom, sharp entrance, easy run, and strong sheer. Carvel planked of thick white oak or longleaf yellow pine secured to bent oak frames, and an outboard rudder that would withstand constant grounding on hard sand, oyster and rock-bound beaches. The beam was wide and carried well aft, the gunwale was full at the bow to give flaring forward sections. The midsection was formed with a rising straight floor, rather slack bilge, and flaring topside. Heavy black locust square thole pins were installed for rowing and sculling. The entire hull and sail rig was similar to the Bahamian dinghy as described in the book *Bahamian Sailing Craft* by W.R. Johnson of Nassau.

Originally yawl boats were fitted to carry sail on an unstayed mast; the common loose-foot spritsail or leg-of-mutton sail was the most popular. Interior surfaces were painted with creosote, dead oil or pitch and usually a white painted exterior with green gunwales. Antifouling bottom paints were omitted because of the frequent "haul outs."

After World War I, these attractively designed little workboats built in the Bahama Islands of the British West Indies were replaced with Bay-built, smaller and more economical yawl boats. This model had a square stern, straight sides, flat bottoms and mostly fitted with powerful second hand automobile engines housed in a much larger motor box and with a reduction gear... resulting in a lot of noise and burning of fuel, churned-up water, and speed; described by naval historians and architects as "ugly."

Four-masted schooners in the crowded Baltimore harbor were usually pushed by their yawl boat from their loading wharf to a fresh water berth at East Jones Falls Street. The water discharged here originated in Lake Roland and flowed eight miles down Jones Falls and killed any teredo worms that may have been in the schooner's wooden hull, especially if the vessel traded regularly in the West Indies. After this deterrent against worms, the schooner may have been again pushed by its yawl boat to one of the nearby shipyards to have the bottom coated with antifouling paint... thus saving a tugboat fee.

Except for use by the remaining oyster dredging skipjacks (and the passenger schooners in New England and Maine) numbering 30 in 1981, this once popular little boat is extinct. The originally designed beautiful yawl boat having its origin in the Bahamas does not deserve such a successor, or demise. Swedish: *julle.*

EFFIE A. CHASE
EFFIE A. CHASE
BARBER

PUNT

The punt was a small, flat-bottomed, open, square-ended boat built originally in colonial days as a "poor-man's" workboat. It is to be held in total contradistinction to the graceful and well designed wherry built for wealthy plantation owners of the same era. One of the first printed references to a "punt" appeared in the *London Magazine* of July 1736 by an itinerant observer in America: "we stepped into a small Punt (a very small and dangerous Sort of Canoa), liable to be overturn'd by the least Motion of the Sitters in it. The Negroes manage them dextrously, with a Paddle...we had nearly gained the Vessel when two stupid Hogs (porpoises) came Souse against one side of the Punt and overturn'd us just upon the Back of a Shoal." This was a "hogg's trough" type, the forerunner of the log canoe, dug out of one chestnut or white pine log with blunt-ends shaped like the lip of a spoon and finished 12′ to 15′ long and 2′ to 4′ wide. Although hewn out of a single log, the timber itself was not of a diameter sufficient from which to cut the punt's full beam. That was attained by spreading the sides with thwarts (transverse wooden seats) after the hull had been made pliable by a few hours of boiling water, then throwing in hot rocks, and, as the wood softened, forcing in the spreaders.

The first boat builder in colonial Virginia pit sawed logs into useable boards for the economical and easily built punt; "a workers' box float." The boats varied in size, owing to the needs of employment; frequently known as "scows." A typical river punt had a nearly flat bottom fore-and-aft until close to the ends, where the cross-planked bottom was brought up rather sharply to the end logs (bow and stern transoms). The two sides were not parallel but were sprung so that the bow and stern were somewhat narrower than the hull at midships. Sides had a little flare, with weak sheer and bottom rocker; fitted with a short deck at both ends and a narrow covering board along each side with a low coaming, housing double thole pins. Watermen considered punts as baby "work-horses" to perform only menial tasks. They were ruggedly built of any kind of easily available wood. Virginia's Eastern Shoremen built a 24′ × 6′ scow-lighter called a "beach punt;" flat-bottom (sloping-up at bow and stern), double-ended, propelled with a sculling oar.

In addition to being a popular rowing workboat, alterations were made permitting various other uses:

1. For duck hunters. The famed punt-gun, notorious for its slaughtering of ducks was originally placed in a punt. This was to insure safety for the gunner when handling his huge weapon, especially at the recoil; and for more duck storage space. Sportsmen hunting over the Susquehanna Flats used a "sinkbox;" an oblong-shaped affair about 6′ long permitted the gunner to lie, sit or stand in the box; and fixed to the outer edges were wooden wings and canvas flaps to squelch the waves. See *gunning skiff*, page #42.
2. For fishermen. A covered compartment was built amidships, extending the full width for storage of live bait, crabs or eels, as the compartment was flooded with river water circulated through holes drilled along both sides of the punt.
3. For oystermen. Punts were used at extreme low tides, for hand picking of oysters off the shallow water-covered oyster bars.
4. For street pavers. During the cobblestone street era at Georgetown, Alexandria, and Baltimore, large punts were used by watermen to search-out and pick-up cobbles in fresh water estuaries on the Western Shore.
5. For sales usage. Up until the 1900s when a foreign seagoing vessel dropped anchor in a Chesapeake Bay harbor, "bumboats" (punts carrying peddlars) crowded around and supplied the crew with fruits, merchandise, and illicit and tax-exempt items such as alcoholic beverages and prostitutes.
6. Shipyards in 1981 still use punts as floating platforms to accommodate caulkers, painters and workers on the exterior of hulls and wharves.
7. To many cruising yachtsmen the term "punt" was a colloquial name for a Dutch *praam* or dinghy which naval architects designed as a tender for ease of rowing, towing, sailing, lightering, for stowage on deck and for landing on sandy beaches. The size of this type of punt was based on the size of the yacht and the number of crew members. German: *punt*. See appendix #136.

Dhiru Thadani '81

SUSQUEHANNA ARK

Oxford's main street is Morris Street, in tribute to Robert Morris, who came here in 1738 and whose son was the great Robert.... who became Agent of Finance for the Continental Congress, founder of the Bank of North America, and owner of many thousands of acres in the Genesee country of western New York State. One of his dreams was to have Maryland and Virginia men of wealth to build homes there and establish themselves as *the* aristocrat-owners of vast estates.

To accomplish such an ambitious program, Morris obtained sturdy, dependable yeomanry from Europe which provided loyal workers for the Chesapeake landed gentry. Marketable products of the fabulously fertile Genesee land could only be shipped by water on the Conhocton, Tioga, and Susquehanna Rivers to the Chesapeake Bay; thence to Baltimore. In 1794, Morris's skilled land promotors heard of Pennsylvania-Dutch millers near Huntingdon (on the Juniata River, a branch of the Susquehanna) having "floated a large wooden box fully packed with about 30 tons of barreled flour passed the Conowago Falls in safety and tied up to wharves at Port Deposit (a 175 mile trip), transferred the barrels to a shallop which sailed 50 more miles to Baltimore."

Immediately, settlers in faraway New York and Susquehanna valley turned to Baltimore as the most "advantageous market" for better prices of their lumber and farm produce...50% higher than those obtained at Albany or Philadelphia. This spurred Morris to promote the building of New York's first "ark" as the 75′×16′ box-boat was gloriously dubbed. A boatyard was established near their office on banks of the Conhocton River near Bath (400 miles from the Bay) and hopes generated to make the river a great artery of commerce for his gentlemen farmers.

Homemade ark-building started with a fervor: durably constructed hulks shaped like a canal barge, heavy timbers extending the entire length of the bottom served as keels and shock absorbers; of the roughest and strongest workmanship and fastenings; a "cast, unpolished and unwieldy box" with flat-bottom, high perpendicular sides; triangular bow and stern; with the center oblong section roofed-over to shelter bold and daring passengers.

Lengths varied from 60′ to 90′: width 15′ to 20′; depth 3′ to 5′; drawing about 2′ of water; carrying about 50 tons of cargo. Each of the two tapered ends was equipped with a 30′ long sweep (oar) which two men manipulated to govern the boat's course, as arks had no rudder. They bounced-off rocks, grated-on shoal bottoms and tumbled-over falls and rapids, being propelled by fresh water current and steered by sailor-farmers.

Arks could not easily ascend the river to return home; being torn apart and sold as lumber for $15 at Port Deposit. However, a few were towed up-stream by oxen or horses aided by windlass, block and tackle, and struggling white laborers.

Time and energy was devoted to rendering the entire river and branches safer and easier to navigate. In dry seasons, driftwood was piled around exposed rocks and burned until they were very hot; water was then thrown over the rocks splitting them for easy removal. Baltimore merchants built canals alongside the rock-strewn portions of the river to give arks a smoother down-stream trip; Philadelphia merchants built dams to prevent ark travel and force farmers to use roadways eastward to their markets. Rivalry was rampant.

During the peak-year of 1822, there were 537 arks to arrive at Port Deposit, from which $1,337,925 worth of goods was transshipped by sailing craft to Baltimore such as: grain, ore, castings, cattle, horses, hogs, leather, straw, paper, agricultural products, sheep, pig iron, paper, pork, bacon, seed, bark, sumac, hay, flour, potatoes, whiskey, tallow, planks, poles for ship spars, shooks, oars, coal, slate, hats, and pots. Arks returning home carried: oysters, salt fish, rags, tobacco, furniture, clothes, dry goods, marble, stone, nails, and household equipment. Four roundtrips a year could be expected. Travel was only at a time of high water, usually in the spring and late fall. Wrecks occurred along the way and their cargoes sold at low prices to scheming salvage workers. For over 50 years, these arks were the favored transportation of the non-tidal Susquehanna; losing to sedimentation, roads and railroads by the mid-1800s. English: *earc*.

TOBACCO-BOAT

The early colonists reflected enthusiasm for their "well watered lands where Planters can deliver their Commodities (tobacco) at their own Back doors...but for the convenient water carriage, it would be impractical to Carry on the making of Tobacco." Bulk shipments to Europe were not permitted after 1698, and the size of the hogshead in which cured tobacco, assembled in hands (small bundle of tobacco leaves) was tightly prized (packed by a lever) for transport and standardized at 48″×30″. Experience in packing raised the average weight carried in a single hogshead from around 600 pounds in the 1660s to just under 1000 pounds a hundred years later. Hogsheads from tidewater farms were delivered directly to the wharves for loading aboard ship. Plantation owners in the Piedmont areas above the fall line, harnessed oxen or horses to axles in the flat ends of the hogsheads and converted them into large wheels which were delivered over "rolling roads" to tidewater wharves. This was time-consuming, expensive, and damaging...thus encouraging water transportation.

About 1740, a rather unique water carrier for tobacco was perfected by Reverend Robert Rose, then living on the James River about 125 miles upstream from Richmond. He and his associates contrived to build two large dugout canoes each formed out of a solid tree of 50′ to 60′ in length, and an inch to the foot of length in the breadth of them. Two of these canoes were clamped together by means of crossbeams, pins and heavy cordage; two pieces of wood being placed lengthwise upon the crossbeams, five to ten casks were rolled onto this floating platform; which from three to six men would convey with ease the distance of 150-or-more miles to market, without the use of horses. Another advantage resulted from this construction method in returning home: the canoes admitted of separation, and as they were seldom overburdened with heavy return freight, two men could manage each canoe, coming home against the current.

These tobacco-boats went down river in groups of three; upon return, if the river was rough or flooding, two out of the three boats sold for lumber and the combined crew worked the third craft upstream with profitable freight. The rate of conveying tobacco by boat from Lynchburg (near the Reverend's home) to Richmond (165 miles) was 30 shillings ($5 in colonial money). It was principally Rose's slaves who operated these craft, expert at "running rapids and rolling the hogsheads around the falls" at the fall line where the hogsheads were loaded aboard seagoing ships bound for England, or on nearby tobacco warehouses; returning upstream with payloads of salted fish, molasses, rum, and "notions" from the West Indies or England. Floods (especially that of 1771), labor costs, and time created a demand for boat replacements that could be built quickly and cheaply.

By 1800, the *Rose-method* of water transportation (lashing of 2 canoes together) had disappeared from upland waters being replaced by a larger and improved vessel designed by Anthony Rucker of Amherst County, Va known as a "James River bateau, Tobacco boat, or Market boat." It was a square-ended scow built of thick wooden boards sawn at local mills. Length from 40′ to 80′, beam of a hogshead height (4′), so the barrels could be "scotched into place with ease." Over each gunwale was built a walk-board for the 3 crew members to use their sweeps in quiet water or iron-tipped poles in rough "white water." It featured upright sides and a flat-bottom which sloped at each each "so as to ride over the waves with less resistance than blunt ends." Refinements in hull design resulted in a boat shown on appendix #139; patented in 1821.

As canals were built, shipping from the Blue Ridge Mountains increased with thousands of barrels of flour and hogsheads of tobacco coming down the Potomac, Rappahannock, York, and the James to Georgetown, Fredericksburg, Aylett, Retreat and Richmond. By 1830, there were over 500 tobacco-boats working 1500 crew members on the river above Richmond.

Rucker's tobacco-boats on the James River succumbed in 1840 to mule-drawn barges when 146 miles of canal was opened between Lynchburg and Richmond; reducing the time from 10 days by the tobacco-boat to 30 hours by canal. Potomac's tobacco-boats died shortly after 1850 when 185 miles of the Chesapeake and Ohio canal was opened between Cumberland and Georgetown. The tobacco-boats and natural fresh waterways solved inland transportation problems for over 100 years. Carib Indian: *tabaco*.

Robert Rose

Anthony Rucker

WHERRY

The Tobacco Society, the landed gentry of the Chesapeake Bay, created an increased wealth and trade during the 18th-century. And as soon as each plantation owner was able to afford a "fashionable water taxi," he ordered an English-built, open, rowing wherry. This was a symbol of prestige, similar to owning a two-door Mercedes-Benz 450-SLC ($45,000) auto in the year 1981. In 1751, if the ambitious Robert Carter of Nomini Hall, Va; planter, manufacturer, factor, and trader, wished to visit his rich neighbors (several miles away) for a discussion in science, religion, music, and "other vastly delicate tastes"...he would dress-up for the occasion, then with his young squire would be conveyed there in his custom built 24′ wherry rowed by his own four-man uniformed black crew. The coxswain was usually white. His larger and more ornate barge was reserved for marine parades.

Beautifully designed with a graceful and sweeping sheer, the wherry was constructed of the finest premium woods from nearby forests; painted with color combinations that would be vivid even by modern standards. Bright colors were applied to the exterior; red, blue, green or yellow and sometimes black, but for unknown reasons rarely pearly gray. Sheer strakes and rail caps were bright finished, or if painted, they would match the owner's favorite color. Blue sterns, red rudders, black and yellow alternating strakes, red or pearly gray interiors, Spanish brown stern sheets, gunwales and bends with yellow or blue mouldings predominated. Turpentined oars with red spoon blades tipped yellow; painted square looms between the tapered handle and the leather; thole pins with lanyards made of flax. The rudder was turpentined, and controlled by a colorful yoke secured to the rudderhead, (Adversity to blue color applied only to workboats; a wherry was considered a pleasure boat.) Yoke ropes were braided Irish linen. After all, this was *the* floating image of status and must attract more comments than other images in nearby waters.

The American wherry was probably copied by English builders of the famed Norfolk sailing wherry, the swiftest and most graceful of all craft on smooth water. The art of wherry building was wrapped in the obscurity of a "closed family guild." Like so many great craftsmen of the past, wherry builders were not communicative; each boat was a work of art and better than the predecessor.

A typical wherry imported by American plantation owners was 24′ between perpendiculars, a 5′ U-section moulded beam, and a depth of 1′9″, of conventional lapstrake construction. Wide whitecedar planks copper fastened to natural crook white oak frames, encircled round what may have been described as "full sides and flaring bows." (Steam was not used to bend frames until 1736 according to Wescott Abell in his book *The Shipwrights' Trade*.) This formed a concave "entrance" by gathering the tapered strakes and housing them in a rabbet incised in a sturdy oak cutwater; the stern end being similar with a straight high tucked stern and a small wineglass transom. Steering was accomplished by means of an outboard rudder hung with pintles and gudgeons, a yoke and rudderlines. The sides with raised sheer flared sharply outward at the oar ports, to outrig them for more efficient rowing; all so embodied in general form of a Mediterranean galley.

The combined features of a wide plank keel, and being practically double ended on the water line, adapted the wherry to be berthed on the beach, and hauled ashore after use and left standing without supporting shores. The 4 to 6 oars, each 9′ long had tapered handles, square looms between handles and leather with spoon blades 30″ long. Originally, sunken rowlocks on higher coamings were used for a more decorative sheer. Later, wherries had single locust thole pins; with these a rope grommet was fastened to the oar and was dropped over the pin. When eventually sold for use in fishing or as a workboat; a centerboard (off center) and a spritsail was added, square or round looms on the oars, and a tiller replaced the rudder yoke and yoke ropes.

In a little over a century, the colorful wherry (and the barge) witnessed the greatness of the Golden Age of the Tobacco Society on the Chesapeake Bay. Its demise symbolized the passing of selfwilled persons and their autocratic social order. English: *whyrry.*

BARBER

BARGE

A most misused term is "barge," meaning anything from a small punt to a gunboat, to a European barge rowed by 40 uniformed oarsmen. Early settlers called any roomy, flat-bottomed craft a barge. The British Navy fought two "Battles of the Barges"—at Cageys (Kedges) Straits on the Eastern Shore in 1792, and on St Leonard's Creek of the Patuxent in 1814; using open round bottomed 30′ whaleboats fitted with one sail and oars. Maryland's naval barges for defense were square and double ended, fitted with deep bulwarks, sweeps and a gun port: schooner-rigged at Cageys Straits and sloop-rigged on St. Leonard's, 50′ to 75′ long.

Glamorous barges for peacetime were designed and built on the Bay for Chesapeake's Tobacco Society—a throwback to Thames River barges for conveyance of royalty, ambassadors and other important personages—an English tradition lasting over four centuries. Barges for Chesapeake gentry were used for guests and mini-parades by the great families such as Maryland's Somerville, Galloway, Paca, Tilghman, Brooke and Sharpe, and Virginia's Carter, Tayloe, Lee, Washington, Byrd and Fitzhugh.

The English love of pageantry grew in the time of Henry VIII (1509-1547). Before coaches were introduced, royal and state processions in London were waterborne. Earlier progressions had been on horseback, but the Thames offered a convenient alternative. So processions by water grew from London up river to Westminister or down to Greenwich, becoming the pattern of city life. The royal residences adjoined the river, and town house gardens of the nobility stretched down to waterside, each with its own landing stairs and architecturally glamourized wharves.

The election of a new Lord Mayor brought distinguished European visitors, members of trading guilds with their barges, such as the "Grocers, Mercers, Stationers, Apothecaries, Tallow Chandlers, Drapers, Fishmongers, Goldsmiths, Skinners, Taylors, Haberdashers, Salters, Ironmongers, Vintners, and Clothworkers." Company insignia and shields were hung on the sides, flags and pennants were flown and ornamented awnings or tiltcloths were erected, making a brilliant spectacle of the once common barge. With increasing prosperity, each company's barge was designed with more attractive sheer, lengthening and carving of the hull, splendid wooden cabins beautifully ornate with stained glass windows, colorful painting and gilding.

The barge master steered with a curved carved tiller, while looking ahead and over the "house" at his eighteen or more oarsmen. Eight musicians wearing "cloaks, dress hats with feathers complete" were seated aft. A *royal* bargemaster wore a scarlet cutaway coat, embellished with royal insignia in silver braid on the front and back, kneebreeches, buckled shoes, white silk stockings, and a cocked hat. Oarsmen were attired similarly but a bit more subdued. All hands wore peaked jockey's caps of black velvet. The barge-era topped in 1772, when the Corporation of London fitted-up a 150′ spectacular barge, holding some 300 persons, most splendidly decorated for utmost magnificence. Because of increased steamboat activity the last to be attended by royalty was at the opening of the Coal Exchange in 1849.

With this sort of maritime heritage, each family leader of the prosperous Chesapeake Society wanted the *biggest-and-the-best barge* to remind them of the grand-old-times when sovereigns and nobles used the Thames as the high street of London. They hoped their neighbors might do likewise.

Records at Mount Vernon state: "Barges were kept in readiness by George Washington and his 'neighbour Digges' across the Potomac. Upon signal they would respond with their private barge manned by Negroes in checkered shirts and black velvet caps; the vessel being captained by a white servant."

Robert Carter of Nomini Hall, Va had a barge 41′ long with 7′ beam, rowed by ten Negroes and captained by a white barge master. Carter, being a "cultivated man of vastly delicate taste," needed this barge for the numerous social obligations imposed upon him as a member of the Chesapeake aristocracy. This type of British splendour started to decline at the end of the Revolutionary War... the last record of a ceremonial barge was when George Washington journeyed from Princeton to New York City to deliver his first inaugural address; "On the morning 23 April 1789 he arrived at Bridgeton NJ; here, a specially designed and colorful barge rowed by 13 pilots in white uniforms, conveyed him across the Upper Bay to the city, arriving at 2 pm." Latin: *barca*.

BARBER

SCHOONER

The historical and economic implantations of the Chesapeake's first specialized trade...that of slaves, was carried on largely by 2-masted schooners. Their employment as naval vessels as well as illicit traders assured this type an insidious popularity in early colonial days. The prototype originated in Holland or England.

Schooners developed rapidly on the Chesapeake Bay. They were in great demand because of their practicality and speed. A popular type was referred to as "Virginia-built" even though Maryland builders contributed to its development; it evolved into the famous Baltimore clipper. During the Revolutionary and 1812 War eras schooners were employed as blockade runners on the lower Bay because of their speed. Following this adventuresome period, schooners were altered in design to become a popular workboat. They became smaller, slower, full-bodied, and while designed primarily for cargo carrying, they remained active in the passenger trade. Roads were few and poorly constructed, and waterways constituted the main arteries of trade and travel, especially in the lower Bay until the early 1940s.

During the first part of the 19th-century, shallow-keel with round stem schooners were common. Continuous silting of all estuaries demanded even shallower draft vessels. Soon after the 1812 War, centerboard schooners were built with wider beams and very shallow draft. By Civil War times the round stern had given way to the more handsome square stern and clipper bow, becoming the most popular vessel on the Bay and carrying every type of cargo: lumber, bricks, cordwood, fertilizer, farm products, oysters, fish, crabs, in short, anything that had to be moved—the schooners did it.

With increased shoaling of estuaries, the loaded centerboard schooners would be pushed upstream on high tide to their wharfed destinations...to rest upright on low tide during the transfer of cargo...unable to move until change-of-tide. This was most troublesome in the early 1900s when many tomato and fish canneries and freight depots were located at the head of tidewater.

Prior to the use of steam as a means of propulsion, schooner packets ("water stages") were used on the river to carry passengers and freight to coastal cities. Ships originating at Washington, Georgetown, and Alexandria served East Coast cities such as New York, Philadelphia, Charleston, and Savannah. Advertisements in local newspapers guaranteed a passage within a fixed time schedule or "your money refunded." Even after power craft gained a foothold on freight and passenger trade, the schooners continued to be employed. Schooners were the "errand-boys," the short-haul and long-haul freight-droghers and passenger-buses for many years. Perfectly suited for their task, the versatile schooners contributed substantially to the rural community life on Chesapeake Bay.

Orginally, a 2-masted schooner was characterized by the fore-and-aft rig of her principle sails, foresail being somewhat less in area than the mainsail, and both *gaff* sails. Seagoing schooners usually carried square topsails and sometimes a topgallant on the fore. A baldheaded schooner carried no topmasts. A hermaphrodite schooner carried no headsails. The largest 2-masted schooner working on the Bay was *Harriet C. Whitehead,* (120×31×8) with a crew of four handling two topsails and four headsails.

Numerous 3-masted schooners were built on the Bay, but only ten 4-masters. The first 4-master, *William T. Hart* (205×38×20) was built in 1883 at Alexandria, and the last *Anandale* (227×42×22) at Sharptown, Md in 1919. Many of these 4-masters sailed coastwise and to the West Indies carrying phosphate, lumber, animal bones for fertilizer, and logwood for dye and drugs. Pilot schooners were built for speed in pilot service and nefarious offshore trade. Schooner barges (267×46×24) fitted with three short masts, gaff sails and a jib, designed to be towed in fleets of two or three during WWI; built (1918-19) at Quantico, Va.

Between the Civil War and WWII, most localized bulk freight on the Bay was carried by the hundreds of 2-masted schooners; their sailing route favored the western shore with its many sheltered anchorages. By 1930, the Chesapeake schooner fleet had dwindled to a little over 200 in number. The last commercial schooner *Anna & Helen,* perished in 1958 by sinking in Crisfield's harbor. Danish: *skonnert*. See appendix # 138.

BARBER

SCOW

Early 17th-century wills and inventories mention "galliots" and "flats"; numerous advertisements for the sale of these vessels appeared during the 1700s in the *Maryland Gazette* at Annapolis and *Virginia Gazette* at Williamsburg. In the *Alexandria Gazette* of 16 October 1785 one such advertisement read: "A twelve-Hogshead Flat, ceil'd, she has a small Anchor and Cable, a middle Thwart nailed with Spikenails, sealed tight, fastened with four knees, swims low before, her Outside pay'd with Turpentine, two masts, and has a full built stern." Many ads stressed that "they are oak-ceil'd for you to carry ore."

At the time of early settlement on the Bay, there was a need for shoal draft rowboats to carry bulk cargoes such as tobacco hogsheads, hay, bricks, building stone, and sand. Virignia's Eastern Shore relied at first on the Western Shore for shipment of its produce to Europe; thus demanding an economically built ferry called a "galliot." This was an open, shallow, log-built scow with spoon-shaped ends, ketch rigged with two Dutch lateen or sprit sails; they ventured short distances and only with a favorable wind, as there was no centerboard to reduce leeway.

A type used all over the Bay was the economical "flat"...similar in shape to the "tobacco boat." Though originally designed for carrying tobacco, the rectangular hull was altered to have blunt yet curved double-ends; flat-bottom, oak ceilings, open deck with platforms at bow and stern and leeboards on both sides. Sloop- and schooner-rigged with auxiliary sweeps made the *flat* a popular workboat up until the Civil War.

For the first ten months of that War, the Confederates controlled a 22-mile stretch of the Potomac (between Hallowing Point and Aquia Creek, Va) with long-range guns and 20,000 men. Union military engineers built *invasion-scows* to ferry their soldiers across the river from Maryland to drive the rebels out. The vessel was a box-like platformed scow with vertical sides, and a rising bow and stern; easily rowed, towed or poled, carrying 40 men and 2 cannon. Several were built in Alexandria, but used only in practice-trials, as General Lee pulled his soldiers to the Rappahannock on 9 March 1862.

After the War, a third type was designed called a "scow-sloop or-schooner." The rectangular hull was frequently refined to have taper at both ends, flaring sides, some sheer, deep transoms at bow and stern blunt or curved ends, cargo rails, leeboards on both sides, but the bottoms rarely had any fore and aft rocker. There was no fixed pattern, almost anything was acceptable for slow transportation of unpackaged cargo in an economical vessel sailing relatively protected waters of the upper Bay, and estuaries such as the Potomac and James.

Scows were widely employed at Maryland stone quarries at Port Deposit on the Susquehanna and on both sides of the Patapsco River in Baltimore. They served Virginia at granite quarries in Petersburg, Occoquan, Richmond, and Fredericksburg; slate and pyrite at Quantico; sandstone at Aquia; and green sand marl on the Potomac, Rappahannock, Pamunkey and James. Quarries near Georgetown DC, exported granite from Little Falls and Rock Creek. The more enterprising scow-skippers carried cordwood, bricks, railroad ties, and hay from the many tidewater landings. Scows were tough competitors with longboats for the cordwood trade on the Potomac to Washington, and on the James to Richmond.

Lengths of scows ranged from 40′ to 65′; beam from 13′ to 20′; draft from 2′ to 5′. Bulwarks sometimes averaged 3′ amidships. A 60′×20′ scow may have a bowsprit extending 8′, a 55′ mast with two shrouds, a sloop rig carrying 1730 square feet of canvas sails, and one or two leeboards. It would be steered by an 8′ tiller or a wheel with blocks and chains secured to the after end of a huge rudder. Crew was quartered in a 7′×7′ cabin with 6′ headroom. The carrying capacity was 28,000 bricks or 75 deadweight tons.

The last scow-schooner on the Bay was *Morning Star* (65×18×4) built in 1892 at Greys Creek (on Magothy River); general freighting out of Hampton, Va until 1925. The last scow-sloop was *Elsie* (56×14×4) built at Philadelphia in 1874 for carrying Jersey marsh grass (hay); rebuilt 1890, sailed out of Havre de Grace for over 50 years. Dutch: *schouw*. See appendix # 139.

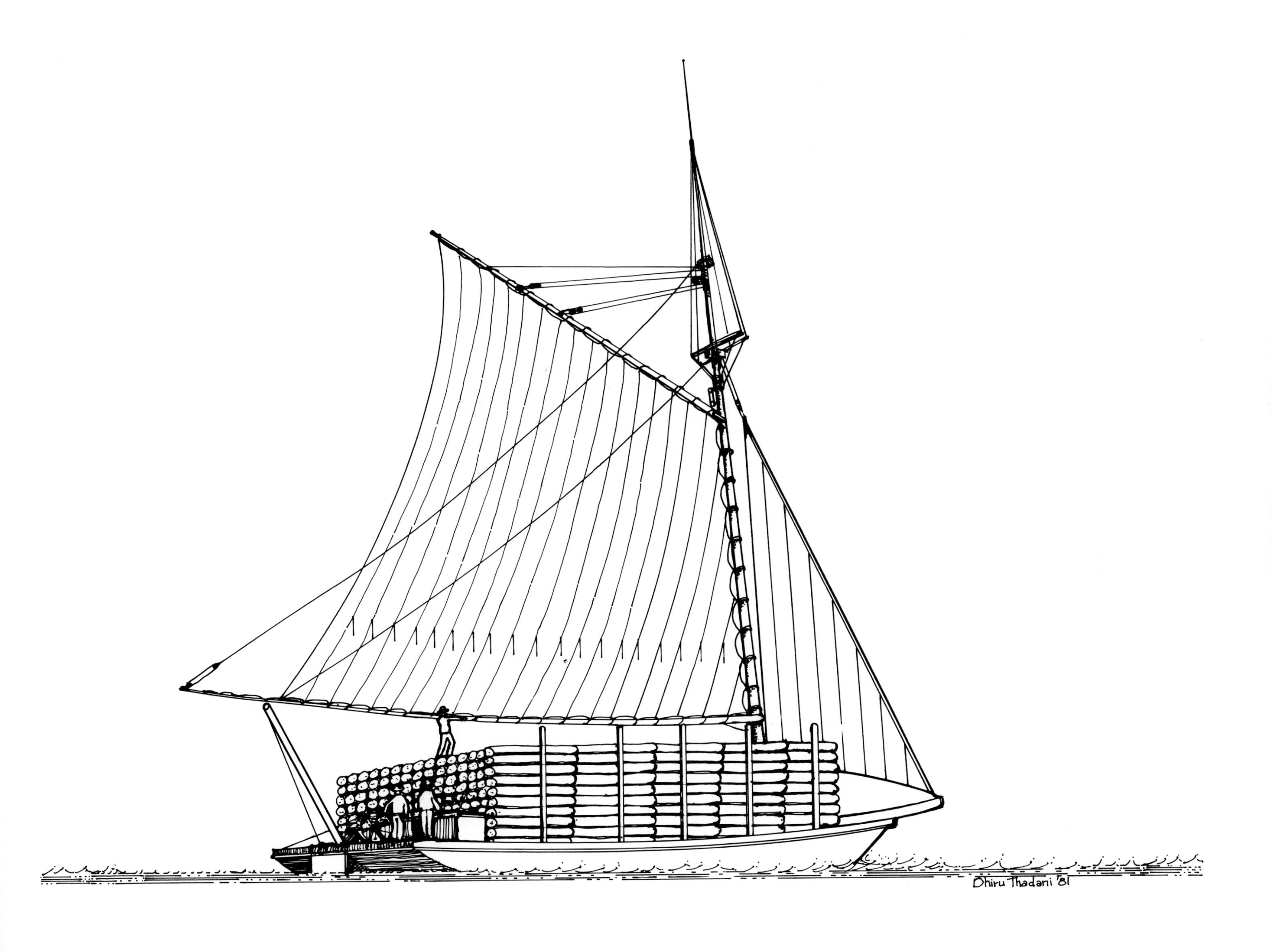
Dhiru Thadani '81

SHAD-GALLEY

The Bay gained national fame for its excellence of shad and herring; huge catches were made for food and fertilizer. A plantation which included a favorable shore for shad fishing was considered to have an asset of real importance, and specialized gear was developed. Where a natural fishery existed, haul seines could be used; the catch pulled up onto the beach. The haul seine is a net set with one end anchored on shore and the other carried by a boat in a great circular sweep out into the river and returning back close to the starting point. The seines were set from a "shad-galley," a large many-oared boat with a large platform in the stern supporting the net. After being set, the net was hauled ashore by horses or hand powered capstans with the fish caught in the bight.

A US Fish Commission report of 1890 notes: "A typical Potomac River shad-seine rowing galley carried about 1220 to 1500 fathoms (7320′ to 9000′) of seine made 30′ deep at the channel (or hauling) end and 12′ deep at the shore end, the mesh being 2½″ to 4″. The boats rowed 20 oars single-banked and, depending on their length, 14 to 24 square-loomed oars, double-banked. (Two opposite oars are pulled by rowers seated on the same thwart.) Nets were carried in the stern and most boats had a net roller on top of the transom.

"A shad-galley was a very long open rowing boat having a long sharp entrance, a short full run to a very wide transom stern. Although this transom was curved, bowed and raked out, the stern post was set nearly upright. The sheer was rather straight and keel long, straight with some drag. The midship section had a slightly rising straight floor, easy bilge and a slight flaring topside. To give longitudinal strength, the boat was braced by a metal 'hogrod' truss passed over the thwarts. The two quarters were free of thwarts to facilitate net storage. Atop a 7′ mast, a kerosene lamp was installed to attract fish.

"The shad galley was no mean rowboat. Lengths were from 40′ accommodating 8 oarsmen to 75′ for 20 oarsmen, maximum beam of 12′ and maximum depth 3′9″. Planking was lapstrake of northern whitecedar. Bent frames, keel, rudder, and deadwood were of white oak. The boat had no centerboard."

Built by Yankee craftsmen who established boatyards on the Potomac soon after the second war for Independence (1812), shad-gallies were modeled after those built on Long Island Sound; being popular in the upper Bay and the larger rivers of the Western Shore for over one and a half centuries.

The Potomac boasted of the largest shad fisheries in the United States. A meticulously kept log of two leather-bound volumes was kept by George Chapman of Charles County, Md, from 1814 to 1824. From it a brief summary of the fishery located at Chapmans Point, about 2 miles upriver from Indian Head wharf follows: "Fishing for shad began in late March lasting until early June. Rowing, setting the nets and seine hauling ashore was done exclusively by Negroes, usually at high slack water (day and night) twice daily including Sundays. Shad sold for about 3¢ to 6¢ each and not by weight. Slaves were rented as seine haulers for about $4 a head, per week. Seine managers for $50/season. Additional wages were paid for Sunday work and no wages for sickness or bad weather. A fishing camp, stable for horses and packing house was located ashore where the men lived. Larger craft using sail and oars transported the catch immediately to Alexandria or the fish were salted into barrels. The complete trip usually took two days, returning home with food, salt, fish barrels, clothing and foul weather gear."

The 1835 *Gazeteer of Virginia* states: "The immense Potomac River fisheries employs 6550 men at 158 landings; 1350 men to operate 135 row-galleys; number of shad taken in one week season totals 22,500,000, using 995,000 bushels of curing salt and 995,000 barrels." This was the peak year for shad-galleys as drift nets were introduced in 1836 and by 1875 there were 3350 in number. Pound nets came into being in 1870, with galleys being used as net-tenders. By 1904, the last shad-galley on the Potomac was hauled ashore at Otterback's fishery, Stoney Point, (near Occoquan) Va. The few based at Havre de Grace died a few years later. Several survivors were restored during early 1900s by the Old Dominion Boat Club at Alexandria for downriver picnics. English: *galeye.*

Basic recipe for planked shad. Fire-up green hickory logs in a dug trench. Nail split-shad to peanut-oil-soaked oak plank; sprinkle with salt/pepper. Lean plank against rack favoring heat; leave for 1 hour; turn board end for end. Baste shad 3 times/hour for 3 hours with sauce (3 pts melted butter & 1 pt lemon juice.)

J. DeGrasse '82

GUNBOAT

By 1800, the United States had a respectable navy, but the quasi-war with France, plus the attitude of Jefferson's administration discouraged any further improvement. All naval vessels were sold by 1801 except ten frigates and a schooner. The period that followed was eventually termed "Jefferson's gunboat mania."

Captain Edward Preble and other naval officers advised the President that small gunboats were an efficient substitute for the larger ships-of-war. It was a gunboat era as vast sums of money were to be saved by this "new policy." Even Bonaparte assembled an enormous fleet of such craft for invasion of England. Russian gunboats trounced a Turkish fleet, sinking many ships-of-the-line. Lack of such craft had severely hampered American operations at Tripoli, where the frigate *Philadelphia* ran aground while trying to perform what was properly a gunboat's mission.

Quoting Jefferson: "at times, when Europe, as well as the United States, shall be at peace...not more than eight of these gunboats should be kept afloat. When Europe is at war, treble that number, to be distributed among our harbors...Only when our country is at war, that the whole number would be in active service. At all times, those gunboats unemployed would be withdrawn into places not exposed to sudden enterprise, hauled up under sheds, covered from sun and weather, and kept in preservation, with little expense from repairs or maintenance."

Commodore Samuel Barron of Hampton, Va wrote Jefferson: "Gunboats...are the proper vessels to afford the most effectual means of defense and annoyance within the rivers of the United States. The small draft of water enables them to take positions as to attack...with impunity, vessels of any size, and are enabled to approach or retire as may best suit, to discomfort their enemy and protect themselves.

"My residence having always been on the Chesapeake Bay enables me to remark more particularly on the effect of gunboats opposed to ships-of-war on the Bay. The Middle Ground, the Horse Shoe, and Willoughby's Point are proper positions for gunboats to repel attempts to enter the Chesapeake. Near each river (James, York, Rappahannock and Potomac) is a flat which affords a safe position to annoy, without fearing the near approach of large ships into that river. Ten or twelve gunboats would be sufficient..."

Captain Thomas Tingey, commandant of the Washington Navy Yard wrote: "The efficacy of gunboats for defense of our coasts, and harbors, is obvious to every militarist..."

During the years 1803-07, Congress authorized construction of 278 gunboats, of which private and naval yards at Norfolk built 21, Baltimore 10, and Washington 9. Frames, planks and masts (spars of all types) were placed into storage with intention of completing the boats in event of war. This bright idea was never put to test...the seasoned premium-grade timbers proved too attractive to Bay builders and were converted into fishing craft.

The few gunboats built for the Bay varied in size; averaging 60′×17′×6′, manned by 25 to 45 men. *Gunboat #5* built at Baltimore by William Price for the Navy (50×17×4) was manned by 3 officers, 15 able seamen and 5 marines. Rigged with a single-masted lateen sail, it was armed with one 24 pounder gun at the bow on a slide. The gun could be trained only ahead; though the slide was pivoted at the forward end, its traverse was limited to 30 degrees. Most of the boats were sharp-sterned; decked with a small hatch abaft the mast and a small trunk cabin aft with a hatch and skylight. With bilge keels they were capable of being hauled ashore with a capstan or "crab," staked out on the beach. Rowing was done with 15′ oars by the crew standing on deck. They were fast sailers; bilge keels acted as leeboards, so they were weatherly in spite of shoal draft. Larger gunboats were built with 2 guns, one forward, one aft, both mounted parallel amidships on what was called a *Hawkins Wheel*—a circular, grooved platform from which guns were pointed in both directions; permitting one gun to fire from either side while the other was being reloaded.

Service aboard these boats was so unpopular that sixteen were publicly auctioned, 12 June 1815 at Portsmouth Navy Yard. "Jefferson's gunboats" became a phrase to summarize an unhappy subject to disrepute the third president. English; *gunne bote.*

Addendum: See the 208 page book *Navy of the US,* compiled by G.F. Emmons in 1853 for other rowing/sailing armed Bay craft.

LONGBOAT

Referred to as the "Potomac Longboat," it was hailed in the *Alexandria Gazette* of 1815, as a "new type of economical vessel being built in the Hunter Shipyard of that town... for any use as required on the river."

For over a century, the longboat was the most popular type of vessel for bulk cargo delivery from Potomac ports to the ever-growing Nation's Capital. The original hermaphrodite schooner rig was 2- or 3- masts; carried gaff sails, no headsails or topsails; leeboards and shallow draft; designed for practical and profitable employment on the more protected waterways of the Bay. A single jib was added during the 1870s.

In the days before central heating and cooking by manufactured gas and electricity became commonplace, wood-burning fireplaces and ranges reigned supreme at Washington, Georgetown, and Alexandria. The quantities of cordwood consumed by residential, commercial, and industrial plants demanded astronomical conveyance facilities from riverside forests to cities' wharves.

For years, large fleets of longboats were employed by firewood companies. As time was of no concern, only sail power was used and careful watch was made by the skipper for every favorable tidal current to help his slow-moving and always over-burdened vessel. The wood was piled so high that the sails were shortened to their cargo reef points and the captain or cook steered mainly by "guess and by God." Returning down river the craft would be loaded with bricks, fertilizer, bagged flour, and general produce. Other upriver payloads were Aquia Creek building stone, Occoquan riprap, and white crystalline sand from the shores of Saint George's Island to glass factories at Georgetown and Alexandria.

President Lincoln's Proclamation 27 April 1861 to blockade Southern states caused the Navy to commandeer all river boats and these little droghers became in great demand for supplying 200,000 men Army of the Potomac at Aquia Creek, and coaling depots at Saint Inigoes, Piney Point, and Belle Plain... though coal was smuggled under darkness to Southern sympathizers. Tandem-towing by Navy tugs proved disastrous as longboats were not designed for towing-stresses.

During the 1890s and early 1900s twenty or more of these vessels could be seen unloading every day at Washington and Alexandria wharves. Generally known as "wood-boats," these craft were so humble in their design and construction that little or nothing of their nature is recorded. Fortunately, Henry Hall in his *Report on the Shipbuilding Industry* described the Potomac River longboat *Union* which he saw at an Alexandria wharf in June 1881; "These craft are peculiar to the relatively quiet waters of the Potomac River when compared to the open and rougher waters of the lower Chesapeake Bay. Generally the longboat is an undecked centerboard schooner with fore and aft sails and a large jib; built of second-rate timber and a minimum of running and standing rigging; measuring from 50′ to 80′ on deck with a 13′ to 15′ beam. It is shallow, flat on the floor, round sides, straight body, and sharp bow, with quarter decks and a cabin aft, drawing only 18″ of water light and 3′ when loaded with 60 to 80 cords of wood or 25,000 bricks."

Though the most lowly of boats, a very colorful paint job enhanced its character. The boats were painted green in a 12″ band along the waist, with a brown stripe above and below it. Above the stripe a 6″ white band to accentuate the sheer. Below, the lower brown stripe, the paint was white or a very light pink, known as "flesh color." The boat's name was painted in black on the stern.

Henry Hall described the method of loading a longboat, "The cordwood is laid fore and aft on the frames until the hold is full. The gunwales are then piled up with sticks laid transversely. The space within is then filled up with 8 foot sticks, laid athwartships as high as convenient."

Cordwood was sawn into 16″ lengths and machine split in several pieces at city wharves by firewood dealers. One hazzard to log handlers was poisonous yellow jacket wasps which were attracted and energized by resins of freshly cut yellow pine.

Henry Hall's epilogue: "Longboats are only fit for quiet waters ... too clumsy for rough seas... a poor man's dump-cart." In spite of his misjudgment, they served for 118 years; the last being the 58′ *Fannie* sailing from Alexandria in 1933. English: *longe bote.*

BARBER

GUNNING SKIFF

This little craft was a sophisticated, highly specialized and well designed skiff for legal gunning of ducks, geese, swans, bobolinks or *reedbirds,* and blackbirds on the shoal waters or *flats* of the Bay. Originally built by the finest marine craftsmen of-the-day; the same men who built gilling skiffs, pungies and bugeyes. There was sufficient room for one man and one gun (first, the flintlock until 1825, followed by the percussion cap, muzzle-loader and finally the breechloader). The gunner would kill enough for his family to "enjoy a mess (meal) of ducks" for one day only. In the early days it was "no duck—no dinner."

The gunning skiff was light, easily rowed, of overall length 16′ to 18′, beam 3½′ to 4′, draft was 2″ unloaded. It was built of ½″ whitecedar or cypress planks, copper riveted to white oak frames and stems, with plank boards running the entire length to reduce friction. Height of sides varied with the expected design load, with a minimum of exposed freeboard (not over 6″) and hardly any sheer. Bow and stern were both sharp to reduce wake drag, and water gurgling noise; a flat-bottom provided stability. Small metal runners were secured to the bottom for wood protection and to aid in skimming over smooth ice using hand-operated ice-creepers. When equipped with a removable sprit sail, a shoving paddle was used as a steering oar.

All sorts of hand-propulsion ("white ash breeze") were used: shoving paddle, hand paddle, sculling oar, and the deep water rowing oar on thole pins. The shoving paddle would slide silently through the water *feathering upon the return* and for poling on hard bottom. Little hand-paddles (20″×6″×½″), used with only slight wrist motion, were preferred when skiffing-to or in close-work near the waterfowl.

Skiff and gun were painted white; even white clothes and hood were preferable,—ducks were not distracted by white colors. Sometimes, a gunner preferred gray-green. The only other color was a small black *sight* placed at the end of the gun barrel to aid in pointing the gun.

With the accelerated prosperity of the Gay Nineties, a demand developed for wholesale duck marketing; satisfied only by mass slaughtering of ducks and geese. Chesapeake Bay waterfowl became nationally associated with epicurean dining, served with wine and Straus waltzes. This gave rise to defiant outlaws with deadly traps; corn baiting, live decoys; lights for night-hunting; swivel, battery and pipe guns with a distorted standard of morality that "God gives us ducks so's we (hunters) can live"...this was encouraged by unprincipled wildfowl commission merchants.

Most market hunters called "ploggers" averaged 10,000 ducks a year with a lifetime total of over 500,000 ducks..."gunning for the gentry" it was called. Sport hunters generally killed only the legal limit in number.

The gunning light was and still is the single most deadly, devastating method ever devised for blinding the fowl; skilled hunters would quietly catch the blinded bird by hand (no shooting); then strangled, tied by the neck and towed behind. Blinding was first caused by use of a candle made of beeswax or spermaceti; replaced by a kerosene flame enclosed in a wooden box with two mirrors forming a "V."

Along with blinding lights came various death-dealing guns. The famous punt gun imported from England (one or two per boat) each weighing between 100 and 180 pounds, length 12′, diameter of bore up to 2″. Recoil shock was absorbed by packing several sacks of sea oats or pine needles in the skiff about the walnut gun stock.

Other types were developed; the three most popular being the *Delaware ducker* built by craftsmen near Philadelphia, about 15′×4′, round-bottom, lapstraked, double-ended, usually painted white and fitted with a small sprit sail. *Patuxent River rail skiff,* built at local yards, about 14′×3′, flat-bottom with sloping sides, double-ended and square-sterned, and painted a "dead grass" color inside and out. The latest and most nefarious type called *Poachers skiff;* built on the Eastern Shore, 14′×4′, square ends, flaring tapered sides and arc-bottom, painted brown. Each type had platforms fore and aft to accommodate a stand-up hunter and a pusher. Push poles have a tripod-like arrangement called "crowfoot" on the end to prevent the pole from sinking in the mud bottom. Other specialized types were: *sneak skiff, ice box, sink box* and the *bushwacker*. See *punt*, page #22.

FLATTIE

A flattie is a sloop-rigged sharpie with a mostly flat-bottom hull. It was originally used for carrying produce on Maryland and Virginia placid tidewater streams; and to a limited extent, in oyster-dredging, crab-scraping and duck-hunting in relatively protected or shoal waters. Before the Civil War the Chesapeake Bay flattie was also called the "Hampton flattie," reflecting its first use on the Bay around Hampton, Va. Flatties were in use on Pamlico and Albemarle Sounds of North Carolina, employed for shoal water fishing and trapping and usually manned by black boatmen...no duck-hunting, or use of guns was allowed by the local white men.

The flattie hull was wide beam with some dead rise aft in the run; it was rigged with a jib-and-gaff mainsail. The mainsail was secured to the gaff with a marling hitch; to the boom with spiral lacing; to the mast lacing was done downward, making one complete lacing on each side alternately. Without a bowsprit, the jib was tacked to the stemhead, a configuration known today as the "knockabout rig." Lengths ranged between 16′ and 40′. A popular standard of dimensions which was followed by many flattie builders: length 27′6″; beam 8′6″; draft at the stern 2′4″. The centerboard increased the draft an additional 3′. The main cargo well (hatch) was about 6′ long and 5′ across with a hatch cover. The open steering hatch aft was about 4′ square.

The planking installation varied as to the builder. Some were cross planked forward and herringbone aft, while others were planked fore-and-aft the whole length of the bottom, with a complete framing system. Keelsons were either laid up with planks or hand hewn in one piece; they were made from longleaf yellow pine which had been soaked for months in a salt brine trench at the boatyard as a wood preservative treatment. Planks and most everything else was of loblolly pine soaked with pitch, with fastenings of black iron.

Chesapeake flatties were created in an effort to produce a wide type of sharpie that would sail well, though they were usually short-canvassed. A flattie's worst point of sailing was to windward in a short sea—true of all burdensome types. A wide flat-bottom hull is often slow when loaded, and, when paying off on a new tack, the boat falls off badly before gathering headway. This led to many capsizings in a fresh breeze, if the handling was careless or slow. The deadrise aft helped to prevent these knockdowns. During the turn of the 19th-century, a more efficient flattie development, called "stick-up rig" appeared in the late 1890s. The rig was striking, consisting of one leg-of-mutton mainsail set on a mast that raked sharply aft. A sprit instead of a boom. There was a short mast in the extreme bow, which raked sharply forward; on this was set a small leg-of-mutton sail (as a jib) sheeted to the cockpit coaming—a very efficient rig. These stick-up rigged flattie skiffs were particularly suitable for weatherliness in a fresh wind, and some were said to be able to go to windward in strong winds under the stick-up sail alone.

The larger flatties were employed as "handscrapers," meaning that they dredged oysters using manually operated "winders," (winches), to haul the dredge. The smaller ones were used for crabbing. Smaller flatties were built up until the 1930s in Coan and Yeocomico Rivers, Va, mainly for crab-scraping at the mouths of these two rivers: of lengths 16′ to 20′, it carried one sprit-rigged sail. A few remain active even today (1981).

When restaurateurs in New York and Philadelphia demanded instant delivery of ducks by-the-thousands, hunters on the lower Eastern Shore would remove their flattie masts and sails and install a seven-barreled 12-gauge battery gun (one flattie at Smith Island had a twelve-barreled 12-gauge battery gun) for profitable slaughtering.

As the boats wore out, sails and masts were removed and the hull converted into lighters to be (gently) towed for transportation of whiskey jugs or large casks filled with fish, oysters, or ducks.

The building centers for smaller craft were (and still are) located from Bishop's Head on Fishing Bay and the neighboring Maryland islands south to and including Accomac County, Va for working on Tangier and Pocomoke Sounds. The larger flatties were built over the entire Bay, and declined in popularity about the turn of the last century, being replaced by the skipjacks. English: *flat.*

BROGAN

During early 1600s, oysters were used as a food only when other supplies failed. Later, when colonists, following the Indians' example, made oysters a regular part of their diet, all one needed to do was to wade or pole a boat of some sort into shoal waters over an oyster bar and rake up as many as desired.

For years it was "every man for himself" oysterwise. Then about 1760, the practice of individual food gathering waned, to be replaced by specialized providers of various life necessities. This led to establishment of a new business—that of the professional oystermen. By 1780, oysters became such a favorite that many inns and taverns specialized in serving them. The boats to supply the markets were log canoes of that period.

Such was the situation when a momentous event occurred, one which was to have a lasting effect on the industry and on its vessels. During the early 1800s a New England schooner came into the Bay, her captain offering to buy all the catch the small oystermen could supply. Oyster beds of Northern States had been exhausted, and the tremendous, virtually untouched beds of the Bay attracted numerous New England skippers. In addition to buying all available local oysters, the Yankees began to "fish" for their own lading using their notorious "dredge," then unknown on the Bay. To compete, Bay canoes gradually were built larger. To prohibit the Northern "foreigners" in schooners equipped with huge dredges from raking up *all their oysters,* both Maryland and Virginia legislatures by 1820 passed laws prohibiting use of *all* dredges, thus protecting Bay tongers.

By this time oyster consumption was shifting from small river communities to Baltimore, Norfolk, and Washington. In 1830, dredging of oysters was approved *only* for Maryland and Virginia residents. Oyster packing houses were established and by 1836, oysters were being shipped by a "line of wagons to Pittsburgh supplying even the West with fresh 6″ to 8″ oysters."

Later, a new practice was inaugurated. Schooner "buy boats" from the North or nearby cities were sailed to the actual oyster grounds to buy the catches of the individual oystermen for something less than wholesale price. In order to get a full wholesale price, the more enterprising oysterman continued to sail his canoe to market. He quickly found that it was too small a boat to carry a profitable load, and that a trip in an open canoe in winter months was hazardous and uncomfortable. A new and even larger type of craft was the remedy that suggested itself.

In its earliest form this new vessel was little more than an enlarged open log canoe with keel, 35′ to 40′ in length, with a tiny cabin forward. As the craft grew in size, a number of alterations took place until a new variation, the "brogan," was evolved. A standard brogan became a large centerboard canoe, usually of 5 logs, from 40′ to 45′ long, having a narrow deck with washboards around an open hatch. A cuddy forward housed two straw-filled bunks and a wood stove. There was a fixed bowsprit; standing rigging with deadeyes supporting a fixed foremast; a smaller removable unstayed mainmast; both sails leg-of-mutton. Invention of deep-water tongs in 1887 by Charles Marsh of Solomons led to substitution of a gaff "square sail" on the foremast, thus permitting the gaff to be used as a derrick boom. The largest of these, *Mary & Virginia,* (54×16×4) was built at Pocomoke City by William Jones in 1885.

In April 1905, George and Robert Barrie wrote: "We passed through a large fleet of brogans off Swan Point Bar (near Rock Hall harbor), two oystermen in each. Instead of using tongs, they use what is called 'patent tongs'; being broader than the former and operated by a rope which draws the rakes together and then is used to hoist them; a small spar with windlass at the foot and a monkey-gaff complete the outfit. The operation consists of one man lowering the open tongs to the bottom; then several jerks on the rope bring the jaws together; then the other man turns the windlass, the tongs come up and the contents are dumped on the culling board."

Every oysterman could handle an axe and adze well enough to hew out a passable canoe or brogan, but competition demanded a larger vessel. Realizing if a brogan were made larger and given more sail area it could easily haul a dredge, some person added a couple of extra wing logs, put a deck on his enlarged dugout, and with that the bugeye was born. Scotch: *brogue.*

BARBER

PUNGY

"The Pongees, or oyster boats... are the most elegant and yacht-like merchant vessels in the world.... It is remarkable that these vessels are intended for the lowest and most degraded offices (carrying manure, oysters, and cordwood): are of elegant and symmetrical proportions." This is an observation made in 1852 by an English naval officer, a Captain MacKinnon, RN, while visiting Baltimore. Bay shipbuilders of the early 1800s modified the forms of a true Baltimore clipper, but still retained the graceful appearance in their newest creation the "pungyboat." Naval architects called the craft a "pungy"; while watermen continued the original name "pungyboat."

It is believed this craft, first designed in the 1840s, was a definite and distinct type; a shallow-draught keel vessel, a schooner rigged with two tall raking masts and a main topmast.

Pungies had full flaring bows, raking stempost and sternpost, long lean run, deep draft aft, flush deck, a log rail except abaft the main rigging where an open quarter rail is fixed, fine lines, designed for swift sailing; and a minimum of standing rigging, with jiggers on the standing part of all halyards.

The pronounced rake aft of the two masts ensured that sails would be lifting rather than depressing when running before the wind. It brought the leeches of the sails nearer to the vertical, and thus the unsupported side of the sail was relieved of the pull exercised on it by the actual weight of the sail. The sail set better and was easier to make. The rake made for efficiency and greater ease in supporting them by shrouds and rigging. (See *bugeye* chapter.)

At the conclusion of the Civil War, the Maryland legislatures, importuned by pungy owners, passed a bill allowing the use of an oyster dredge in the Bay and the Potomac River in waters over 15′ in depth. The pungies were the best of local craft and powerful enough to haul enormous dredges across oyster bottoms. (They were ultimately replaced by the handier, cheaper, shallow-draft bugeyes, and later the skipjacks.) When dredging season closed, pungies turned to general freighting on the Chesapeake. Here they were restricted, for their deep draft would not permit them to sail up shallow rivers where bugeyes and centerboard schooners could sail with ease and rest upright on the bottom at low tide.

Pungies were seaworthy, carrying oysters to New England and influenced the design of down east fishing craft. At the turn of 19th century, pineapple importation from the West Indies to Baltimore was at its peak... Baltimore was known as the greatest pineapple center in the world. The first week in April through July saw many pungies and seagoing schooners racing to the Indies, returning in about 30 days. By 1912, this profitable trade had diminished to only a few vessels. However, records indicate more pungies sailed exclusively on the Bay that year than other types of vessels.

The last pungy engaged in freighting was *Amanda F. Lewis* (67×22×6/8) sailing out of Coan, Va; owned by Eugene Fallin and captained by Gus Rice. During the summers of 1932-7, the author and his sea scouts sailed on this vessel which hauled canned tomatoes, empty cans, lumber, and wheat, from Coan River to and from Baltimore, Norfolk and Washington. "Dirty freight" such as petroleum products, cordwood, or road paving materials were not tolerated aboard; decks scrubbed every morning. Esoterical cooking was demanded as noted in chapter *Vignettes.*

Our 1935 log reads: "15-July, load wheat into the *Lewis* off Kinsale bridge. 16-July, a S wind to Baltimore; return to Coan on 23rd. On 24th, leave for Humphries Railway, Carters Creek, Va. Anchor in Great Wicomico with schooners *Ida May, Federal Hill, Mildred, Minnie & Emma,* and *W. J. Stanford* for 3 days waiting for wind. Arrive at railway on Saturday; no work allowed on Sunday (this place is dead). Monday, 28th, we (scouts) scrape barnacles and sand hull using canvas scraps and beach sand. Baltimore copper paint (fishermens red, $5/gallon) applied by yard workers, as we watch. Return to Coan on Wednesday, 29 July."

Amanda F. Lewis was kept in immaculate condition; no Irish pennants; pointed reef points and stops; and greased spars. She had flesh-colored topsides, bronze-green bends at the sheer, a white rail and beautifully colored trail-boards and stern carving on the transom. A gold ball was carried atop her foremast, crowned with a wooden anchor—the last of the aristocrats of the Bay. Capt' Gus and his beloved *pungyboat* retired in 1939. Old French: *pungere.*

Addendum: In 1982, a replica of the 64′ pungy *Mary and Ellen* (built in 1881 at Baltimore) was built at Deltaville, Va.

BARBER

DORYBOAT

The Potomac River doryboat and her predecessor, the "black-nancy," are the only two small sailing craft with origins on that river; the larger longboat was also a native. The 2-masted, leg-of-mutton rigs of the dory and nancy were developed from foreign-lateen and shallop rigs; otherwise they are the river's true-born children. Both sails were laced to the mast, the foresail being larger than the main, loose-footed with a "spreet" instead of a boom and gaff.

Their quiet and undercover origin traces back to the Civil War; all vessels and boatyards on the Bay were closely watched by the Federal Navy which destroyed hundreds of local craft. As the Potomac was considered the boundary line between the North and the South, the nancies were especially vulnerable. The black-nancies were used for smuggling and necessarily painted or stained black; they were considered to be a "poor-man's boat." Flat bottomed, straight with sides of one plank of local pine or gum in lengths of 18′ to 27′ and with beam usually 1/3 of length, they were always painted brown-black (this being the cheapest paint color). Instead of paint, a good grade of preservative called "East Country tar" was applied to interior and exterior wood. It was distilled from local pitch pine trees and of a brown-black color having a strong pungent odor. This kind of preservative was used on many Bay vessels up until World War II. The smaller boats were cross-planked; larger boats planked fore-and-aft with ribs. It was a completely open boat, with no deck or cabin, a fair sailer with centerboard; generally used for oyster-tonging and crab-scraping. Inexpensive cotton sails were tightly wrapped around the mast while tonging. Immediately following the Civil War, small-boatbuilding prospered especially on the lower Potomac in Maryland. Here hundreds of oystermen in black-nancies tonged and dredged off Maryland's protected shores between Lower Cedar Point and Bretton Bay even during the winter's strong northwest winds. The last nancy was built in 1890, *Brooklyn* (27×10×2) carrying 44 bushels of oysters; sailing out of Saint Patrick's Creek, Md for 25 years.

About 1880, oystermen began to demand a more sophisticated design than the popular black-nancy. A new type on both sides of the river was developed called the "Potomac River doryboat." (This dory had no connection in any respect with the *doree* of the French fishermen on the Gulf of Saint Lawrence or the well-known *banks-dory* of Maine and New England fishermen.) A deadrise model, planked lengthwise with 1″ longleaf yellow pine and a complete set of white oak frames about 18″ on center; this doryboat had local cedar sides that were steamed, twisted and curved to form a rounded surface forward with a moderate sloping bottom forming a wide "V." The heart shaped stern was undercut, sloping upward and rounded, resembling a shield. Large doryboats had cabins. Their width, centerboard, thole pins for rowing and rig reminded one of the black-nancy, but it was a far better sailer, fast, and easily handled for fishing, oyster-tonging and dredging, and for crab-scraping as far upriver as Maryland Point.

Between 400 and 500 doryboats were built in Wicomico, Saint Clements and Bretton Bay estuaries at the turn of the century. The largest and last of these was the *Marie Estelle;* 39′11″ long; built in 1931 by Walter Cheseldine at White's Neck Creek, Md and suitable for carrying 68 bushels of oysters to Washington.

Costing an average of $100 for a boat and $20 for the sails, the doryboat became the most popular of all-purpose craft on the river during the early 1900s. Doryboats were built only in Southern Maryland, though many were sold for work off Tilghman Island and Virginia's Potomac shores.

In contrast to the "pirate color" of black paint or "tar" on the nancy, the doryboat had white sides, the gay stripes of green, red and yellow below the gunwales (rubbingstrake or "bends") from bow to stern. Interior wood surfaces were finished using East Country tar.

The last oystering doryboat, *Shamrock* (30×9×2) worked out of Saint Patrick's Creek, Md until 1931; then converted into a trot-line crabber. In 1970, Capt' Sam Bailey of River Springs, Md restored her to her former glory—the author being her first "captain." French: *d'oree.*

BARBER

BUGEYE

During the Civil War, oystering was practically discontinued in the Bay, because of naval operations. At the conclusion, Maryland legislature, importuned by oystermen, repealed the law of 1820 and passed a bill allowing use of the dredge in the Chesapeake Bay proper in waters over fifteen feet in depth; the same bill prohibited use of steam power. The effect was to assure the longevity of sail on the Bay, to encourage the use of vessels larger than the brogan and eventually to development of the bugeye.

At first bugeyes built of logs called "chunks" ranged from 50′ to 60′ in length. The largest chunk-boat *Louise Travers,* (72×20×6), built in 1896 at Solomons had a 14″ keel 64′ long. The later ones were framed and planked, and measured up to 85′ in length. The bugeye had a round bottom, double-ended hull, with raking stem and sternpost, a straight keel, centerboard, permanent clipper bow, long head, and bowsprit. It had two permanent tall raking masts with foremast placed far forward, setting a jib and triangular foresail and mainsail, the foresail being the larger. Sails, rigging, and hull shape were similar to the brogan, but larger and with a centerboard and a deck. To provide more deck space aft for the main sheet horse and to protect the rudder from damage, J.T. Marsh of Solomons designed a square overhanging platform "duck-tail" on his bugeye *Alexine* in 1880... which was eventually copied by most Bay builders.

Rudders with beautifully carved tillers were the means of steering until about 1892, when Messrs. John C. and Simon Lake (of submarine fame) designed a new and practical gear; a compact wheel axle, gear, and yoke attached to the rudder head. A horse-shoe (pointed skyward) was secured to the after side of the samson post "to encourage fair winds."

Up until 1908, most bugeyes were painted "pungy style" with dark green bends, white rail and "flesh" colored sides. Later, most were painted white with gray bends, with decks apple green or sky blue. A few were painted black, keel to rail, and were suspected of being pirates since that color made them less visible at night.

The rake of a bugeye's (and skipjack's) mast was about 2 inches to the foot for various reasons: (1) Its sail plan was derived from the raking yards of the Arabian lateen rig, simply following an old custom. (2) It made gybing easier. (3 Sails would come down easier "on the run" while off the wind. (4) Hoops would not jamb. (5) The craft worked better to windward as it was easier to get a suit of sails to fit, than on a plumb vertical mast. (6) Pitching and diving were reduced. (7) The foremast halyards could be used for block and tackle lifting, being located directly over that hatch center. (8) It freed the hull's middle section of spars and rigging by placing the foremast well up in the bows, keeping clear of the cabin; also the foresail's center of effort was brought into its proper relation with the whole sail plan.

Brewington lists 5 credible origins of the word "bugeye." His favorite: During the early 1700s Scotch immigrants to the Bay used a vessel of similar hull form for their smuggling called a "bucklar." Comparisons resulted in the name "bugeye."

As a late development in Chesapeake maritime history, the bugeye had few opportunities to become involved in early historical events. It did, however serve as pirate-craft in oyster wars between Maryland and Virginia, and in stealing privately planted and tonger's oysters. More exciting was whiskey smuggling during the Prohibition era (1918-1933).

The bugeye proved sufficiently seaworthy to voyage off-soundings in the pineapple trade to Porto Rico (1885-1910, circa). Of the few bugeyes used in this, one was the 61′ *Mary E. Foble* of Dorchester. For most, there was always plenty of work to do at home dredging and running oysters in fall and winter; hauling lumber, fertilizer, grain, coal, building materials, fruit and vegetables in spring and summer.

Building of bugeyes centered in the villages of Solomons with a total of 58, and Oriole with 55; Somerset County totaled 86. The first chunk bugeye (1867) was the 57′ *Coral* of Somerset; the last (1909) was the 75′ *C.I. Miles* of Oriole. The first framed bugeye (1879) was the 52′ *Carrie* of Solomons, the last (1918) was the 57′ *Anna Florence* of Chester, the largest (1906) *A. von Nyvenheim* (85×24×6) of Champ. The 54′ *Edna B. Lockwood* was restored (1980) by the Chesapeake Bay Maritime Museum sailing out of Saint Michaels.

BARBER

PURSE and STRIKER BOATS

Menhaden are the fish with a hundred names from "alewives" to "yellow-tailed shad," and a hundred uses from fertilizer for farmers to *potage consomme* revered by French chefs. Historian Mark Catesby in 1731 called menhaden: "excellent Sweet Fish, and so excessive fat that Butter is never used in frying... much esteemed by the Inhabitants for their Delicacy." William Byrd of Virginia in 1737 wrote: "Fat back... a small but good fish, as fat as butter. (It) affords a splendid fish when... baked."

Menhaden were originally harvested by haul seining from ashore; then later by purse netting from sailing vessels which were replaced by steam propelled vessels each having two striker and two purse boats; carried aboard in davits.

George Brown Goode in 1887 described the fishing method: "Half the seine, then 280 fathoms long and 100 feet deep was put into each purse boat. The steamer cruises with men at the masthead looking for fish. When a school is raised they put striker-boats (without net) on them, with one man in each; they are quick men with sharp eyes. They row close to the school of fish, observe its course, and by signs they direct crews of the two purse boats (with net) how to set their purse-seine. If the fish get scared, they drive them with white pebbles, which they carry in their boats. If the fish turn to run out of the seine, they throw the pebbles before them, and as they pass through the water the fish turn and swim in an opposite direction. After the fish are surrounded, the purse crew and strikers work together to get the seine around the fish. In sailing vessels the fish (caught in the purse) are hoisted from the net by hand and have boats take the fish from the fishing-grounds to market, while the purse crew stay on the 'grounds' with a separate vessel. Steamers, however, go to the grounds, catch their fish, hoist them aboard by steam and when the day is done take them to the market, and the same men who catch them, discharge them."

Steamers carried the crew, gear, and catch between factory and fishing grounds, and served as a base from which the purse (seine) and striker boats operated when on the grounds. Steamer lengths varied from 100′ to 175′ carrying from 200,000 to 1,000,000 fish.

The purse boat was of rugged, round-hull construction, gunwales, thwarts and ribs of white oak; carvel planked of whitecedar; length from 28′ to 34′; beam 6′ to 7′; draft of 2′ to 3′. Small platforms were built about a foot below the gunwale in both stern and bow ends and extended 2′ to 3′ from the center. Captain and mate occupied the stern platform of their respective craft while directing fishing maneuvers. Each of the two boats had four thwarts; one aft and three forward (of the center of the boat). Half of the total seine was stowed in the stern, forward of the aft thwart (to balance the weight of the oarsmen forward). Equipment included 16′ oars with metal oarlocks, rope, anchors, and bumpers for each end. Steering was accomplished by one oar in a metal oarlock at the stern. Standing oarsmen varied from four to twelve, dependent on the net size.

The striker boat was a small round carvel-bottom boat, with a sharp bow and a square stern built of oak ribs and cedar planking. The midship section rounded, rising floor, a slack bilge, and nearly upright topsides. Owing to its light weight, it rode the sea like a cork. Length 13′; beam 4′ to 5′ and draft 2′; rowed with two 7′ oars by one striker man who stood while rowing.

In 1865, the Bay's first menhaden schooner was a floating-factory from Long Island. In 1867, Elijah Reed of Brookline, Me with two schooners established the first land-based factory at Back River, Va and another in 1874 at Cockrells Creek, Va. By 1900, the Fairport-Fleeton-Reedville harbor had more schooner-traffic than Baltimore.

During the early 1900s, there were 60 to 70 fish-factories in Virginia on or near Cockrells Creek, Dymers Cr, Dividing Cr, Indian Cr, Prentice Cr, Corrotoman R, Reedville, Fleeton, Harborton, Kinsale, Lewisetta, New Point Comfort, Whitestone Point, Tangier Island and six on the ocean side. Maryland had factories on Janes Island near Crisfield, Fishing Island on Manokin River, and at Solomons. In 1981 there remained two active fish reduction plants both at Reedville employing about 30 vessels. English: *purs, striken.*

Recipe for cold smoked menhaden (page # 106). Mix diced fillets with diced boiled potatoes and apples; mix with a little vinegar; chopped chervil, parsley, tarragon and fennel; serve as a salad. Or soak fillets in milk, cut into thin strips and lay upon a mound of diced apples, cucumbers, beetroots and thin slices of peeled lemons; moisten with a bit of vinegar.

Dhiru Thadani '81

POTOMAC ARK

At the beginning of the Civil War, the Atlantic Blockading Squadron imposed a scorched-earth policy on all Chesapeake Bay boats, and especially those on the Potomac River, which was considered as the boundary line between the North and South. Inspection of each and every floating vessel was mandatory and to make sure the job was well-done...those vessels in question were destroyed beyond repair, scuttled and burned...and this went on for almost four years.

At the end of the War, shipbuilding activities suddenly boomed, and particularly flourishing were shipyards along Alexandria's waterfront. Six 3-masted schooners and one 4-masted schooner (the first on the Bay) were built here, in addition to numerous 2-masted schooners and longboats. Most craftsmen working at the many city-based marine railways were New Englanders who found housing ashore unavailable to them because of the continued "Southern detestation of Yankees."

And so a demand for inexpensive houseboats for shipyard workers and professional fishermen was met by the "arkwrights" whose initial and successful effort was the famed and popular "Potomac Ark." Specifications for their standard model called for a scow-like vessel, 20′ long, 10′ wide and a draft of 12″, flat-bottom, flat-sides, square sloping ends with superimposition of one room with ceiling height of seven feet. The ark had Eastern redcedar clapboard siding, red painted standing-seam tinned flat roof, two windows, two doors, lighted by a kerosene lamp or candles, with a coal-fired stove installed for heating and cooking. No engine or sail...only sweeps or poles with a tripodial-end to prevent sinking in the mud. Arks were anchored out or tied to ramshackled piers along the river's edge usually on the western shore, to get protection from cold northwest winds. Secluded inlets such as Battery Cove gave shelter from floods and ice gorges.

Shipyard workers found arks to be convenient lodging when moored near the job. Fishermen discovered arks to be ideal for economical living quarters as well as adequate space for their workshop and barrel storage. Then too, the occupants were free from real estate tax, municipal building codes and health regulations (there were no toilets aboard). Sturgeon fishermen maintained 12 arks in Quantico Creek; 5 were in Mallows Bay for salvage workers on the 212 WWI wooden troopships there until the late 1930s; Gunston Cove had 7 arks used by Eastern Shore eel fishermen, muskrat-trappers and frog-giggers.

By early 1920s, an estimated tax-free 1000 arks lined the Virginia shores from Little Falls to Quantico, having been forced out of Washington's crowded harbor. During winter floods and ice gorges, the arks were brought ashore and jacked-up, resting safely on blocks.

As pollution increased, fishing and shipbuilding decreased, arks were sold-off to gamblers, yacht clubs, bootleggers, floating tomatoe canneries or sawmills down river. Ark colonies grew—the largest being at Bull Town Cove...a small Maryland harbor directly across from Mount Vernon, where 15 more-or-less arks were located from about 1890 through the 1930s. Each ark was engaged in a business catering to passing sailing vessels on their way to-and-from Washington, Georgetown and Alexandria. It became *the friendly meeting place* for all river-folk because of its prime location close to the main river channel.

One ark was a ship's chandlery; others offered general merchandise, food, clothes, haircuts, drugs and medicine, gaming tables, whiskey (rum during winter) and maybe an effeminate social service or two. During the slot-machine era in Southern Maryland (1934-1968), one such ark was packed with these gambling devices. Sympathetic police enforced the law with kindness and toleration. Friendly farmers living on surrounding hills provided an effective bulwark, too, as the Cove was never raided.

During WWII, ark colonies were rejuvenated for sensualistic business and located near military establishments such as the Pentagon, Torpedo Plant, Naval Research Laboratory, Fort Belvoir, Fort Hunt, Fort Washington, Naval Powder Factory at Indian Head, Quantico, and a few were snuggled-away in headwaters of Upper Machodoc Creek near the Naval Proving Grounds at Dahlgren. After that War, US Public Health officials and do-gooders got rid of this auspicious craft. English: *earc.*

N.B. A little male frog being *propositioned* is shown in the lower right hand corner of the drawing on page #57.

J.F. DUNDIN

SHARPIE

Tradition has it that sometime in the early 1870s, a New Haven, Connecticut sharpie named *Frolic* was found adrift on the Bay near Tangier Island. Local boat builders immediately copied the *Frolic* making modifications to suit their needs. For the next fifty years, Tangier Island skiffs resembled the sharpie, though this did not influence the design of the larger oyster boats. Steadiness, reasonable carrying capacity, low building cost, good sailing and rowing qualities were desired. Prior to the arrival of *Frolic,* the log canoe appears to have been the most popular in Chesapeake oyster fisheries, probably because of the ease of handling oysters in the smooth unobstructed interior.

Originally, a sharpie was a one-man, one-masted boat with a maximum length of about 26′. During the 1880s the builders had two standardized lengths: one about 35′, capable of carrying between 150 and 175 bushels of oysters and worked by two men; the other between 26′ and 28′, for carrying about 75 to 100 bushels and usually worked by one man. Both types were equipped with 3 mast-thwarts (or partners) thus permitting the use of one sail (on the center partner) in the stronger winter winds and two masts (in the foremost and the aftermost partners) during other seasons. Although its unstayed masts were a bit larger in diameter than those in other boats having stays, the ease with which masts could be shipped and unshipped was advantageous. Then, too, sharpies were safer as unstayed-masts spill the wind out of the sails quicker in a knockdown.

Sails generally were leg-of-mutton shaped with a sprit boom supported by a snotter rove to the mast. The early boats had the sails laced to the masts, and hoisted by a single part halyard; by the 1890s mast hoops were used. Reefing was effected by a reef band parallel to the luff instead of the boom. Some boats had wooden clubs at the clews, which permitted more sail area.

Because there was no standing rigging and the masts revolved, the sheets could be let go when the boat was running downwind, so that the sails would swing way-forward. In this way the power of the rig could be reduced without the bother of reefing or furling. When the wind was light, oyster tonging was performed while the boat drifted slowly downwind with sails fluttering. The tonger, standing on the side deck or the stern, could tong or nip oysters from a "thin bed" (shallow water) without having to pole or row the sharpie. This was especially true over large shoal areas such as the Tangier and Pocomoke Sounds.

In 1886, C.P. Kunnhardt of New York showed in his book *Small Yachts,* detailed drawings of a 2-masted, gaff-rigged sharpie designed as a terrapin smack (38×9×2) complete with well and cabin. In the late 1800s there were many such craft in the lower Bay, supplying time-honored restaurants as New York's *Louis Sheerys, Delmonicos, Restors,* or the *Waldorf-Astoria;* Philadelphia's *Bookbinders* or the *Bellevue-Stratford;* Washington's *Occidental*...and where terrapin used to be a trademark, Baltimore, the center of Maryland's culinary arts.

Originally the sharpie hull was flat-bottomed, planked athwartships; though in the late 1890s, the V-bottomed hull gradually replaced the flat-bottom. It was long, rather narrow, straight-stemmed, round-sterned and economical to build. Sharpies were surprisingly handsome and a graceful boat in spite of their straight sides, for the sheer was well proportioned and the freeboard low. The sharp raking transom allowed a long balanced rudder of lengths from 4′ to 6′...a typical feature of a sharpie. They were half-decked, as they were narrow craft and inclined to sail on their sides.

Both pivoted long and shallow centerboards, or daggerboards were used, with metal lifting handles; an oyster shell jammed into the trunk wedged the board in place.

Because of the flat-bottom or shallow V-bottom construction, sharpies were unable to stand years of work in exposed waters. For those over 38′ in length, metal tie rods under the mast thwarts reinforced the hull. When weakened and ready for beaching ashore, many were reinforced and transformed into lighters carrying fish, crabs, oysters, ducks, or whiskey jugs in quieter waters; while others during the 1930s were converted into impractical yachts. German: *scharf.*

POUND-NET SCOW

The first colonists neglected to bring from England either efficient fishing gear or knowledge of how to capture the "strange fishes" of the Bay. Spears and hooks became the standard method for a daily catch, followed by small weirs or traps made of "bark of certain trees," deer sinews or a tough kind of marsh grass and reeds. Eventually linen nets were perfected and designed for haul seining.

To increase the size of fish catch, the pound-net for entrapment of fish was unsuccessfully introduced to Virginia's Eastern Shore in 1858 by fishermen from New Jersey. Another attempt was made in 1870 at the mouth of the James River, fishing for shad and alewives; and again in 1875 at Mobjack Bay where tremendous quantities of fish were taken. Mathews County, Va fishermen, being wholly unacquainted with the pound-net, were jealous of the strangers from New Jersey and watched them for several weeks, and after seeing the great number of fish trapped by this new and imported method, at once informed them that they must take their "traps" and leave the Bay, "once-and-for-all." Upon refusal, the Virginians destroyed the stakes and nets; whereby the Jersey fishermen migrated to the more friendly Eastern Shore. By 1880, there were several hundred pound-nets located in the lower Bay. *Commercial Fisheries Review, May 1955* notes more historical details.

A sailing vessel called "pound-net scow" was developed during the late 19th-century for driving poles for support of pound-nets in the construction of fish weirs. The scow was used to carry the poles out to the location of the fish trap site and the poles driven into place from it. For this, the scow carried a small manually operated piledriving rig which could be set up after it came to anchor; the crew set up a pole and then, with the rig, drove it into place. A protective iron cap was secured at the pile top to prevent crushing of wood fibers. Finally, a lighted lantern was hung at the channel end of the traps and one at the shore end.

Pound poles were cut from nearby forests; loblolly pine, longleaf yellow pine, pitch pine, or red oak, and stripped of bark for protection of nets. If used in strong salt water, they were impregnated sometimes with creosote or dead-oil (distilled coal-tar) for protection against teredo worms. By law, poles were to be removed at the end of each fishing season; generally this law was not enforced.

These vessels were decked over without cabins, since they did not stay out overnight. The traps were commonly located close enough to port so that the scows went to and from them in a single working day. Frequently called "stake boats," they had vertically-sided, rectangular hulls with rather short curved rakes at bow and stern. The boats ranged from 25′ upward to 50′ in length and from 6′ to 10′ beam. Both sloop-rigged and cat-rigged versions used a boomed gaff mainsail.

Two unusual features distinguished these scows. (1) A deep slot in the stern was used to pull stakes or poles at the end of the season, which required a rudder hung off-center; a hand-winch for pulling the poles was located over the slot. (2) Two projecting timbers at the bow were secured to carry the stake-driving rig; these timbers also steadied the stake when ready to drive.

The driving rig consisted of two upright timbers and a crosspiece, the driving hammer (a block of cast iron) rode on the uprights, and a block (pulley) on the crosspiece took the manually-operated hammer line. The heels of the two timbers socketed into the projecting timbers at the bow, a foot or so forward of the hull, and the uprights were supported by two light timber stays leading aft to the deck. When driving stakes the boat was moored with four anchors with lines belayed to timber-heads or cleats on each bow and quarter. Pound-poles (or "stakes") were carried fore and aft on deck or on both sides of the hull. The pound-net scow had a large centerboard amidships. In lines, these scows were primitive, having neither sheer, flare, nor rocker. There were two pump boxes, one at each rail with a wooden plunger. These boats were reported to have been quite fast and weatherly, but never sailed in head winds or rough water. After introduction of the internal-combustion engine, the sailing pound-net scow quickly disappeared. Old English: *pund.*

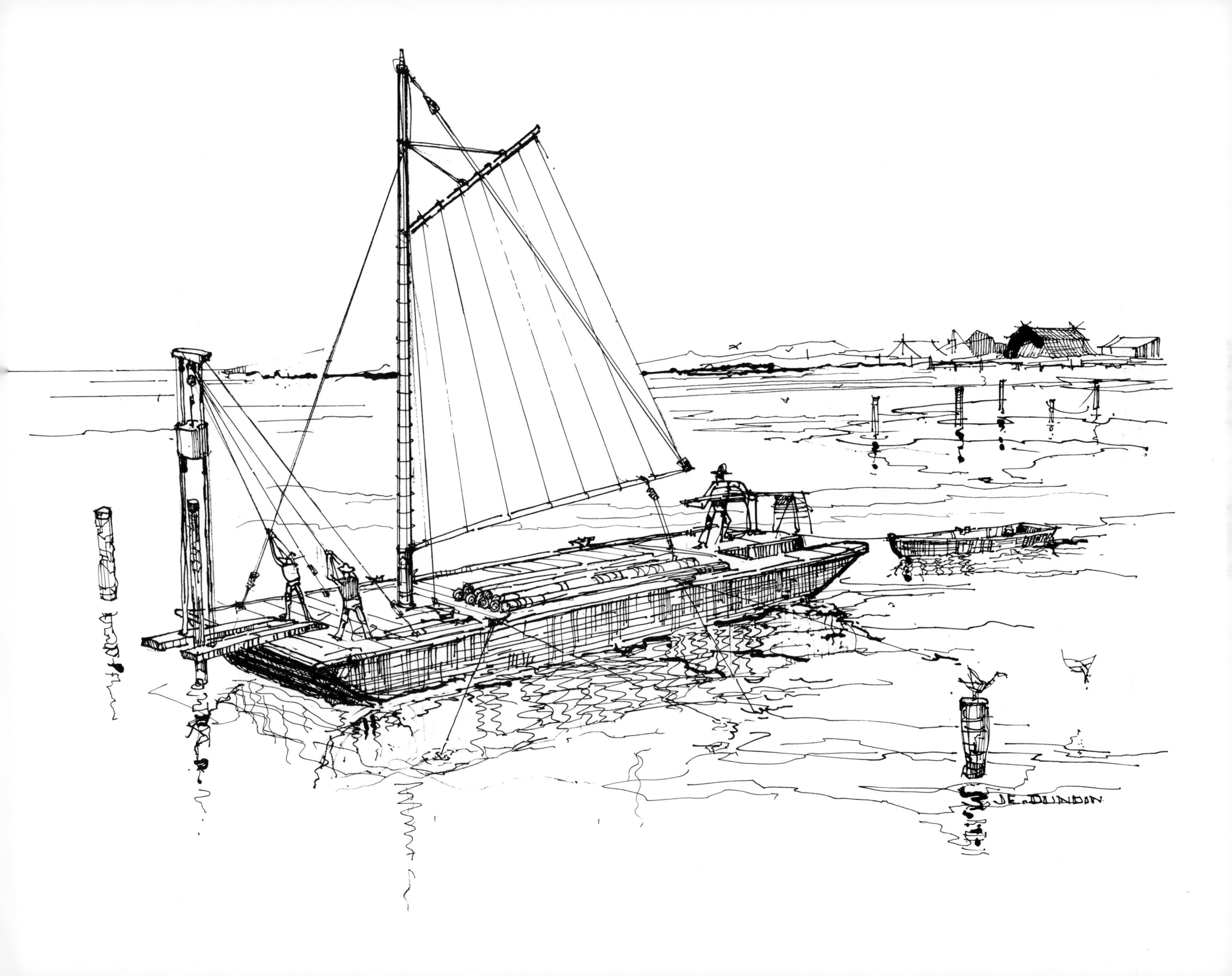
JE. DUNDON

GILL-NET SKIFF

Spearing, hoop nets, and fyke nets were the earliest European methods for catching fish on the Bay, to be followed by seines which were nets used to encircle fish and close all escape routes. The circle of net was pulled smaller and smaller until the trapped fish were concentrated. This became the most important fishing gear until about 1835, when the gill-net was introduced to Bay fishermen by Baltimore linen thread companies to be followed by pound nets in 1870.

A gill-net *gills* fish. Swimming fish come upon a gill net set in the water, and try to swim through the openings. The openings or meshes, are large enough to allow a fish to get its head through but not its body. When a fish tries to back out of the net it is usually caught behind its gill covers, causing anesthesia. The size of mesh determines the size of fish caught, the most popular being shad, striped bass, trout, and catfish. Other native fish were herring, bluefish, hickory shad, croaker, flounder, jumping mullet, spanish mackeral, spot, white and yellow perch.

Fishermen use many methods to fish gill-nets, and they know which method is best for certain fish in certain waters. A *drift-gill net* is set at right angles to, and across the direction of tidal current of larger rivers, and allowed to drift; thus intercepting fish migrating upstream. It is not anchored, and catches more fish than a fixed net. A fisherman in a gill-net skiff periodically lifts portions of the net and checks for captured fish. Drift-gill nets were set at slack high-water at the beginning of an ebb current; the season lasted from early March through mid-May; the men worked day and night every day including Sundays. All estuaries were fished in tidal fresh or brackish-waters with largest catches being made on the Potomac, James, York, and Rappahannock rivers and the upper Bay from Havre de Grace eastward and south to the mouth of the Chester River. An *anchor-gill net* is anchored at both ends, and set in shallow water touching bottom and only when the buoys attached to both ends of the net are visible above water. A *floating-gill net* is anchored at both ends, and set in deeper water supported by floats where the net does not touch bottom and the floats are visible on the surface. A *stake-gill net* is supported at various points along the net by upright wooden stakes. A *run-around-gill net* is set in a semicircular pattern near a school of fish; fishermen "tossing pebbles" frighten the fish into gilling themselves in the meshes: although the net is fished as an encircling gear, the fish are "gilled."

The traditional rowing skiff was used for this work until about 1885 when a "foreign import" took over. The craftsmen in the many boatshops along the Delaware River near Philadelphia built a well designed combination rowing and sailing gill-net skiff. It was noted for fine qualities; easily rowed, towed and sailed in smooth or choppy waters, dry and safe even when heavily loaded. Shipped by railroad to Widewater, Va for Potomac fisheries; to Richmond for fishermen on the Western Shore of Virginia; and to upper Bay fishermen by boat through the Chesapeake and Delaware Canal or the Philadelphia, Baltimore & Washington Railroad. A few were built at Havre de Grace.

Gill-net skiffs were built in lengths from 19′ to 23′; beam 6′ plus with scantling keel and offside centerboard; slack bilged with curved flaring sides and a skeg. They were propelled by a loose-foot spritsail, fitted with four galvanized iron rowlocks, and steered with tiller and rudder. They had short foredecks and side decks tapered toward the stern. The coaming was not carried abaft amidships which enabled nets to be hauled from aft. Whitecedar ¾″ planks were carvel-built, copper-fastened over bent white oak frames at 10″ on center. Keel, deadwood and stem were oak. They were finished "like-a-yacht." Fast sailers in spite of a small 150 square foot sail; in fact a "joy to handle" said Laurence Monroe who worked the Potomac's *Nanjemoy Reach** with a one man crew for nearly a half century. These boats gradually faded out and by 1981 the beautiful gill-net skiffs had disappeared from the Bay.

Another import called "Yankee skiff" of similar size and construction; rowed with oars between thole pins (no sail) by one man who sat far forward. Brought on schooners from Staten Island in the 1870s, these skiffs are still (1981) used for oystering in the lower Bay. English: *gille.*

*The 10 mile stretch between Maryland Pt and Mathias Pt is at right angles to prevailing winds (which are *up* or *down* the river). Sailing vessels usually *reached* through here (Nanjemoy Reach) instead of *tacking* or *running free*.

STURGEON SKIFF

The most productive sturgeon waters on the East Coast were the Delaware and Hudson Rivers. The third was the 50 miles of the James River between Hopewell and Pagan River, centered at Sturgeon Point: known as "Charles City bacon," the greatest catches were off Wards Creek in 68′ depths and Sturgeon Point in depths of 87′. Potomac River was fourth in production, extending 25 miles between Hallowing Point and Riverside, with caviar factories at Liverpool Point.

Fishing was done by two or three men in a 1- or 2-masted boat known as a "sturgeon skiff" (in contradistinction to a shad-galley which required many oarsmen to drag the fish-filled nets). Built lapstrake and carvel of whitecedar; bent white oak frames; wide rail caps, with a low coaming from about amidships forward. The stern supported about 3′ of decking for use in working nets and gear. With length 24′ to 34′ on the keel, a large centerboard, and about 8′ beam, the sturgeon skiff could carry a ton or more of fish.

In heavy weather they worked under foresail alone, at which time the mainmast and sail was struck and stowed. Sand bags were carried as ballast, along with 12′ white ash oars with square balanced looms for rowing in calm weather.

Rigged with sprit sails laced to the mast, both loose footed, and foremast was taller than the main. Some boats carried leg-of-mutton sails with sprit booms and club-ends; sharpie fashion with the mainmast as tall or taller than the foremast.

Most skiffs were rigged with a boomless sprit, to allow an open uncluttered work-space for ease of handling the big fish. Economy of gear and running rigging (omitting gaff and boom) and general handiness of the rig made it a favorite in waters where squalls and sudden shifts of wind were common.

Some of the later sailing skiffs at James River fisheries were fitted with small naptha engines and screw propellers. A few installed side (paddle)-wheels powered by an engine; the wheels were damaged when hauling fish into the boat. Philadelphia boat builders specialized in sturgeon skiffs to work on the ruffled waters in the tidal currents of the Delaware Bay, and in addition shipped them by railroad to Widewater, Va on the Potomac, and to Richmond on the James.

Sturgeon were caught where the river is deepest and narrow with large-mesh, drift gill-nets, usually 1500′ long, 21′ in depth; three nets being secured together depending on the width of the channel. Fishermen went out about 2 or 3 hours before slack water and put their nets overboard. As the fish fed in deep water, the nets were weighted so as to reach the bottom. Wooden buoys, when "bobbing" would cause the fishermen at once to take in that section of the net, haul the fish into the boat and reset the net. If the fish was over 10′ long, he was dragged over on nearby shoals to "lash himself out." When hauled into the boat, they seemed to lose heart and were generally rolled in like a log.

The value of the Atlantic sturgeon is legendary. In 1609, the Virginia ship *The Blessing* returned to England with a shipment of pickled sturgeon where it became a luxury food. The firm, hard, and coarse meat makes good eating, whether baked, barbecued, boiled, dried, fried, pickled or smoked. The eggs which look like buckshot, are processed into well-known and expensive caviar. Isinglass is prepared from the bladder and is used today principally for clarifying wine and other beverages, and to a limited extent in the manufacture of court plaster, special cement and waterproofing compounds.

The "great sturgeon era" of both rivers (James and Potomac) spanned 1870 to 1925 with the average catch of 130,000 pounds yearly. During a typical fishing season (March through August) about 300 fishermen and 100 persons were employed at 20 plants ashore. Equipment included over 250 drift gill-nets, each averaging 31,500 square yards in size. The last active sturgeon fleet was pulled ashore to die in 1926 near Monroe's caviar factory at Liverpool Point, Md on the Potomac River.

Epilogue: The great sturgeons of the Chesapeake estuaries will never return, due to overfishing, pollution, and the dredging and damming of those rivers used for spawning. They were strange appearing fish; armored like the knights of old; records note many were 14′ long weighing almost a ton. Their behavior was sluggish when feeding on the bottom; during spawning they roll, splash and leap up to 7′ from the water. English: *sturgiun*. See appendix #137, and a 5-page history in *This Was Potomac River* by the author.

CRABBING SKIFF

The Eastern Shore has long been noted as a prolific breeder for distinctive models of sailing craft. Though the bugeye, skipjack and log canoe are the best known of all Bay craft, the "crabbing skiff" was the most numerous and well represented by 15 different hull forms and 6 sail rigs...all produced on the Bay between 1880 and 1920.

Usually under 20′ in length (a few were 28′), these boats were found in every waterfront hamlet on both the Western and Eastern Shores of the Bay and estuaries from the Susquehanna Flats to Norfolk. A native waterman began building "his special model" after long experience with local weather conditions and his personal whims. Eventually he developed definite ideas as to what was best for "his" waters which came to be accepted as the preferred local type. However, the highly individualistic Baymen were often not content with the neighborhoods' favorite and so he imported models from other areas. This resulted in a variety of hull forms (and rigs) employed in a single locality, for use by crabbers, oystermen and duck hunters. There was no orderly progression in design-development which may be traced from model-to-model. Flat-bottom, V-bottom, or a combination of both with 1- or 2-masted rigs (on unstayed raking masts) were all in use and appeared to have sprung into existence at about the same time. Probably there were a few with an arc-bottom.

Literally thousands of these skiffs were built, making it almost impossible to accurately identify any one type such as a *Smith Island Skiff,* a *Hooper Island Boat,* or a *Cambridge Sloop,* as all of the 15 recorded models were built "wherever there was a demand." Building was centered in Maryland at Smith Island, Bishops Head, Crisfield, Deal Island, Champ, Oriole, Wyngate and Nanticoke; in Virginia at Saxis, Tangier, Justiceville and Onancock.

When employed for illegal duck hunting, a flat-bottom, double-ended skiff was used, with sails stowed upon approaching the wildfowl flock. Soft shell crabbers using scoop nets preferred flat-bottom, square-sterned boats with leg-of-mutton sail which was wrapped or tied around the mast while the crabber waded along the water's edge with a dip net and towing his skiff, or by standing-in-the-boat quietly rowing or poling. A dip net consisted of a circular bow of iron (about 12″ in diameter) with a cotton mesh bag from 6″ to 8″ deep knit around it, and a wooden handle about 5′ long. Double-ended skiffs were favored by many "polers."

Soft shell crab and terrapin "scraping" (dredging) was the main usage of the popular crabbing skiffs sailing at about one to two knots over the flats (shoals) especially on the lower Eastern Shore. A scrape is a rectangular or triangular iron frame about 3′ wide to which is attached a bag-like pocket of cotton webbing about 3′ to 4′ deep. The bottom scraping-bar does not have teeth, like an oyster dredge. One or two scrapes are dragged over the bottom and taken aboard every few minutes after covering 100 yards or so—the contents (grass, shells, crabs) are sorted over. The season lasts from May through October when skiffs were converted for oyster tonging and duck trapping until spring—thus being worked-all-year-round.

Hard shell crabs were obtained by one man using trot-lines. The lines average about 450 yards in length and are anchored at both ends; made of cotton and baited at intervals of 3′ to 4′ with chunks of fresh or salted beef tripe, eels, hog jowls or ears, or hogchocker fish. The line is slowly hauled hand-over-hand from the bow, or over a roller on the gunwale side of the boat pulling forward at the same time; a short handled wire-scoop is used to transfer the crab (which is holding-on to the bait) into a barrel in the boat. Lines are overhauled 10 to 20 times a day, generally starting shortly after midnight—though crabbers today (1981) work any time of the day or night. A skilled crabber with rhythmic movements of his arms, legs, and body can scull his boat with one hand and scoop crabs with the other hand...and sing at the same time.

Crabbing skiffs are well described by Howard Chapelle in *Yachting* magazine, June and October of 1943; and in a 24-page reprint by the Chesapeake Bay Maritime Museum. French: *esquif.*

Addendum. Chesapeake landings provide over 50% of US crab meat.

a. Lump (back fin)—all highest quality meat from body portion.
b. Flake (regular or white)—all meat from body except lumps.
c. Claw—all meat from the claw appendages.
d. Mixed white (special)—a mixture of lump and flake meat.
e. Deluxe—not an official marketing standard; anything goes.

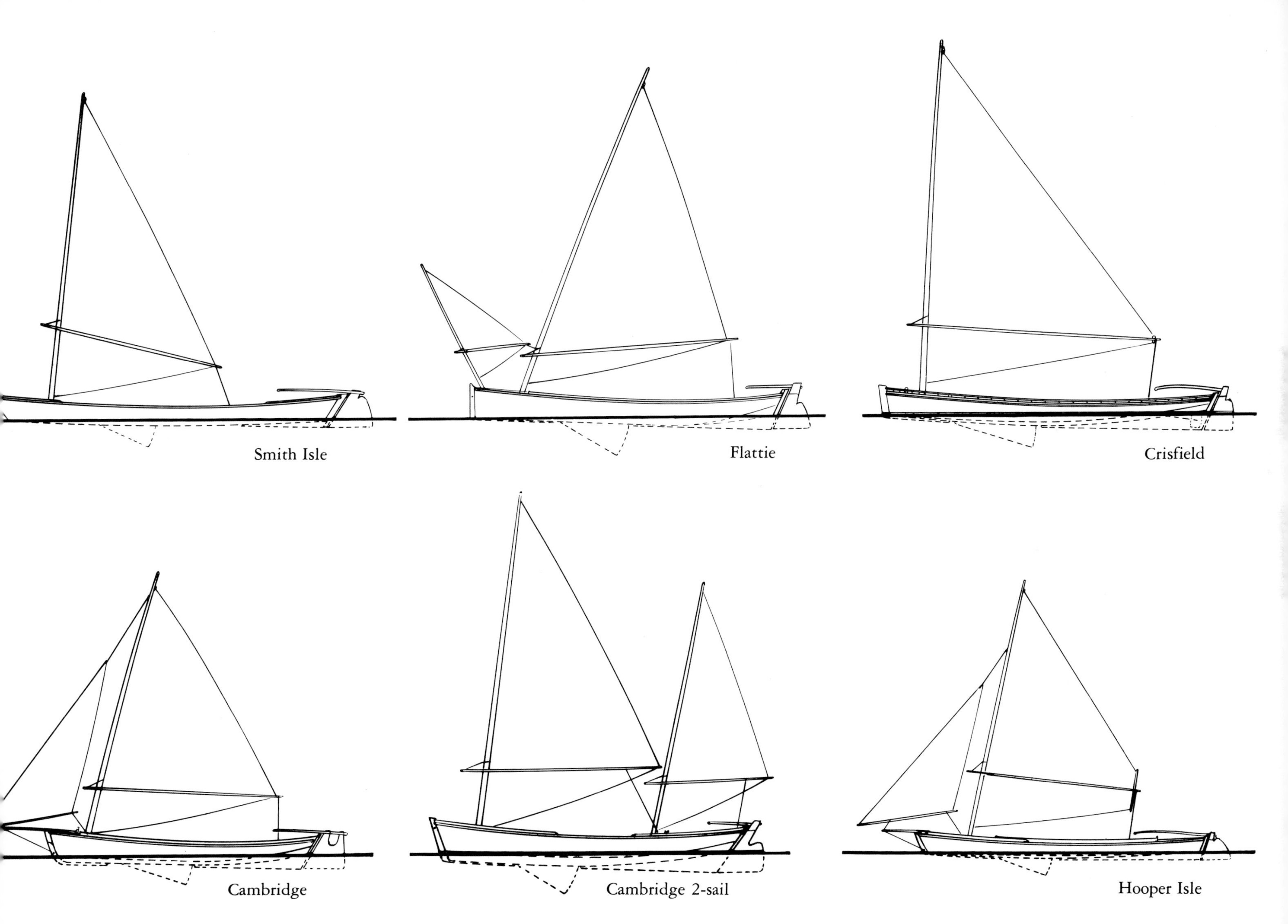
Smith Isle
Flattie
Crisfield
Cambridge
Cambridge 2-sail
Hooper Isle

LIGHTER

During the latter part of the 1800s a special form of lighter or "inglamourous barge" between 45′ and 60′ long was used on the lower Potomac. It was designed to quickly and efficiently transport freshly caught fish to Alexandria, Washington, or Georgetown. The daily catch was shoveled aboard and at a fixed hour a number of the lighters were picked up at various locations by a steam tug and towed to the cities' fish wharves. And there were always a 3- or 4-masted schooner between Lower Cedar Point and Alexandria wanting a "cheap tow" up-river; the lighters being towed astern. On their return trip the lighters were loaded with bricks, salt, building stone, rip-rap rock, any type of bulk or heavy, unspoilable cargo easily available at city wharves.

Lighters were of flatiron shape with a flat-bottom. They were rockered aft only in profile, with little flare to the straight sides and wide at the stern, the greatest beam lay just forward of the transom which was rather upright. A rather sharp bow and raking stem headed a long entrance and short but easy run made for fast towing. Longleaf yellow pine "flitch sawn" for greater strength was generally used in all the building members. No sail or engine power, local maneuvering was provided with one or two long white ash sculling-sweeps used at the stern oarlocks, thole pins, or in the slot with open top on the port side of the transom. When being towed, the lighter was steered with a powerful outboard rudder and tiller.

A small cuddy (cabin) aft provided shelter for the one-man crew who slept on a straw filled canvas mattress alongside an iron stove, fueled by pea-coal. There was no head (toilet), or ports for fresh air. Bilge access amidships was provided through a long hatch with several covers. Strong towing bits were placed forward and on the quarter decks. The boats were coated on the exterior and decks with local pine pitch known as "green-tree tar," instead of paint. The interior had an uncoated natural wooden bottom and ceiling as...osmosis by paint or tar would spoil the fish. These lighters were roughly and strongly built, assembled with extra heavy black iron fastenings. The hundreds of fish lighters built in Alexandria's shipyards measured 52′×16′×6′. Their popular usage up-and-down the river continued until the 1940s.

Thirty-six different species of fish were caught in pound nets during the peak year of 1929 and are listed in order of importance by weight as recorded by the US Bureau of Fisheries for the one hundred year period of 1880-1980. Most of these fish were transported by fish lighters on the Chesapeake Bay and its estuaries:—alewives, squeteague or *sea trout,* croaker, butterfish, shad, striped bass, white perch, catfish, bullheads, flounder, whiting, spot, mackerel, scup, bluefish, black drum, gizzard shad, eels, carp, yellow perch, hickory shad, bonito, king whiting or *kingfish,* red drum, mullet, skates, sea robin, tomcod pike, black bass, sea bass, cobia, spanish mackerel, sunfish, tautog, popano, sturgeon, etc.

Tobacco, molasses and pig iron lighters were used until the early 1900s. They were large, open, flat-bottomed barges, for loading and unloading seagoing vessels wherever shallow water prevented them from coming close to shore. The longest lightering trips on record were on the Patuxent River; pig iron castings in lighters poled from wharves near Muirkirk, 26 miles down-stream to Pig Point (Bristol Landing) where larger vessels waited, anchored in deeper water.

A smaller (not over 20′ long) and shallower-draft boat was used expressly for grain lightering. In this case, the grain carts were horse-driven right out into the shoal water up to the wheel hubs, and the grain sacks hand-passed from the carts into the lighter (which was secured to the cart). When full, the lighter was poled or sculled laboriously out to a schooner anchored in deeper water. The bags were lifted from the lighter by block and tackle supported by a boom and emptied into the larger vessel's hold, where a crewman shoveled the cargo to ensure proper storage—a real back-breaking job. Grain carried to market by sailing ships brought a higher price than grain carried by power vessel as fumes from gasoline or oil tainted and polluted the grain. Though grain is generally transported by truck today, these shallow draft lighters will continue in use so long as pound-netting of fish in the Chesapeake remains profitable. German: *leichter.*

Dhiru Thadani '81

RAM

A 3-masted, schooner-rigged vessel with a wall-sided, flat-bottomed, shovel-sterned, barge-like hull with centerboard, fitted with a clipper bow and spike bowsprit—carrying a bald-headed gaff-rig; length usually 125′ to 135′. This was the largest of all traditional Bay craft, deliberately designed for canal trade; a completely developed type.

During the early 1880s, a vessel was needed to carry large cargoes of rough lumber from forests on the Carolina Sound and lower Chesapeake Bay to industries on Delaware Bay, and the cities of Philadelphia, Baltimore, and Washington. A ship bound to Philadelphia had to pass through the Chesapeake & Delaware Canal, and herein lay the determining factor in this design. Width of the canal locks at that time was 24′, and thus the newly designed vessels had a beam of 23′ and a few inches.

A probable origin of the ram design is noted in John Lyman's uncopyrighted *Log Chips* of March 1952: "J.M.C. Moore copied the lines of the schooner-rigged canal-type craft which carried coal through the Delaware & Raritan Canal and the Schuykill River Canal to Philadelphia." In 1870, Moore migrated to Bethel in Delaware and became superintendent of the Lewisville Marine Railway. Thirteen years later several Schuykill River barges sailed through the Chesapeake & Delaware Canal carrying coal; one vessel, the *Reading Railroad #34,* (106×19×8.6) was refitted at Seaford, (about four miles from Moore's yard). He probably studied the lines of this barge and six years (1889) later built the first ram, *J. Dallas Marvil* (112×23×8); followed by twenty-one more rams from his yard. Building of rams centered in two Eastern Shore localities on the Nanticoke River at Bethel (called Lewisville prior to 1880), and Sharptown, Md, beginning in 1889. Four rams were built at Sharptown, two at Baltimore, one at Pocomoke and one at Madison, Md. The last (1911) and largest, at the Bethel yard was *Granville R. Bacon* (133×32×12) to be chartered mainly for carrying coal from Norfolk to Bermuda. During 1906-7, two 4-masted rams were built; the 155′ *Judge Pennewill* had two centerboards, one forward and one aft.

In their shallow-water trade of lumber from the Carolina Sounds, rams usually returned south with fertilizer or coal. Many entered coastwise work carrying stone, lime, road building materials, lumber, or animal bones for processing into fertilizer. During WWI, *Joseph P. Cooper* (150×28×10) sailed with a hold full of oak barrel staves from New Orleans to Cadiz, Spain in 34 days.

Rams at Bethel were built for specific captains who sold 50% of the shares to repay the building cost. The first ram, *J. Dallas Marvil,* cost $7638 in 1889. One of the last, *Joseph P. Cooper,* cost $20,500 in 1905. Shares in rams were profitable; usually a return of 5% to 20% annually.

Construction time was about 90 days in most cases. Yards averaged 3 to 4 vessels per year; built by approximately 15 men working 10 hours a day and 5 to 6 hours on Saturday. Carpenter's and caulker's wages were 15¢/hour; yard forman 25¢/hour and superintendent Moore paid himself 30¢/hour.

A ram's construction was: keel of white oak, 10″×12″×35′; ribs 8″×8″ @ 18″ on center; flooring 8″×10″; planking 3″ to 4″ thick of longleaf pine; other members comparable in size. Salt was put in the sides, between the flooring and planking; requiring two bushels to fill between frames; up to 2′ the deck. Douglasfir masts shipped by railroad to Baltimore were towed to the yard in four pieces, then hewn to tapered round shape by use of an adze.

Builder J.M.C. Moore, being superstitious, did not allow a keel laying, a launching, or a vessel to leave his shipyard on a Friday. Originally rams were painted black or brick red; by the year 1900, a light gray became the popular color trimmed in white.

Due to low bridges, only a few had topmasts requiring extra crew to handle topsails. No amount of sail could drive this box-like hull beyond a certain slow speed. Three men could easily sail a ram (skipper, mate and cook) with a gasoline donkey engine to handle sails and a powered yawl boat to assist in calm weather.

By 1930, there were 17 of the original 29 at work. The last survivor, *Edwin & Maude* (126.5×23.8×8.8) built in 1900, was renamed *Victory Chimes,* and refitted in 1954 as a cruiseship where she still (1981) sails out of Camden, Maine.

BARBER

SKIPJACK

The last type of working sail vessel developed on the Bay was the skipjack. Maritime authorities indicate this craft was better known as a "two-sail bateau," and that the V-bottom hull was developed from flat-bottom skiffs such as the flattie or the sharpie. Originating on the Eastern Shore; an archaic English word meaning, "upstart," or "inexpensive yet useful servant." The name "bateau" (French for *boat*) was derived from Huguenot boat builders at Ross Neck on the Little Choptank prior to the Revolution.

When first built, bateaux were under 36′ in length, had a *sunk-platform* (self-bailing cockpit) for rowing room, necessary to propel the boat with sweeps in a calm. Hand winches, or "winders" were used for lifting dredges. The change to larger vessels with flush-deck and gasoline-powered winders took place between 1903 and 1910.

The full form and sail shape of the skipjack is attributable not to hydrographic but to economic conditions, the depressed period of the early 1890s and the decline in oyster production at the same time. Almost any waterman could and did build skipjacks. Then, too, they needed a boat larger than the popular sharpie-schooner to carry more cargo. The sharpie was copied with increased beam and a raking mast. Skipjacks were simple in design, requiring no special tools and little hardware, rigging and equipment; hence they were cheap to construct when compared with other vessels. Furthermore, they were inexpensive to operate; one man could sail a skipjack in a pinch, even taking care of the dredge as well in mild weather.

The skipjack's hull was shallow, wide, and V-bottomed, and had a low angle of deadrise, raking stem, and square stern. It was fitted with a centerboard, clipper bow, long head, carved trailboard, and bowsprit. Bottom planking was laid on athwartships; side planking was fore-and-aft with frames. One tall raking mast, set far forward, carried a jib and triangular mainsail; a cabin and sleeping quarters were added around 1890. Standing rigging with deadeyes and hemp lanyards came into use, along with increased size and wider use of power winders. If ballast was required, the many cemeteries close to sinking shores furnished stone tombstones to be fitted tightly next to the centerboard trunk; brick ballast was never used—like blue paint, it was "unlucky."

The first skipjacks, those of the 1890s, were small; they were used near home, selling their catch of oysters or crabs to buy-boats hailing from cities or local wholesale houses. By 1901, the skipjack had developed to a size large enough to carry its own catch to Baltimore, Norfolk and Washington; these were equipped with a cabin complete with straw-filled mattress berths, a wood-coal stove, and kerosene lamps. By 1915, their size peaked; with *Robert L. Webster* (60×20×5.8) built in swamps near Oriole, Md.

Sharply raked masts, as a tradition of the skipjack and bugeye design had numerous advantages; more useable deck space resulted with the mast positioned well forward. The rake located the mainsail's center of effort to its proper position. Mast hoops tend to jamb less than on straight masts. A triangular sail on a raked mast spills wind easily making for steadier sailing. The center-of-effort on the sail moved very little forward when the sail was reefed, thus giving a minimum of lee helm and easier steering. Finally, the main halyard was vertically over the hatchway so that it could be used in hoisting-out oysters or freight stored in the hold. When loaded with oysters, skipjacks had a reputation for speed and weatherliness, although the flat angle of deadrise causes pounding when the boat sailed on the wind with a slight heel. Two-masted double-ended skipjacks with bugeye rig and proportion were built at a few yards south of the Choptank.

Chapelle (when writing a skipjack history for *American Neptune,* October 1944) estimated over one thousand of these craft were built... basically for oystering. After the 1931 ban of dredging in the Potomac River, many skipjacks were left to die in estuarine swamps of Tangier Sound and the Potomac River. By 1981, there were 30 skipjacks licensed to work the few remaining oyster bars on the Chesapeake—the last commercial sailing fleet in the United States. See appendix # 121.

Addendum: In 1981, a dredgeboat was usually manned by a captain and a crew of six; one of the crew doubled as cook. All hands worked on a profit-sharing basis; the boat received one-third of the day's income for maintenance. After fuel and food was paid for, the remainder was divided equally between the captain and crew.

BARBER

LUMBER DROGHER

Because of stiff competition, many 2-masted schooners in Maine and New England were forced out of the coastwise trade during the early 1900s. The Chesapeake Bay offered a haven where they continued in profitable freighting Carolina and Virginia lumber to Washington, Baltimore and Philadelphia. A typical schedule involved sailing light or with coal or fertilizer down the Bay bound to a lumber port. On the way to Carolina the schooner would go through the Albemarle and Chesapeake Canal and then traverse the Carolina Sounds to her destination, returning home loaded with lumber. These down-east vessels had a solid chunky appearance, and differed completely from the sleeker Bay-built schooners; built by shipwrights accustomed to turning out deepwater ships for coastwise and offshore trade which demanded heavily-built vessels.

These schooners averaged a cargo of 100,000 board feet of rough lumber; longleaf yellow pine for structural timbers and shortleaf for general building purposes. Occasionally they carried other woods: red oak piling, white oak barrel staves, and loblolly pine for pulpwood and cordwood. Steamers from the West Coast brought Douglasfir; laths of Sitka spruce from British Columbia; red spruce from Maine and other woods to Baltimore or Norfolk; here the lumber was loaded aboard sailing droghers for delivery to Bay ports.

Cargoes were usually handled by the crews aboard the vessels rather than longshoremen. Lumber was taken over-the-rail and stowed directly from shore-based sawmills; then discharged back over-the-rail at the unloading port. Long pieces of timber were loaded through "lumber ports" (an opening in the hull just below the hawse pipe.)

The lumber was of standard sizes and because of its trimmed edges, it stowed well both in the hold and as a deckload. It was laid fore and aft, beginning in the hold. Once that was full, the hatches were clamped on and covered with tarpaulins, and the deckload started again being laid fore and aft up to the height of the bulwarks. Above them, however, the next tier of boards was laid athwartships projecting out several feet beyond the sides of the schooner between the fore and main mast rigging. The next tier was then laid fore-and-aft, beginning at the center line, and from then on the tiers were stowed alternately fore-and-aft and athwartships until the deckload had risen to a height of 4′ or 5′ above the main rail, "winged out" 3′ or more beyond the hull on each side.

No positive lashing was possible, and other than the alternate direction of the tiers, the only fastening ever given were a few spikes driven at random down through top courses of boards, the last tier having always been laid athwartships. There was always anxiety, particularly in winter. Spray froze in the crevices and in bad weather the vessel could get iced up to a dangerous degree. There are very few records noting that part of deckload being lost; the vessel would not sink because the wood acting as flotation, and the trips were relatively short and the vessel was not driven hard.

Loading a lumber drogher was slow and painful as the boards had to be handled one at a time, and before long, uncalloused hands became raw from the splinters. Gloves were useless and expensive as they wore through in a few hours, and it was simply a matter of endurance until hands became sufficiently calloused. In the meanwhile liberal applications of grease (usually mast slush) and wrappings of old rags helped to ease the pain.

Difficulties in loading of lumber were experienced on wharves at Salisbury (Wicomico R, Md) and Walkertown (Mattaponi R, Va) because of exceptional spring tides ranging 3.6 and 4.5 feet respectively.

During the early 20th-century, at least twenty New England lumber droghers earned their keep on the Bay. The well known 2-masted schooner *Robert McClintock* (96×27×8) operated out of Baltimore as a lumber drogher for 50 years. Built at Norwalk, Connecticut in 1858, she came to the Bay in 1892. She was heavily built, fitted with fore- and main-topmasts, carrying a crew of seven; her cargo was heavy timbers, railroad ties and iron rails. Converted to a diesel barge in 1941 and during WWII, she went into the Caribbean trade.

The last was *Maine* (105×28×8.5) built in 1886 at Bath, Maine. She migrated to the Bay in 1913 under the ownership of Mary A. Carter of Washington, matriarch of one of the largest "lumber families" in the tidewater area. This schooner was retired in 1945 at Baltimore after delivering a load of lumber from North Carolina— a useful life of 59 years. Dutch: *drog(h)er.*

R.T. MILLER
'82

THE GREAT FOREST

Even before the days of the Armada, England saw in the New World an opportunity for relief from dependence on the Baltic for masts, spars, and naval stores. Though many European voyagers approached America with minds full of prospects of sudden wealth from gold, they recognized the needs of England's shipping as an argument for establishing colonies. "If we may injoy any large Territorie of apt soyle, we might so use the matter, as we should not depend on Eastlande for flax, pitch, tarre, mastes, etc.," wrote a gentleman interested in Virginia, about 1580. The same idea was expressed in the writings of Gilbert, Raleigh, John Smith, and nearly every Englishman who described his American impressions at the time. During the last years of Queen Elizabeth's reign, the timber phase of the problem also came into prominence, for the depletion of England's forests had begun to alarm the Navy, and men saw that America could furnish substitutes for English oak as well as Baltic masts. To relieve "the great and pitiful waste of our English woods... we may help ourselves out of Virginia," suggested a writer in 1615. Seven years earlier, the political value of such a supply as a cause for establishing Virginia was suggested in the words of one Strachey:

"Nor lett any man suppose that materials of so good a navie as may be framed for planckes, masts, pitch, and tarre... are of no value, or not worthy the exposure of a colonie (Virginia) for politique endes to be established there, since Muscovia (Russia) and Polonia (Poland) doe yearlie receive manie thowsandes (of English currency) for pitch, tarre, soap ashes, resin, flax, cordage, sturgeon, masts, yardes, waynscot, firrs, glassie, and the like."

It is small wonder that the forests of America roused these considerations in Englishmen who saw their country totally dependent on foreigners and especially the New World for many of the essentials of sea power. In North America, the Atlantic coast presented an almost unbroken forest from Labrador to Mexico, and Chesapeake Bay forests were the most desirable... with trees native to the north and the south.

The first cargo of masts (and sassafras roots), if not of timber of any kind, from the colonies was a cargo of "fower score" masts from Virginia in 1609 in "a ship of 300 tonne burthen called the *Starre* (sent thither... upon purpose fitted, and prepared with scupper holes to take in masts)." The English commented on the large size of the masts, which were so large that they had to be cut down to fit the vessel's hold.

Father Andrew White, S.J. described the forests of 1634: "Fine groves of trees appear, not chocked with thorns or undergrowth, but growing at intervals as if planted by the hand of man, so that you can drive a four-horse carriage wherever you choose through the midst of the trees. The many hickories, the oaks, so straight and tall that beams sixty feet long and two and a half feet wide can be made of them. The cypress trees, growing to 80 feet high before that have any branches, and three men with arms extended can barely reach around the trunks. I speak of pine, laurel, sassafras and other trees which yielded balsam and fragrant gums, trees useful in every way, for building, shipbuilding, for making planckes, pitch, tar, turpentine, sinegma (ginseng), perfumes and plaster."

The tidewater country of Delaware, Maryland, and Virginia was covered with large, tall trees suitable for shipbuilding; the excellence of the timber was repeatedly mentioned in reports of the early discoverers, thus attracting the King's mast surveyors. The dense and continuous forests on both Eastern and Western shores contained an enormous supply of many species of trees, generally with straight trunks, although yielding a great deal of usable crooked timber.

For over three hundred years, the Great Forest of the Chesapeake Country furnished thousands of sailing vessels continuous employment in transportation of rough or "undressed" lumber, cooperage (casks, barrels, etc.), veneers for baskets, pulpwood, bark for uses in tanning, wharf piles, railroad ties, millwork and veneer, fence posts, shingles, laths, and cordwood. By the mid-1800s most of the original trees were cut and used for naval stores or shipbuilding.

Floating wood-fired sawmills were in widespread use until the early 1900s. Originally the best trees suited for a specific purpose were cut; of the 97 available species, only 26 were used for shipbuilding and are described in the Appendix.

THE ROYAL NAVY established in 1685 the title "Surveyor General of His Majesty's Woods" for their marine inspectors to grade standing trees for use as shipbuilding timber. Written reports by those men assigned to the Chesapeake Bay country were:

1. Oaks growing in a warm dry climate are harder and more compact, and are less subject to rot than those in temperate climates. Oaks between sixteen and twenty inches in diameter are the most profitable. (Marylanders hid the best oak from the surveyors for their cooper friends to make barrels for port and beer.)

2. Trees growing in the margin of a forest or isolated are harder timber and of better quality; making excellent knees.

3. Trees in the middle of a forest are not so hard, but are of a long body and straight grain; the best for planks.

4. Trees growing exposed to the east, though subject to be crooked, are very hard and very durable.

5. Trees growing exposed to the west or the setting sun are less hard than those of the contrary exposure.

6. Trees of a northern exposure have a larger and taller growth, though of a softer wood.

7. Where part of the top branches are dead, this is a sign of rottenness at the heart.

8. Large and deep fissures in the bark indicate internal weakness.

9. If the bark is covered with moss or mushrooms, the interior is damaged by rot.

10. A tree is of good quality if all the leaves are green continuously until late fall; and the bark is fine, clear and level from the ground up to the large limbs.

11. If sap distills through the pores of the bark, the tree is dying.

THE KING'S SURVEYORS standards used for cutting, evaluation and protection of shipbuilding woods were:

1. The color of cut pine should be a uniform clear yellow; concentric circles of the body of the tree even with alternate layers of a brilliant yellow; full of pitch or resin. And a minimum of fissures or knots.

2. Trees should be cut between the middle of September and the following middle of April. This wood should be placed under a dry shade as soon as hewed for use, or put into a basin or trough dug into the ground and filled continuously with strong salt water or brine...for a minimum of six months.

3. Advise the shipbuilder to build a roof-over his vessel under construction to protect the timbers from sun, snow, and rain; and to leave off a few planks until the vessel is ready for launching, in order to allow a free passage of air into the hold.

Epilogue. To many thinking men during colonial days, it became evident that the Bay forest resources were rapidly and wastefully being depleted. All of them knew that westward and northward great timber reserves still existed. Rarely was their attitude that of "Woodman, spare that tree," but yet with the memory of England's sad plight still fresh in their minds they failed in stopping the indiscriminate felling of trees and expressed no alarm. Their militant and unremitting attacks upon one of the finest forests in America has been successfully continued for centuries resulting in the destruction of living evidence of a prized American heritage. It is sad.

Addendum. The average life of a Bay workboat was 25 years; about one ton of iron (for bracing, bolts, anchors, etc.) was required for each 100 tons of shipping. Though some of this metal was imported from Europe, the major portion was supplied by the local charcoal iron industry, which consumed 8 cords of hardwood for every ton of "knobbled iron" produced for shipbuilding.

SHIPBUILDING

Prologue. The first sailing vessel in North America was built in 1562 by Frenchmen on St. John River, Canada. The first built by Englishmen was the pinnace Virginia *(38 × 13 × 6) on Kennebec River, Maine in 1607.*

When Lord Baltimore's colonists reached Chesapeake Bay in 1634, the shipbuilding industry had already been well established. Twenty-seven years before, when Virginia colonists founded Jamestown, they put together a shallop which had been transported from England in knockdown form. One of the Virginia Company's main objectives was production of naval stores, ship timbers, and vessels for export. Members of the prestigious Shipwright Guild (chartered in 1605 by King James to supervise shipbuilding in England were sent over in 1610.

Vessels had been built on both shores of Virginia, and as fur traders pushed northward into what was to become Maryland one of them, William Claiborne, had setup a shipyard on Kent Island. Here in 1631, William Paine built the pinnace *Long Tayle,* the first boat built solely on the Bay.

Three years later, Lord Baltimore's colony was established on the Western shore at Saint Mary's; the settler's first act was to assemble a "barge which was brought in pieces out of England." The inferior quality of this boat and the difficulty in chartering vessels from Virginians, caused Leonard Calvert to write his brother in England: "you must cause boates and hands to be procured of your owne here and not put yourselfe to hyer them for that will eat you out of all your profits and even your principall..." Every settler was advised to bring from England "necessaries for a boat of 3 or 4 Tunnes; as Spikes, Nayles, Pitch, Tarre, Ocone (oakum), Canvis for a Sayle, Ropes, Anchor, Iron for the Ruther (rudder), and as servants to include a "boat-wright."

It was not long before the colonists realized that land along the Bay offered many types of wood suitable for boat building; "The Timber of these parts is very good, and in abundance," states an early account, and continuing, "it is useful for building of ships...and brave ships may be built without requiring any materialls from other parts. Masts for ships the woods will afford plentifully." Actually there was little need for Bay colonists to build or own large ocean going vessels. Their chief product, tobacco, was in such demand in Europe that English and Dutch merchants were only too glad to send their vessels loaded with manufactured goods for a return trip of tobacco. One small and specialized group of colonists, the Indian traders, required sailing and rowing craft of smaller size for extended trips up the river to their customer's villages. Builders of small boats were gradually established on nearly all the peninsulas jutting out from the woodlands of both provinces.

Construction of large vessels on the Bay began during the last half of the 17th-century, following a series of catastrophes in Europe that reduced the number of vessels coming to the Chesapeake. This shortage of bottoms plus a series of subsidy acts by Parliament made ship-owning profitable, particularly if they were home-built. Hundreds of English axmen, sawyers, adzmen, and augermen emigrated to the Bay.

By 1697 a census of vessels built since 1689 indicated that Bay shipbuilding industry was on a firm foundation. Unfortunately, exact yard locations were not recorded. While small craft still dominated in numbers, seagoing vessels as large as 450 tons, such as pinks and brigantines were being built for English owners; sloops and shallops for local owners. Lists indicate that all rigging, iron, sails, and even the sailmakers and carpenters, came from England.

The Peace of Utrecht, signed in 1713, closed Queen Anne's War and England was given territories in Canada, the West Indies, and the Mediterranean; and the right to supply slaves to Spanish colonies in South America. This opened new markets not too far distant from the Bay, markets which needed the lumber, iron, tobacco, grain, barrel staves, pitch, and salted meats produced on the Bay to be paid for with rum, sugar, molasses, cocoa, indigo, wines and coffee the Bay needed. Other incentives were the growing Atlantic slave trade, smuggling and privateerings—all demanding smaller vessels to engage in intercolonial and West Indies traffic. In consequence, Bay builders catered to the demand for ships with speed, maneuverability, and ease of escaping capture thus resulting in high profits. This developed the clipper-schooners that became famous during the Revolution as "Virginia-built schooners," and at the peak of their development during the War of 1812, as "Baltimore clippers."

Shipbuilding became a widespread industry, as all yards (during early 1800s) had the combined advantages of deep water and vast quantities of suitable timber nearby for the construction of small and large craft. The greatest difficulty seems to have been to find skilled labor, but by importing English shipwrights and training apprentices this problem was gradually overcome. The fact that Potomac River yards had more marine artisans than any other river on the East Coast aided in the site selection for establishment of the new Capital City in 1790 and the Washington Navy Yard in 1799.

Secretary of Navy Benjamin Stoddert wrote to General Washington stating: "No place farther south will admit of the same degree of security against the enemy. No place to the northward or eastward will afford timber so good, so cheap, or in such abundance. I might add all other materials for building and arming ships." With each of three invasions on the Bay by the British fleet in 1755, 1776 and 1814, their ships returned home loaded to the gunwales with valuable ship timbers.

For over three centuries the Chesapeake has been particularly suited for wooden shipbuilding. Timber was at hand in great quantity and was of good quality. Though the hamlets and villages in the area were not large, many of them supported two or three shipyards, each capable of building vessels up to about 100′ on deck. Labor was cheap and not wholly dependent on the yards for a living; the workmen partly sustained themselves through farming or fishing. Thus workmen would remain close-to-home when the yards were inactive so that the ship-building yards were not permanently abandoned as a local industry in time of economic depression.

Industries supportive of the shipbuilding trade were relatively close at hand in the Chesapeake country. Iron fastenings and fittings, flax sailcloth, wooden blocks, caulking material, cordage, and tar could be had at nearby sources. Bladensburg, Georgetown, Alexandria, Annapolis, Baltimore, and Norfolk boasted of ropewalks, sailmakers, and blockmakers. Even Washington had 3 ropewalks by 1814.

The Navy Yard purchased the best stands of oak, pine, cedar and cypress on the Bay to insure a source of ship timber. The commercial shipyards of New York and New England sent their buyers here to scour the forests for suitable timber for frames, stems, hooks, and knees. These agents furnished Bay shipbuilders with rough moulds to which timbers were shaped when hewn in the woods, then dragged by oxen to their yards, and finally shipped by sail to Northern builders' yards. Thus the frames of many New England Clippers of the 1850s came out of Maryland and Virginia woods. After the Civil War, the shipyards on the Bay by experience knew exactly what was wanted, and furnished partially-finished frames for complete vessels to Yankee shipbuilders. Oak and yellow pines formed into rafts were poled down the estuaries to nearby mills and yards for planking, decking, and spars.

Of the thousands of wooden sailing vessels built in the Bay shipyards, the two largest vessels were *Minnesota,* a 44-gun screw frigate (250×52×24) of 3200 tons built at the Washington Navy Yard in 1855; and *Anandale,* a 4-masted schooner (227×43×23) of 1630 tons built by Alonzo Conley in 1919 at Sharptown, Md.

The Civil War inflicted almost total disaster to the Bay shipbuilding business, inasmuch as the Federal Navy systematically destroyed many floating craft and kept *all* builders under strict surveillance. Following the War, river traffic increased tremendously, encouraging watermen to work at fishing and boat building. The building of seagoing vessels gradually faded out, to the advantage of the smaller yards which continued building for farmers, fishermen, and oystermen. The years 1870 to 1920 were "boom-times for boat builders on the Chesapeake" which is best described by Henry Hall in the appendix of this book.

During the twenty or thirty years prior to WWII and with the increase in the use of the internal combustion engine, most of the yards on the Bay gradually lost their craftsmen skilled in wooden boatbuilding. After that War, a few wooden boatyards continued to remain in business, their output chiefly being pleasure boats or making repairs to small commercial craft. Most watermen still build skiffs for themselves and sometimes perhaps a few for sale. This practice continues to the present time; however, most of the work has lost all semblance of the original character.

MARITIME ARTISANS

Accounts from Chesapeake shipyards over a period of two centuries show 21 trades directly involved in the building of a sailing vessel. Shipwright related trades received approximately 45% of the total expenditure. Cordage was second largest with 21%, and iron at 16%. Because some merchants used old sails on hand while others imported new ones from New England or Europe, the percentage for sails varied between 2 and 14%. The joiners bill accounted for 2%; small boats and barrels at 2%, and 1 to 2% each for blocks and painting. Other accounts received, varied up to 8%.

A typical shipyard never employed a naval architect (probably never heard of one)...as wooden half-models were generally used. Usually the yard was composed of one large building with one railway or side-launching ramp, and frequently workers of the same family (brothers, sons and cousins) with each having his own specialty. Small yards had only an uncovered area alongside a tidal swamp; launching only on a full moon at spring tide. During colonial and federal times, sails, cordage, and paint were imported from England.

Tasks which called for specialized tools in the hands of exacting craftsmen were gradually replaced by machines whose products were sold at big-city chandleries or lumber yards. Eventually all that became necessary to build a boat was to have a dedicated shipwright with practical experience and the ability to organize the various trades...resulting in a happy launching reinforced by the traditional christening and guzzling of dark West Indian rum.

The large shipyards at Baltimore, Norfolk, Newport News, and Alexandria had several railways complete with lumber sheds, loft buildings, mill shop, paint and treenail shop, blacksmith and machine shop, and a joiner with a carving shop. The typical small yard was composed of 3 or 4 men who "did everything" except sewing sails.

A description of the specialists, their work, and their predecessors work from colonial days to the mid-twentieth century follows:

Shipwright. English maritime trade guilds dictated that the *shipwright* perform all work on structural timbers of the hull. The ship's *carpenter* did the non-structural work leaving the "cosmetic" finishing work to the *joiner*. However, in small yards, the *boatbuilder* did everything even the caulking, rigging and painting.

The master shipwright in larger yards made the plan of the ship, prepared the timber, organized and carried out the construction work, and supervised the launching. He was the shipyard foreman; if something went wrong—it was his fault. He knew exactly what type of tool was to be used for what purpose such as the axe, adze, hammer, maul, chisel, gouge, caulking iron, mallet, pitch ladle, treenail maker, auger, plane, clamp, screw driver, cramp, puller, scraper, punch, etc.

Logger. The master shipwright went into the forest and selected the trees, a contract would be drawn up with the land owner, and arrangements made with a logger for felling, lopping, and carting the logs to the shipyard. A felling axe was used for timber cutting; a topping axe for lopping; a two-handed crosscut saw used for cutting in the woods, and a heavy hatchet for trimming. Horse or oxen pulling a *pair of wheels* transported the timbers to the nearby water's edge. Rafts were made by the logger and the timbers floated to the shipyard.

Barker. At the shipyard, the tree bark (especially white oak) was split by a barker with a barking-axe, carefully lifted out, stacked and dried, and eventually ground into a powder for use in a solution for tanning leather and preserving sails.

Sawyer. Sawyers worked in pairs (one in a dug-pit and one on the natural grade level) with the senior member called *tiller-man* on top. In the pit was the *box-man* wearing a broad-brimmed hat for protection from sawdust. Sawing was done with pitsaws in a sawpit at the shipyard; if the ground was too soft or wet in a pit, an elevated-trestle was erected. Increased business caused the establishment of sawmills powered by a horse-gin or a windmill; steam came later. Ripsaws, crosscuts and tenon saws having deep gulleted teeth were used. Many Eastern Shore yards had *pickle ponds*—a fresh water pond where rock salt had been dumped. This tended to preserve the timber, and wash-out the sap to facilitate better and quicker seasoning.

Augerman. This craftsman had to possess a steady hand, and exacting eye, and above all be 100% sober at all times—drilling long holes in wood was his task. His work ranged from 12′ holes in centerboards using a dowelling auger (and several slip-in hafts) to ½″ diameter dowel holes for short treenails. Different species of wood had different characteristics and the augerman had to know what type of auger was most suitable. A hole of ¾″ (minimum) in diameter was drilled vertically in mast-heads for several feet in depth, filled with kerosene (as a preservative) and corked; then capped with the mast truck.

Trunnelmaker. A *treenail* was one of the principal fastenings used in wooden shipbuilding up until the 1920s. It was a stout wooden pin of locust or white oak, driven into a hole bored about one-eighth of an inch under the size of the treenail. The ends were then split, caulked or wedged. Originally the pins were shaped with a froe (cutting knife) and mallet; a small knife or spoke shave was used for trimming to shape.

Later a treenail maker's plane called a "moot" was used; it was a heavy tool in which the central boss was of cast brass. It had a radiused lead-in, and a blade set into the side of it. The moot was turned round the roughly-shaped treenail to "round-it-off." In the 17th- 18th- 19th-centuries, Bay treenail makers exported millions of these wooden nails to England. Eventually this became a big-business in which steam-powered lathes replaced hand shaping.

During the 20th-century, wooden fastenings for structural timbers were replaced by galvanized metal bolts and screw-nails capped by wooden *dowels, pellets, plugs or bungs* for planking work. Dowels have the grain of wood running lengthwise, the others have the grain running across the diameter.

Joiner. This craftsman only worked in light wood construction such as hatches, coamings, skylights, decks, doors, cabin paneling, trim, mouldings, etc. He took a roughly sawn board and made it into a finished piece of wood joinery ready for painting or a finished coating; even the captain's furniture and cabinets in the cabin were his work. His tools included everything from a cutting axe to a small finish nail punch.

Pumpmaker. Originally a bilge pump was a squared-off timber with a hole (or barrel) in the center. Elm wood was generally used because it has very strong grain and is resistant to water immersion. The tree often suffered from a heart rot (hence the tendency to be blown-down) which made it easier to bore out. The maker's tool was a cross-handed auger with a long shank capable of extension by adding sections. His skill consisted of keeping the hole straight all-the-way through. The plunger was a wooden shaft with tin and leather fastenings forming a one-way flap valve. The bilge water passed through the valve on the downstroke of the plunger, and was lifted on the upstroke. When sufficient water had accumulated on the top it poured out of a lip on top of the pump barrel and over the ship's deck. Centerboard craft usually had pumps in pairs, one on either side of the keelson, and worked with a rocker arm over the top. After the Civil War, metal pumps with diaphrams were used on larger vessels. Smaller craft used a portable galvanized iron pump inserted in a small square well leading down into the bilge.

Blacksmith. The word"smith" implies that the craftsman worked in metal. At large shipyards there were four kinds of smiths; a heavy-work smith, a light-work smith, a tinsmith, and an anchor-smith. All smiths had many ingenious tools suitable for their particular trade such as hammers, swages, fullers, flatteners, peins, tongs, drifts, punches, strikers, sheers, soldering irons, etc.

The heavy-work smith fabricated straps and bands used in structural framework of a vessel. The light-work smith did the chain plates, irons, bands of all sorts for the bowsprit and spars; hanks for the jibs and steering gears, the boom horse and traveler bars, even the traditional horseshoe which was secured to the after side of the samson post (the horns turned up to keep luck from running out).

The tinsmith made the lamps, oil cans, "Charlie Nobles" (galley smoke pipe), windvanes...anything that was made of sheet metal. The anchor-smith "beat-out" the anchors...and many a discarded buggy axle became an anchor for a Bay sailing boat. All these smiths became fabricators of tongs, nippers and dredges during oyster season.

Chains, patent-stern metal work, and steering wheels were generally imported from chandlers at Baltimore or Norfolk.

Glazier. This highly specialized art was practised by very few men on the Bay. The circular shaped "bulls-eye" glass was the cheapest of heavy glass...it admitted some light through the deck, and was framed in a lead band or "bar." Heavy flat window glass for cabin and skylight installation was introduced a short time prior to the Civil War and was fabricated on the metal frame with a metal grill on the exterior to protect the glass from wave action and fracture from normal handling of the boat. Glazed ports and portholes were always fixed in the frame as hinged windows were expensive and unpopular.

Sparmaker. Timber came to the sparmaker as a squared-off log. Eastern Shoremen preferred the heartwood (the center of the tree) which became the center of the mast, while the Western Shoremen swore by the quartersawn log. The center-cut mast tends to twist-in-time in a clockwise direction (looking up).

Spars were not made on a lathe; only various types of adzes were used. A log was squared-off to the largest diameter; then tapered (square) to the finished diameters; then cut to an octagonal shape; and finally rounded to the "set" as the finished spar was called.

A well shaped mast had a curved entasis called "spar taper" instead of a straight taper to the top. The augerman bored all holes in spars. Bowsprits were tapered on all four sides; and bent-down or "hogged" forward to give a more pleasing appearance to the traditional flowing sheer lines of the hull. Spars for Bay craft were of one piece; built-up spars were generally made for large seagoing vessels.

Mast hoopmaker and cooper. Coopers have been important persons on land and afloat since the first settlers. A "wet cooper" made barrels and larger casks to hold liquids such as rum; the "dry-cooper" made kegs for dry goods such as tobacco; and the "white cooper" made open-topped tubs and pails for daily use aboard. Casks made for maritime use were: a *rundlet* held 18 gallons, *barrel*-31½g, *tierce*-42g, *hogshead*-63g, *puncheon*-84g, *butt* or *pipe*-126g, and *tun*-252g. Each type of cooper had a large assortment of tools such as axes, froes (splitting knives), adzes, shavers, borers and knives-of-all-sorts. In fact their craft required more tools than any other. Cask and mast hoops were of ash, hickory, chestnut or hazelnut wood; the barrel staves and headings were usually white oak.

To turn out a hoop the hoopmaker had to first "cleave" the green wood with a small bill-hook or froe sometimes called a "splitter." The bark left on one side, but the inner wood was shaved off with a drawing knife. Then the straight wooden stick called a "rod" was soaked for days to make the wood pliable. Frequently, a green sapling was used.

The split rod was then bent on a hoop bending easel. This was a wooden frame consisting of eight radiating spokes with a series of holes bored in each, into which wooden pegs were inserted. The hoop (rod) was bent round inside the pegs to a circle of the required size then clamped and riveted. Parral balls ("beads" or "trucks") were sometimes used instead of hoops and were strung on wire or marlin; also used to connect the gaff jaws before the mast...all were made by the hoopmaker.

Blockmaker. Blockmaking by the use of one piece of wood gradually declined with the increased use of animal glue, thus permitting four or more pieces of wood to be securely joined. The principal parts of a block were the wooden shell and the revolving sheave held in place by a metal pin. The sheave was usually imported lignum vitae, though elm was begrudgingly used. Strops were made of fiber or metal rope, or metal straps. A holdfast bench was required and the proper use of drills, bits, burrs and knives resulted in beautifully made blocks. Sheaves were turned on a hand or steam-power lathe.

The many wooden deadeyes of lignum vitae, walnut, locust or hickory cooked in linseed oil with metal chain plates for standing rigging were another precision-made item fabricated by blockmakers. Metal work was usually done by a blacksmith.

A typical 2-masted gaff-rigged Bay schooner with topsails, complete with halyards, down-hauls, jiggers, sheets, lifts and a few spare *taykles* (tackles) required one hundred or more blocks of various sizes and shapes.

Ropemaker. Professional ropemakers from England emigrated to the Bay shortly after Jamestown was established. Attempts to grow hemp (*Cannabis sativa*), their favorite cordage-fiber plant (marijuana) were made in both provinces; none was successful, except along the shores of the Eastern Branch of the upper tidal Potomac. In Bladensburg, Maryland's first seaport, Christopher Lowndes built a ropewalk and on 26 June 1774, he advertised in the *Maryland Gazette:* "All sorts of Cables, standing and running Rigging of every Sort and Size; also Spun-Yarn, Marline, Housing, Amberline, deep SeaLines, Log Lines, Lead Lines, and any Kind of Rope that can be made of Hemp; likewise Sail-Twine, Whipping-Twine, Seine-Twine, Drum Line (for barrels), etc. Any Person wanting a Quantity, not over Five Ton, shall have it delivered to their Landing on this Bay, at the same Price it sells at the Walk; and Orders shall be strictly observed, both as to Size and Length."

Records indicate that Lowndes had a monopoly for many years on the Bay cordage business; even though the "stuff" was of such inferior quality that many riggers preferred to buy from England until the War for Independence. During that War, Boston with 14 ropewalks supplied many Bay riggers with rope, using hemp fibers smuggled from Holland via the West Indies...and after the War, hemp came from the Baltic countries. Baltimore became the center of Bay ropemaking prior to and during the Civil War with walks scattered all along the Patapsco shoreline, employing well over 120 workers. In 1852, William Brady, sailing master USN, author of *The Kedge Anchor,* a 400 page book of specifications for cordage, blocks and sails notes a formula for preserving standing rigging: "To a half barrel of tar, add 6 gallons of whiskey, 4 pounds of litharge, 4 pounds of lampblack, 2 buckets of boiling beef-pickle...mix well together and apply immediately."

Hemp continued as the most popular fiber until 1830, when the Philippine Islands began exporting their *Abaca* commonly known as *manila.* Their better grades of manila were stronger and more suitable for marine work than hemp. Imported and domestic fibers such as jute, coir, cotton and flax were not popular on the Bay.

Tarred hemp was the best of all treated fibers, even though the term *tarred* is a misnomer. The finished rope is slowly drawn through (using a hand-operated capstan) a large kettle of hot light pine tar. On the Bay, this tar was made by burning longleaf yellow pine wood stacked in a pile 25′×5′×5′ and covered with *pinestraw and sand* to prevent complete burning of the wood. In about 2 weeks the *burning* is completed resulting in a barrel of tar for each cord of wood burned.

Ropewalks are specialized buildings varying in length from 300 feet to a half mile. In this building the *roper* spun the fiber, backing slowly away from a revolving hook turned by an apprentice manning a crank. The roper wrapped a bundle of *hackled hemp* around his waist and fed fibers from it to the twisting and lengthening yarn thus forming rope.

By the end of the 19th-century, ropewalks on the Bay were lessening and by the early 1900s, all cordage for Bay boats was being furnished to chandlers by Northern firms such as Plymouth, Columbia, Fitler, Wall and New Bedford.

Rigger. An artisan skilled in the rigging of ships and the care and use of cordage and wire ropes. A rigger usually took over as soon as the vessel was in the water. First, they stepped the masts in place...then guyed the masts with standing rigging of shrouds, forestays and backstays. Hemp was used until about 1891, when James Marsh of Solomons rigged his bugeyes with steel wire rope. It proved so successful that metal slowly replaced hemp. Hemp lanyards with deadeyes continued throughout the 1930s when replaced by galvanized turnbuckles.

All tasks relative to rope was for the rigger, such as mousing, worming, parcelling, serving, whipping, splicing...everything including the bucket-rope, bobstay chain; rope mat on the cabin floor and bell lanyard. All tasks for the complete rigging ready for the sails to be *bent on* by the crew was the rigger's job. His tools were several sheath knives, beeswax, pliers, marlinspike, marline, sail-cord, fid, serving mallet, needles, linencord, heaver, thimbles, a roping palm, bandages and a bottle of iodine.

Practical marlinspike work was performed by crew members such as: blockmats, rope ladder, baggywrinkles, rope fenders and handles, pointing of reef-points, and the sail stop-bag or stop-box. Decorative marlinspike as executed on square-riggers was generally not practised on Bay vessels.

Sailmaker. During the early years, there appears no record of sailmaking on the Chesapeake. Public notices posted on court houses noted arrivals of "canvis" and "sayles" acquired from England and Holland. As late as 1697, Governor Andros of Virginia reported that 34 seagoing ships had been built in his province, but the rigging and sails "were brought from England"...even though attempts had been made to encourage planting of flax and hemp for weaving of sailcloth.

The first mention in a 1737 newspaper was about a "sayle maker" (an indentured servant) who ran away from his master. A Negro was noted in the *Virginia Gazette* of 1768, "who is a good seaman and sailmaker" and at the same time, the owner offered to house him in a "large warehouse...shedded with a good sail loft" in Gloucester, Va.

The first professional sailmaker to advertise was Samuel Osband of Annapolis in the *Maryland Gazette* of 1753; his competitor William Bicknell, living nearby, advertised two years later: "Notice that any Gentlemen who wants sails made...as Cheap and as well fitted as any brought from Europe."

William Johnson opened the first loft in Baltimore at Fells Point in 1775, and shortly after James Gay and Talbot Thompson began work in Norfolk. Adam Bence advertised in the *Alexandria Gazette* on 8 June 1786 as having sail lofts in Bladensburg and Alexandria ...the first maker doing business in both states.

The two Wars, one with England and one with France created a great demand for sailmakers and by 1801, Norfolk had seven and Baltimore twelve, but practically all cloth was smuggled from England or France, or imported from Russia and Holland.

The first US Navy specification (1800) for "home made sails" was contracted with Levi Shepherd & Son of Massachusetts for "500 pieces of cloth (linen), 37 yards long, 24 inches wide, and 33 pounds weight; warp and filling to be wholly or good hackled flax and in no part thereof of tow (shorter and less desirable fibers)."

In 1810, a company at Ellicot Mills, Md was making coarse cotton cloth, and 15 years later, Baltimore mills were turning out sail cloth.

Canvas goods such as wagon covers, aprons, coffee bags, sails for windmills and sailing vessels were in great demand...and by 1850 Baltimore had 24 cotton mills. Hemp was tried as a fiber for sails, but never attained the popularity of genuine flax which even when soaking wet remains soft and flexible. (The author found wet or wind-filled heavy cotton sails especially in the winter as easy to furl or reef as a tin roof and resulting with 10 torn fingernails; frozen sails were furled with the aid of baseball bats.)

The method for grading sailcloth weights through the War of the Revolution was based on a width of 24 inches and 38 yards long called a "bolt." Eight different weights were specified from #1 weighing 44 pounds per bolt, to #8 weighing 21 pounds; with equal graduations. After the War of 1812, a new standard was adopted. The weight of canvas was based on one unit, one yard long and 28½ inches wide (1026 square inches). Generally Bay workboats up to 30 feet long used #4 canvas (8 ounce per unit); larger workboats used #2 (12 oz.) or #3 (10 oz.) canvas. Four-masted schooners used #00 (20 ounce). Cloths of 8 ounces and lighter were stenciled with a raven-silhouette; heavier cloths were stenciled with a duck-silhouette. As sailmakers took great pride in their craft—they always stenciled or sewed a label bearing their name on their sails at the tack.

Most sails were made with cloths running parallel to the leech because of the method of weaving giving uniform distribution of strain; water ran off the sails easier thus resulting in less mildew and less demand on the threads when frozen. Bolt ropes were sewn on the port side of a sail.

Sailmakers on the Bay developed their preferred clientele and type of sails they needed. The "sharp sail," or so-called Bermuda sail was the favorite for bugeye and skipjack oyster dredgers. The family and descendants of Henry Brown on Deal Island have been making sails for over 90-years; Robert Burgess in his *Chesapeake Circle* wrote an excellent account of this family which is still (1981) in business.

Oakum spinner. "Spinning oakum" was teasing-out the strands of old rope fibers. The threads are rolled or "spun" between the palm of the hand and the knee into long strands. Originally this was done by slaves or convicts. Later, it became something that "all hands" did in bad weather. Commercialized tarred fibers have since replaced old rope for caulkers.

Caulker. Except for the master shipwright, the boss caulker and his men (usually Negroes) were the most respected on a shipyard site. A caulker's iron was used to force stranded oakum into the seams between planks on the deck and ship sides to make the ship watertight. There were about 20 different types of caulking irons; steel, chisel-like tools, about 6-7 inches long, mushroom-headed and their blades were mostly flared—a shape known as fantail. Mallets were of live oak, specially designed with slotted heads that made a bird-like whistle when being used. Caulkers traditionally worked together *tuning* their mallets to ring (when driving the iron into the seam) like a set of matched bells—working in rhythm to keep a uniform fast rate of work (and music). Teams of singing Negroes (members of the Baltimore-based Association of Black Caulkers) dominated the Bay trade, traveling from yard to yard—through the early 1900s.

Strands of oakum were *driven down* into the seams with the caulking iron, and then *hardened down* with a making-iron. Caulking was done from left to right and the *making* was done right to left. Then the seam was filled or *payed up* with pitch "hot from the nearby oven."

Experience was necessary in the making because if the caulking were too tight it could spring the seams and sheer off fastenings; if too slack the seam would leak. Later came the caulking wheel which put in the oakum prior to the hardening-down—thus a lot of time was saved. Later came the many chemical caulking compounds, marine glues, and white lead putty. After the caulking work, came the painting.

Painter. Painting was the last important task performed prior to launching. During the colonial period, an inexpensive way was to soak everything topsides with turpentine which weathered to a dark yellow, and relieve it with several banks of a mixture containing tar and lampblack. The bottom was painted with a combination of tallow and sulfur, resulting in an off-white color; another popular mixture was composed of ox-blood, buttermilk and lime. Seams were *payed* with a concoction of one part tallow, three parts resin (rosin), and one part sulfur, sometimes called "brimstone."

Owners desiring "fancy ships" had them decorated with combinations of red, yellow, green, blue and white paint...all imported from England. If their vessel was to sail the Bay only or to the West Indies—the entire vessel was painted lighter colors. If the vessel was to sail the colder climates or to Europe—the vessel was painted with darker colors, as dark colors generate heat inside and outside for both crew and cargo.

A few painters on the Bay imported their "Paynters Colours ...white lead, red lead, Spanish whiting, Spanish brown, spruce yellow...linseed oyl, nut oyl, etc" from Thomas Child of Boston, who in 1701 was granted the privilege to "mix paynt" by the London Guild of the Painters-Stayners.

Others "mixed-their-own" using imported pigments or those found nearby. Their paint was prepared by reducing lump pigments to powder by grinding in a mortar with pestle. Many natural colored pigments suitable for paint were found in earth deposits in the Patapsco region. Colors and accessories made from local sources were:

Black: burned bones, soot from oil and candle lamps.
Red: iron oxide, red ochre, ox blood.

Green: buckthorn berry, pigments from Delaware Bay.
Indian Red: by heating natural yellow clay to a red brick color.
Yellow: yellow ochre pigments from Baltimore County.
Blue: copper carbonates from Baltimore County.
Brown: mixture of yellow and black ochre from Baltimore County.
Pungy pink: logwood imported from Mexico and West Indies boiled with chalk.
White lead: a complicated method using lead sheets with vinegar contained in a stone-ware pot, and buried in horse manure.
Oil: animal fat, vegetable oil, sunflower oil, linseed oil, fish oil, whale oil.
Thinner: rum, whiskey, urine, oleoresin (turpentine).
Resin and tar: burnt pine wood, especially knots.
Brush bristle: hogs, horses.
White chalk: chalk pigment, white lime from oysters.

During the colonial and federal eras, colors on Bay boats were usually bright red, blue, green, or yellow; sometimes black or yellow. A typical combination might be blue stern, red rudder and oars, black and yellow strakes, red or pearl-color insides, Spanish brown sternsheets and gunwales with yellow or blue mouldings.

During the 19th-century, the "pungy-style" came into vogue; pink topsides, red bottom, white rail, dark green bends and sheer strake, light apple green or sky blue deck and furniture.

During the early 1900s, a complete uniformity seem to be in fashion: red-coppered bottom to the load waterline; stark chalk-white topsides; the bead of the bends of yellow or red; log rails, cabin ends and sides, hatch coaming, white: cabin tops of gray; inside of hatch coaming of red or brown; decks and hatch cover of gray or light buff. Workboats in the lower Bay used a light green for decks, as it is the "coolest of colors." Yawl boat was white with white bottom and the inside to match the ship's deck. Ironwork similar to adjacent wood color. Club ends, boom ends, platform and jaws, mast top, base, and truck, painted white...all the rest of the moveable spars scraped and oiled natural. Carved wood work of very bright colors. Blue colors were used at a very minimum.

An Eastern Shore custom was to add 1 tablespoon of pine tar to a gallon of white paint where used for topsides. Originally, masts were *greased* with boiled animal fat or rancid butter until petroleum greases such as *Sparene, Mastolene, Preservalene,* and *Rex-Magnus* were made for hand applications to masts. Checks (mast-splits) were filled with a mixture of tallow or white lead and Spanish whiting. A popular seam compound was 3 parts cement mixed with 1 part lime and water.

Bay vessels were usually washed-down twice daily, at sunrise and at sunset, accompanied with a light sprinkle of rock salt. Packing salt between the frames above the waterline to prevent rot was not too popular on the Bay as the salt tends to rust iron fastenings and prevents air circulation. To prevent mast rot a vertically drilled hole at the top of the mast was filled with kerosene and capped: and a grease-cup filled with kerosene drained into the mast (above the coat) prevented rot at the deck line.

Teredo navalis called the "worm" since colonial days, caused (and still does) considerable damage to exposed underwater hulls of wooden boats. Beverley's *History of Virginia* in 1705 described the method of attack: "In the Month of *June* Annually, there rise up in the Salts, vast Beds of Seedling-Worms, which enter the Ships, Sloops or Boats wherever they find the coat of Pitch, Tar or Lime worn off the Timber; and by degrees eat the Plank into Cells like those of a Honeycomb." They usually "arise" in early June and disappear around the end of July.

During colonial days, protection against worms was effected by mixtures such as pine tar and beeswax; tar, fish-oil and lime; or suet, resin, fish-oil and chalk; or tar with brimstone. The first practical anti-worm composition was imported about 1860 from Liverpool and called "McIness;" a metallic soap compound with copper sulphate applied hot. This antifouling paint was put on over a quick-drying priming paint of rosin varnish combined with iron oxide pigment.

In 1863, two ship's painters in Gloucester, Massachusetts brought out a mixture of copper dust, naptha, iron oxide, and pine tar, thus becoming the first makers of antifouling marine paint in America. About the same time, Baltimore copper smelters in Canton, makers of copper sheathing had a surplus bi-product called "copper scale." In 1870, Oliver Reeder founded the Baltimore Copper Paint Company at the foot of Federal Hill, combining this pulverized "scale" with Maryland red oxide, refined pine tar, shellac japan and heavy petroleum spirits...the Bay's first antifouling paint. The Reeder family had been active on the Bay and engaged in engine- and ship-building activities since 1813—when Oliver Reeder's grandfather came to Baltimore to install the engine in the first steam-driven ship built at that port. For over 100 years, this firm has furnished most of the Bay vessels with copper and marine paints...the founder's grandson Oliver H. Reeder is still (1981) active in the company.

To be independent of commercial suppliers, the US Navy manufactured its own antifouling paint—a shellac formula developed in 1908 and used for 20 years at the Norfolk Navy Yard which contained red mercuric oxide, gum shellac, grain alcohol, turpentine, pine tar oil, zinc oxide dust, and Indian red pigment.

Marine archives record several money-saving schemes for protection from worms such as: (1) Anchor the vessel in the maximum strength of the tidal current where the worms are apt to be carried-by, before they could attach themselves to the exposed timbers; (2) A Pocomoke City favorite was: "heave the vessel down immediately after the worm-season; burn and bream (cleaning with a torch) the bottom for the teredos which are just stuck into the Plank, and have not buried themselves in it, so that the least Fire in the World destroyes them entirely."

The easiest method was: "run the vessel up a river into the freshes during the five or six weeks that the worms are active, for they never bite, nor do any Damage in fresh Water, or where it is not very salt." George Washington was one of the first to recognize the effects of fresh water and wrote his agents in London to anchor their vessels in Piscataway Creek (just opposite Mount Vernon), as it "was safe and out of the Way of the Worm which is very hurtful to shipping a little lower down." Even today (1981) this is done by small sailing craft on the Bay. Large sailing vessels were "cleansed" (as the watermen called it) at Salisbury, Jones Falls in Baltimore, and the upper reaches of the Elizabeth and Potomac Rivers.

Shipcarver. During the colonial era, carvings of figureheads and other ornamental wooden works on Bay vessels were imported, chiefly from New England. When the 36-gun frigate *Constellation* was launched in 1797 at Baltimore, the head of the Greek goddess *Demeter* was carved by William Rush in Philadelphia, who sent one of his workmen, John Brown, to fit the pieces to the warship's bow. He remained in Baltimore for many years and established a guild of shipcarvers, many of whom migrated to yards along the Bay shores. Every shipyard, no matter how small had one worker proficient in handling carver's knives and chisels.

By the 19th-century, shipcarving on the Bay had evolved into carvings honoring a war hero, a loved one, owner of the vessel, or for whom the vessel was named. The tradition was exemplified by comparatively small figureheads and subordinate trail-boards designed to be seen from the sides. This custom has been preserved on Bay craft longer than elsewhere in the United States.

Traditional shipcarvings characteristic of the Bay were:

Trail-boards. This is a long tapered board which was fastened between the two rails which strengthen the long-head under the bowsprit; characteristically very long and thin compared to other areas and usually made of one inch thick white pine, cypress, or cedar. The entire motif was generally conventional, consisting of geometric designs with ivy or oak leaves, arrangements of American flags and shield or a spreading eagle; with cannons, ramrods or cannon balls grouped around a cartouche or ribbon on which was carved the name of the vessel all of which blended into the whole trail-board design. The board was painted in garish reds, greens, blues, and yellows with no attempt at realism. They were usually removed during off-season for protection from weather, and they were the first item to be stolen when the vessel was abandoned.

Billet-head. A simple scroll carved to fit on the forward end of the long-head under the bowsprit. It was nothing more than a spiralled volute similar to that on violin head.

Figure-head. An ornamental figure that "rode under the bowsprit," positioned like the billet-head. The subject most frequently used was an eagle's head, followed by a sea-serpent, hybrid alligator, ducks, geese, fish, a pointed hand or a blossoming woman with a bulbous bust.

Stern-carving. Generally this was executed on the ship's transom with designs such as a star, fraternal emblem, spread eagle or a balanced big-bosomed woman. The law stipulated that documented ships clearly show their name on the stern, thus this area became a challenge to imaginative and artistic wood carvers.

Quarterboard-carving. Sometimes the vessel's name was inscribed on name-boards and fastened to both rails (the plank sheer covering the frames when they extend above the deck). When placed aft they are called quarter-boards; when forward they are called *head-boards.*

Mast-head figure. Brewington states that this was unique to the Bay, and only on the foremast, as the mainmast flew the wind pennant. Lavishly carved and colorful figures such as a flying eagle, a winged horse, an acorn, a huge ball, a fouled anchor or even a large capital letter as an "A" as on the bugeye *Avalon.* The author crewed on the schooner *Mattie F. Dean,* whose foremast truck was capped by a lavishly carved and colorful bounteous buxom young woman referred to by the capt. as the "femme fatale." The pungy *J.S. Smith* carried a full length figure of a blissful female with a raised hand holding a miniature American flag. Strangely, all of the three above mentioned vessels made a lot-of-money during Prohibition sailing out of Saint Mary's County, Md... which implies that maybe their figure should have been an alcoholic beverage bottle.

One minor carving typical of Bay craft was a motto fastened over the companionway ladder... pious statements such as "In God We Trust," "God Bless Our Home," or "God Save The Poor Sailor."

Outstanding shipcarvers were Otis S. Lloyd of Salisbury, Pepper Langley and John Olson of Solomons, William Geggie of Newport News, Dewey Webster of Wenona, and Hammond Skinner of Woolford on the south branch of the Little Choptank River.

Name-board, 1911
schooner *Thomas A. Jones*

Trail-board, 1940
skipjack *Wilma Lee*

Stern-carving, 1884
pungy *Amanda F. Lewis*

Figure-head
1853

Mast-head figure, 1874
pungy *Mary J. Bond*

Billet-head
1856

NEGRO AMERICANS

The Bay's favorable geography and climate, and the attitude of the colonists made it one of the most desirable areas on America's East Coast for making use of black workers. Thomas Andrey, an English traveler in 1789 wrote, "It would almost seem as if the poor white man here would rather starve than work, because the Negro works." A sort of "slave aristocracy" developed for those who became artisans; that is, those who were ship's carpenters, rope makers, sawyers, loggers, coopers, blacksmiths and especially caulkers... all in big demand at shipyards; originally called "men of colour."

By 1810 aproximately one-fourth of the Negroes living near the Bay were free. They worked in gangs and at jobs requiring rhythm such as caulking. Caulkers traditionally worked together "tuning" their mallets and singing while at work. Laboring on or near tidewater provided a sense of freedom not likely in the fields ashore. Other attractions were easy access to seafood, a yearly cash crop and a job without capital investment; a small homemade boat made it possible for a poor Negro to obtain a livelihood.

Federal discrimination in 1835 by the US Lighthouse Service occurred with regulations, "forbidding Negroes to be hired aboard Bay lightships except as cooks." Traditionally, cooks on Bay vessels were usually Negroes...as they were masters of the culinary arts even though cramped in tight confines of small galleys.

Exposure and hardships that they had to endure conditioned them for all types of backbreaking and monotonous work, and for the toiling at it for long hours. Thus the scraping and cleaning of marine growth from wooden hulls, followed by copper painting was reserved for them. Other "black-work" monopolies existed in the making of barrels and wooden containers for the many cooperages along the Bay; logging; cutting and loading of firewood; and "Negro Lymburners" working at lime mills, burning oyster shell for conversion into lime needed by masons and plasterers.

Their employment on rowing vessels apparently started as uniformed oarsmen aboard colonial barges (see chapter *Barge*). During the wars of the Revolution and of 1812, Negroes served as reserve pilots in Maryland and Virginia Navies.

The Federal Census of 1860 lists over 2000 Negroes on the Bay as fishermen (fish, crabs and oysters;) this declined during the Civil War. After the war forty Negro oystermen claimed a $10,000 loss from the Federal government because the Potomac Flotilla had destroyed their workboats during the frantic search for John Wilkes Booth, Lincoln's assassin. The war's outcome did not change their lives as most of them had been self-supporting.

One of the greatest of blacks, Frederick Douglass (1818-1895, born at Tuckahoe Creek, Md) served as a caulker at the age of 17 for a Fells Point shipyard before his rise to fame. The Association of Black Caulkers was spawned to combat resentment and envy of white caulkers. According to Henry Hall's 1882 shipbuilding report, "a large number of sailing vessels on the Bay are owned and operated by colored men, and in order to secure prompt and inexpensive repairs to their vessels, they organized stock companies and operated their own marine railways."

"Negroes filled the need for strong, active men suited for outdoor work," said George Brown Goode's 1887 US Fisheries report, thus justifying shipyards to hire them instead of casual white labor. "Negroes are not considered good for regimentized factory jobs, but need to be out-of-doors where strength is required." Work was awarded to blacks because of their proficiency in: handling of nets on fishing boats; rowing of shad-galleys; cutting of ice for land-based depositories; lightering of fish, grain, iron and bulk items; stevedoring at canneries and Bay wharves (see chapter *Canning*); crab picking (usually women); oyster shucking; trimming of coal and stowing of logs on large schooners.

Menhaden craft (page #54) employed mostly blacks because of strenuous, exhausting hand labor requiring rhythm and muscle. Numerous steamboat companies out of Washington, Baltimore and Norfolk were owned and operated by black entrepreneurs.

Self-employment was found in crabbing, oystering and especially turtle hunting in tidal swamps, as their fever-proof heritage made them less susceptible than others in mosquito infested waters. Negroes owned and operated the Bay's last freighting firm with eight vessels sailing out of Smith Creek until 1940. Blacks known to the author seemed to be anxious to make the most of their opportunities. Their social position on the Bay was respected as it reflected their ability, puck, and capacity to work... a Utopian Paradise.

THE GLORIOUS OYSTER

French satirist Jean Voltaire observed, "Oysters are lazy. They stay in bed day and night. They never work or take exercise. They are a dainty, easily digested morsel because their idling never builds any tough muscular tissues. They are free from sinewy, coarse grain fibers. They are moist and mellow to the palate. Oysters do not prowl for food. They loaf in bed and wait for their meals to come to them. They are stupendous drinkers; they guzzle about a hundred and sixty quarts of sea water a day; yes, they even have sexual relations without moving a mussel."

Oysters have been heralded as an aphrodisiac—a philtre made of oysters guaranteed seduction so said the promoters of the Virginia Company in the 1600s. Poetry and legend proclaim the romantic virtues of oysters for man's reinforcement with the *filles de joie;* but this book will only note that the Chesapeake Bay contained the world's richest oyster bottoms which gave employment to thousands of rowing and sailing craft for over three and a half centuries.

The oyster domain covered 2300 square miles; oysters grew northward in the Bay to Poole's Island; up the Potomac to Maryland Point, the Patuxent (Pig Point-Bristol Landing), Rappahannock (Tappahannock), York (West Point), James (Jamestown Island), Chester (Quaker Neck Landing), Choptank (Windy Hill), Nanticoke (Penknife Point), and Pocomoke (Shelltown).

Peter Kalm, a Swedish scientist visiting Baltimore in 1754 noted: "Chesapeake Bay oysters are pickled and shipped to the West Indies. The oysters are opened and boiled in their liquor then flavored with nutmeg, allspice and black pepper and vinegar and dumped into a large crock with half of the liquor. The container is then well-stopped to keep out the air and shipped to the most distant parts of the world."

In 1796, Moreau de Saint-Mery of the French island Martinique visited Norfolk and said: "The people here have a great love for oysters, which they eat at all hours of the day and on Sunday. They are sold in open baskets, by the dozen or the hundred, and are hawked through the streets and allys with horrible noises until then at night. Rum is in great demand..."

And it was in 1837, that the English naval Captain Frederick Marryat visited the United States and wrote: "Participating in a Fourth of July celebration in Manhattan; Broadway being three miles long, and booths lining each side of it—in every booth there was a roast pig and Chesapeake oysters."

At the beginning of the 19th-century, Connecticut was the center of the oyster business. Yankee dredge boats having exploited the New England beds, turned to the waters in the southern half of the Chesapeake Bay where they removed large quantities of oysters which were transplanted to their home waters. In 1810, Virginia passed an act to prohibit the operations of these "foreign" dredgers who promptly moved northward into Maryland waters to carry on the same activities. The Maryland General Assembly became concerned and in 1820 passed an act prohibiting the dredging of oysters and forbidding the transportation of Maryland oysters by any boats except those owned by Maryland citizens. Before the passage of this act, Maryland watermen had learned how to construct and operate a dredge; law enforcement was difficult and dredging continued notwithstanding the law.

Oysters became the measure for social status during the pre-Civil War days. There were demands for cooks to prepare oysters at every regal function especially when large gatherings feasted at prominent estates. The country was generated into the throes of an "oyster cult." Express-wagons heavily loaded with fresh 6″ to 8″ oysters from Chesapeake Bay thundered across the Alleghenies; frequently shifting to fresh horses, for delivery of shellfish so far inland that Abraham Lincoln, when he was living in Springfield was able to give oyster parties at which incredible quantities of this bivalve were devoured. Oysters were eaten raw, baked, fried, fricasseed, minced, pickled, spiced, stewed, panned, scalloped, barbecued, in soup, in pies, in stuffings, and riding triumphantly on top of grilled steaks. Every coastal city had its specialized oyster houses, and peddlers hawked oysters in the street. Oyster houses in Boston, New York, Philadelphia and Baltimore were plastered with signs reading: "All the Chesapeake Bay oysters you can eat for six cents." The wealthier a family was—the thicker was their oyster stew. O happy land of plenty, with oyster houses on every corner and first-rate cooks available at the drop of a hat whenever a housewife needed one for an evening! The B&O Railroad helped as in the mid-1850s, oysters packed in ice were first shipped from Baltimore to Buffalo, accompanied by an outburst of publicity. Epicureans proclaimed the Bay oyster as: "the most appreciated of all God's blessings."

Yet,in contradistinction to this joyful statement...the longest interstate and bitter conflict in American history is the "Bay's oyster war" between Virginia and Maryland, which started in 20 June 1632 and is not over yet. As recently as 1959 several fishermen were killed in one of its skirmishes. This conflict was a by-product of favoritism by the English King Charles I, who cut a slice off northern Virginia to make a domain for his friend, Lord Baltimore. The Potomac boundary line of this grant was not along the thalweg (the line of deepest soundings along the course of a river), as is the usual practice almost everywhere in the world, but at the high water mark on the Virginia side. Thus to Maryland, at Virginia's expense, was given all marine life of the river. And to further confuse the situation King Charles I (who never left England) placed a meandering boundary line from Smith Point, Va, crossing the Bay and up the deepest natural center of Pocomoke Sound and River.

George Brown Goode in his 1884 report to the US Congress notes the different classes of oystermen and their harvesting equipment, namely:

Dredgers. "A dredge is a metal frame with teeth along its base, behind which is attached a bag made of chain rings or rope, is drawn along the bottom behind a fishing boat and the oysters scraped into the bag. After dragging a certain length of time, the bag is drawn aboard, by the aid of a winch, and emptied on deck. Forty to fifty bushels may be taken a day from natural beds. Dredgers form one of the most depraved bodies of workmen in the country (remember this is 1884), being gathered from Baltimore jails, penitentiaries, workhouses, and the lowest and vilest dens of Baltimore. They are principally white, many of whom are foreigners and unable to speak a word of English. When a crew which usually consists of about eight men, is wanted, the vessel owners or captain applies to a shipping agent, who then gathers these men wherever they may be found, drunk or sober. As one agent said 'We don't care where he gets them, drunk or sober, clothed or naked, just so they can be made to work at turning a hand windlass.' The agent is paid $2 for each man furnished aboard.

"With such a crew as this, who neither know or care for laws, the captain is able to work wherever and however he desires. Life led by these men becomes of the roughest kind. When sleeping, surrounded by vermin of all kinds; when working, poorly clad and with every garmet stiff with ice, while the wind dashes the fast freezing spray over them, hour after hour winding away at the windlass, pulling up a heavy dredge; or else stooping with backs nearly broken culling oysters.

"Returning from a trip, the men take their little pay and soon spend it in a debauchery amid the lowest groggeries and dens of infamy to be found on Baltimore's spreading waterfront. It is a gratifying fact, though, that even amid such surroundings as these, there are some few and respectable and honorable men in the oyster trade, especially those hailing from Southern Maryland and the Northern Neck of Virginia. Their crews are gathered from nearby farms and are not as degraded as those on Baltimore vessels. The average pay for crew is about $11 a month or $77 for the 7 month season. Pay-off was always in silver dollars as paper money was too easily blown away by the wind. Inspectors estimate over 1000 vessels employ 8000 or more men."

Scrapers. "Scrapers are simply dredging on a smaller scale, both as to the size of the boat and dredge, and is conducted only in shallow water. The crews of these vessels average a maximum of four men each, the majority of whom return home after each day's work, as the boat does not go out of county waters, except to make an occasional run to a neighboring market. Inspectors report about 800 scrape-boats with crew totaling 3200 with a pay of about $18 a month for the 7½ months of work...or $135 for the season. Socially and morally, the scrapers are superior to the dredgers."

Tongers. "Tongs are a scissorlike appliance, consisting of two longleaf yellow pine poles with a toothed bar about a yard wide on one end of each. These poles (up to 30′ long) are riveted together (with a dogwood pin) about one-third of the distance from the toothed bar to the end of the pole. By alternately opening and closing the tongs the teeth dislodge the oysters, which are caught in the basket that is formed when the poles are pulled together, and they are then raised to the deck of the boat and unloaded to the culling board. During the course of a day one tonger may take 7 to 8 bushels.

"Tongers are men of a better class, are better remunerated for the labor, and are less prone to evade laws than the other two classes. Yet, they are as a class indolent and improvident. They live near the water, often owning a small house and an acre of land or so, a log canoe or an interest in one, used in winter for oystering and in summer for fishing. Having secured a house their ambition seems to be satisfied and but little time or money is spent in beautifying or improving it. It is too often the case that tongers, especially many of the Negroes, will work only one or two days at a time and then remain idle until necessity forces them again to earn a few dollars.

"Tonging if pursued as steadily and systematically as the wind and waves will allow, is as remunerative as other trades. Tonging necessitates very great exposure to the cold, though not as severe as dredging. They are generally better clad and seldom work in extremely frigid or gale-wind weather. Inspectors found about 6500 tongers using about 3000 canoes or smaller craft with an average wage earning of $225 a season."

Runners. "Oysters caught by tongers are sold to runner-boats, sometimes called "buy-boats" and by them are carried to a market town such as Baltimore, Annapolis, Washington, Crisfield, Cambridge, Seaford, Phoebus, Newport News, or Norfolk. There are about 300 runner-boats usually schooners crewed by over 1200 men. The runner will anchor near some tonging ground, and an empty basket is hoisted to the masthead as a signal that she is ready to receive oysters. In one or two days she is loaded and sailed to a market. Off of some bars, half dozen or more runner-boats may be seen surrounded by forty or fifty canoes. As soon as a tonger has caught as many as his small boat will carry he sells out to a runner and returns to work. Crew members on runner-boats receive about $18 a month including board."

Shippers. "Three million bushels of Bay oysters were shipped this past year by larger schooners to restock exhausted beds of other localities between Portland, Maine and Albemarle Sound. Delaware Bay alone received about 500,000 bushels from May 1879 to May 1880, in about 300 vessels...purchase price was 4¢ to 7¢ a bushel.

Shuckers and Packers. "The Oysters are delivered to a shucking plant where they are opened with a special knife, the meats extracted, and then washed, graded as to size and are packed in small air-tight cans holding about a quart. These are arranged in a long wooden box designed for this purpose only with a block of ice between each row. (Barrels instead of boxes are used in plants outside of Baltimore.) Daily oyster trains from 30 to 40 cars from Baltimore go to the West as far as Detroit. Canned steamed oysters are shipped further west and to European countries.

"Baltimore packs more oysters than any other city in the world...45 firms employing almost 7000 persons. Shuckers are usually male Negroes, receiving an average of $8 to $15 a week, though 2500 white females are employed at 75¢ to $1 a day.

"Summing up the total of those supported by the oyster trade we have: over 124,000 persons working as dredgers, tongers, scrapers, runners, packers, shuckers, can-makers, ship-yard workers and local marketers." And so ends G. B. Goode's report of 1884.

By 1890, the heavier dredge boats had left few oysters remaining on the bars for tongers, except in waters too shallow for the larger sailing craft. County laws prohibited dredgers from operating in river mouths and in county waters. Dredgers defied the law causing strained relations with tongers forcing the formation of an "Oyster Navy." Using fast schooners equipped with howitzers and rapid-fire rifles, the oyster police were charged with the task of protecting the tongers' "rocks" (oyster beds) from marauding dredgers.

To avoid police, the dredgeboats worked at night. Tongers constructed crude watch-shanties on stilts at selected oyster bars where armed guards could protect their "rocks" from oyster pirates. Capt' Gus Rice (out of Coan River, Va and a friend of the author) was the outlaw chieftain of the Chesapeake Bay dredgers who boasted that no "law-man" could defeat his oyster pirate fleet anywhere between the Chester River in Maryland to Coan River. The Oyster Navy was beefed-up causing Capt' Gus and the pirates to eventually disband and return to more peaceful pursuits such as freighting cordwood and tomatoes.

Howard I. Chapelle, in 1972 cited, "Of all the gifts bestowed by God to the Chesapeake Bay, the oyster probably was the most responsible for the beautiful design and evolution of her watercraft."

Lamentation. The Chesapeake Bay which once contained the world's richest oyster bottoms has been almost destroyed by man's development of efficient fishing gear. Total destruction will probably occur from other human activities other than over-fishing. Most of the formerly productive beds have been damaged beyond reconstruction by the filling of marsh lands for industrial sites; by the construction of thruways, marinas, and real estate developments; dredging for navigational improvement; trash and garbage disposal; by everincreasing discharge of domestic sewage and trade wastes; and by numerous contaminents which reach natural waters as the result of wide spread and nonselective use of insecticides and pesticides. Discharge of radioactive materials from nuclear plants present a new and serious threat. A recent issue of the *Wall Street Journal* said: "The oyster has just about had it."

Culinary History. Professional oystermen, being traditional purists scorned cooked oysters, but achieved an exciting recipe called "torch-bearers"...it goes like this—place 6 to 8 dry oysters in a large metal pie pan. Add just enough 151 proof dark rum to cover oysters; set afire. Flavor the blue-blazing oysters with black pepper and tabasco...and when the fire is out, munch slowly with a certain quiet dignity and ceremony which will accentuate the rum taste and aroma.

THE CANNING INDUSTRY

During the 1880s, Chesapeake Bay canned oysters were known in many parts of the world, and the Bay's canned fruits and vegetables were sold in every state of the Union. Sailboats furnished low-cost transportation from the tidewater farms to the canneries. This all began when Thomas Kensett of New York moved to Baltimore in 1826 and established the first oyster canning factory on the Bay. Square-rigged ships brought tinplate, the principal material for canned food containers from Wales and England. By 1850, Baltimore boasted of five canneries; each canning oysters, fruits, and vegetables.

Canned foods were shipped from Baltimore around the Horn and across the Isthmus of Panama to accommodate California's gold rush. Because of the Civil War, the number of canneries increased during the 1860s from 13 to 34 in Baltimore alone.

The canning procedure was simple as food was processed in sealed cans immersed in boiling water. Then in 1861, Isaac Solomon of Baltimore found by adding salt to the water; the boiling temperature raised from 212 to 240 degrees, which in turn reduced the processing time from 4 hours to 30 minutes... later, he built the first oyster canning factory in Southern Maryland at a site that still bears his name. In 1873, another Baltimorian, A.K. Shriver invented the pressure cooker, which further reduced cooking time. The result was a boom for tidewater truck farming, causing Baltimore to become the national leader in the canning industry with most of the canneries on or close to the Patapsco River.

US Army and Navy canned food specifications on 1870 approved 16 different fruits and vegetables. Those of the Bay region were: peaches, pears, apples, cherries; tomatoes, corn, peas, string beans, asparagus and limabeans. Meats were beef, veal, lamb, chicken, and turkey. Pork stayed home.

Eastern Shore and Calvert County peaches were the most popular fruit. Pineapples came next, grown on the Bahama Islands and loaded on Bay schooners anchored off the sandy beaches near the island farms. Baltimore was the only place in the 19th-century canning pineapples... continuing until about 1910. As a deep water port, this city provided economical sail and steamer transportation to any place in the world. It had abundant local labor, and was easily supplied with metal and accessories for canning, and farm produce from the 185 mile long Chesapeake Bay. In addition, the Bay furnished the internationally known oyster and hundreds of accommodating sailing craft.

Baltimore canners operated on a nearly year-around basis. During summer months, fruits, berries, and vegetables were canned, and during the remainder of the year, oysters were shucked and canned. By 1880, canned or "cove oysters" as they were called, about equaled the "fresh trade" (uncanned) of some 3,500,000 bushels.

During these years, canned foods became firmly established in the American diet. No longer were they luxury items for the wealthy or deep-seamen. Baltimore and the Bay country retained its role as the dominant national canning center throughout the 19th-century.

Labor strikes, machinery boycotts and a publicity campaign against machine-made cans forced Baltimore canners to relocate to points *down-the-Bay.* On Virginia's Western Shore, floating-canneries from Baltimore processed local vegetables, fruits, and seafood for shipment back to their home port. By the 20th-century, truck farming had become of major importance all up-and-down the Bay. Nearly every hamlet or town had at least one cannery, and by 1930, there were over 200 canneries in the Bay country. Sailing vessels would load *empty* cans-in-cartons at Baltimore wharves... deliver them down the Bay to canneries... returning to Baltimore with *full* cans-in-cartons.

Virginia's peninsula between the Potomac and Rappahannock called "Northern Neck" had the most suitable temperature and productive soil for growing vegetables especially tomatoes. Coan and Yeocomico Rivers were shipping terminals for their canned agricultural and tidewater produce to Baltimore. Here, in the 1930s, the author and his sea scouts worked at the canneries and on their schooners (a dying business) sailing from: Walnut Point (A.J. Lewis & Son), Lewisetta (A. Garner), Coan (E. Fallin & Bro.), Lake (A.B. Headley), Cowart's Wharf (W.P. Cowart), Kinsale (C.F. Unruh), Mundy Point (W.J. Courtney), Harryhogan (D. Faulkner), Oldhams (S. Walker) and B & F Delano). In 1940, there were 52 tomato canneries in Northern Neck; in 1982, there were two.

RIVERSIDE STORES

The Bay has many estuaries; these estuaries had many wharves, and on or near these wharves were stores catering to watermen and farmers. For almost forty years, the author and his sea scouts cruised the Bay and knew nearly every storekeeper in the tidewater area. We found that the wharf store was more than a place where merchandise was sold; it was, in fact, a community clearing house. It played a big part in the affairs of churches, schools, lodges, banking, politics, oystering, crabbing, fishing and farming.

Farmers and watermen collected their mail from the post office at the wharf store and came there to hear and talk about the news. There were few radios in the 1930s and newspapers were on sale only on Sundays. Stores were placid islands of community life where the cosy stove sides were forums for domestic affairs and gossip; places where the "natives" came into touch with the outside world and where the outside world came into touch with them.

Every storekeeper was "our friend," and the sea scouts and I knew that through *him* we could establish pleasant relations with the people of the community. We made it a point to request *his* permission to make our boat fast to *his* wharf out front of *his* store. As our progress under sail was slow, a stay near a store for several days waiting for a favorable slant of wind was commonplace.

To us city-kids, the fun of visiting these river stores was a joyous, heady experience—what with looking over their crowded shelves of brightly-colored goods, piles of fat meats, and smelling coffee beans, lard, and peanut butter packed in open tubs... also tempting salt herring and mackerel spiced with celestial odors of sardines and cheese, and the mouth-watering sight of tantalizing glass jars of long sticks of striped candy. My sea scouts gorged themselves on Eskimoe Pies, candy, and sarsaparilla; frequently I was forced to stop their predominately sweet diet.

When a waterman wished to "cuss" the government in the person of President Hoover, (or his successors) or complain to the Lord because of perfidy of politics or weather conditions, there was no better place to take the podium than the store with its nearby wharf. No other place, not even the church graveyard or the polls ever offered quite the same convivial atmosphere for getting drunk. For every fifth tub of oysters tonged; there followed a "drowning of a half-pint of local whiskey" at the store; more so in Maryland than Virginia.

"Putting on a front" was an important matter of the river store business. The invariable porch that faced the wharf was a practical necessity, as most business was done there with watermen, drummers off Baltimore steamboats, and visitors who had just arrived at the wharf. Small hotels frequently sprung up behind the store (the hotel buildings at Leonardtown Wharf, Md and at Coan Wharf, Va still stand in 1981).

Back of the impressive front was generally a rambling two-story building. Along one side of it was a feed, seafood, or ice storage shed roof leaned against the main building. It served as a whispering room during Prohibition Days for merchants and their thirsty customers, who could conveniently hide from other customers' view an occasional crooking of the elbow with a genial drummer who had brought along a little Kentucky Bourbon to give an added bit of appeal to his line of goods. The Eighteenth Amendment era (1919-33) made this room especially important for the covert dispensing of whiskey (rum during cold winters). Women customers were always excluded from this "speak-easy" room because here off-color stories were told in their full ribald version.

Storekeepers in Southern Maryland usually had an antique cash register located in one corner; the post office in another corner; slot machines and a colorful bar in the other two corners... for dispensing of booze and profits. Illegal sale of whiskey stopped at high noon on 5 December 1933; slot-machines had a total demise at mid-night on 1 July 1968.

A wide double door, flanked by heavily barred windows, broke the monotonous faces of the buildings. By day the doors were swung open, with their heavy window shutters pulled aside and hooked to the corners of the houses. At night, strong diagonal iron bars were pulled into place and securely bolted from the inside. Every drummer would remove competitive signs from the scarred entrance doors and then tack up his own. Sheriffs, bailiffs, auctioneers, and US Marshal's nailed their notices to these informal bulletin boards. Between the Garrett Snuff signs and auction notices were posted the invitational funeral handbills that used to be printed up as a part of the local funeral custom. Announcements of all-day political speakings, oyster-shucking contests, and singings and camp meetings found their way to the store doors with seasonal regularity. Some store fronts were virtually covered with nails and tack heads.

Above the inevitable porches were the bold white or red signs painted by medicine, fertilizer, and milling companies which proudly displayed their house-name. Every store had a permanent *Coca Cola* sign, which if removed, was replaced the following day. Occasionally a dignified officious metal sign swung in the breeze to attest to the fact that the building contained a US Post Office.

There were other telltale indications that the age of standardization had arrived. Almost precisely in the middle of each roof line, the stove-chimney flues jabbed their blunt and soot-stained noses upward. They were there ostensibly to draw off smoke from the stoves, but actually they performed the more important function of establishing the approximate geometrical center of the building. Many factors decreed that a huge, potbellied stove should be in the middle of each of the long, rambling buildings: they were placed precisely where the greatest number of people could gather around them, and where it was vainly hoped they would heat four corners of the building with some degree of impartiality. Areas around the stoves, on porches, and underneath nearby shade trees were communal ground, where neighborhood problems could be aired and discussed at all seasons of the year. Here every religious doctrine was given the third degree, and where weather was abused and political parties were taken to pieces. Local oyster dredgers damned Baltimore dredgers; tongers damned local dredgers, buy-boat captains, packers and everybody else.

The external appearance of the average store was as distinctive as the hull on a black walnut. It was the inside of the house that counted. Here again was standardization that was broken only by the degree of general confusion in the arrangement of the stock. Near the door on the right hand, in the place of honor, was the US Post Office with its official oak partition or its homemade bars and its dozen or so locked boxes. In the middle of the oak panel, which hovered protectingly over the postmaster (about 90% were postmistresses) and his (her) paper-rattling and string-breaking activities, was the stamp and delivery window where customers approached the postal department of the Federal government in a spirit of cautious supplication. Customers were kept well out of the working areas of this "holy of holies," one reason being that the storekeepers themselves had a healthy respect for Federal postal laws. Adjoining the Post Office bulletin board was another one on which were notices of planned dredging by US Engineers and a large 1906 map showing Bay steamship routes from and to Norfolk, Baltimore, and Washington.

Beyond the Post Office, to the right, a long, heavy homemade sectional counter extended all the way to the door of the side room. The local carpenters were prodigal in the use of rich, longleaf, yellow heartpine paneling and molding and they built counters to last for centuries. On the back sides of the counters were bins which either tilted in and out or were mounted on runners to be pulled back and forth like drawers. The bins were built to hold flour, rice, sugar, coffee, salt, garden seeds, and dried peas.

Hip-high rows of heavy drawers, with stout knobs and finger pulls, were used to hold all sorts of small or loose merchandise. Ankle-high work shoes, the principal item of men's footwear, came from the factory tied in pairs rather than being boxed, and these were kept in drawers instead of on shelves. Men's shoes and boots, were considered the coarsest sort of merchandise, and it made little difference to the customer if they were scratched or bruised in handling.

Across the aisle in roughly the front half of the store, improved shiny glass showcases in time crowded out the sturdy wooden counters. These were filled with heterogeneous mixtures of fancy merchandise such as ribbons, buttons, needles, pens, collar buttons, knitting needles, hatpins, bow ties and self-tied four-in-hands, hairpins, corset stays, hair rats, pencils, garters, slate pencils, hooks and eyes, bottles of perfume, rings, earbobs, necklaces, dollar watches, chains, scissors, and thimbles.

Aside from their mixed stocks of merchandise and their curious old buildings, the merchants were incidental curators, along with the country newspaper editors, of informal museum collections. Hand-carved painted trailboards salvaged from abandoned sailing vessels adorned the walls of many stores. Unusually large crab and oyster shells, water moccasins, and hornets' nests were hung up outside on the porches for brief displays, or they were placed on more permanent display inside. Deerhorns, stuffed eagles, feathers, owl's claws, queer-shaped eggs, extraordinary pieces of whittling or wire bending, Indian arrowheads and stone axes, Civil War relics, newspapers, odd coins, strange root growths and weird knots from many trees, and other artifacts of wonderment and mystery were left there by their owners for the public to see. At Riverside Md in 1929 there was put on display a stuffed rooster which had two horns and no spurs.

The store became a profitable outlet for a vast stream of tonics, pills, ointments, liniments, and dry-herb mixtures which poured out of laboratories in Baltimore. The benevolent lady, Lydia E. Pinkham, with a properly bloused shirtwaist and a motherly mien, created a bottled formula which is still a boon to all females, and believe it or not to many males working around the Bay.

I remember one particularly marvelous medicine which cured headaches, fullness in the head after eating, dizziness, dots before the eyes, shooting pains through the body, dyspepsia and constipation. One of my sea scouts who was chemically inclined took a sample back to his high school laboratory and found it to be composed of several "exotic herbs" suspended in a generous quantity of alcohol.

The propaganda of the old-time elixir manufacturers sought to eliminate the doctor and discredit competitive patent medicines. This type of do-it-yourself medicine business was probably a reason for the Pure Food and Drug Act. However, the storekeepers conscientiously tried to prescribe for customers who were ignorant of proper medical care and were often without adequate medical service.

There were showcases filled with an array of shirtwaists, paper collars, shirt fronts, bustles, false breasts, corsets, stocking holders, cloth, ladies' hats, shoes, trousers, suspenders, stockings, and socks. Then there were the glass-top counters which were filled with bottles of herb tonics, dry herb mixtures, cans of pomade, fancy toilet and shaving soap, talcum powder, black rubber nursing nipples, fruit-jar rings, shoestrings, shoe polish, fishhooks, lead bars, balls of gum opium, camphor, asafetida, and bottles of morphine. In a corner of these cases, well hidden from both the critical and the curious, were plain little cardboard boxes which contained the iniquitous devices of birth contraception which were called for in private conference behind the closed doors of the feed rooms, and which were smuggled to customers by sleight-of-hand in the most adroit manner.

The back half of the store was devoted to heavy barreled goods and marine hardware: barrels of whiskey, Po-T-Rik molasses, lard, salt, coffee, rice, sugar, vinegar, kerosene, and engine oil. Empty lard tubs were saved for use in work of scalding hogs. One grave offender in this mixed assortment of liquid merchandise was the kerosene barrel. Kerosene (coal oil) was forever getting into the sugar or lard or meat, and horrors of horrors, it even permeated the liquor barrel. Kerosene had a sneaky way of creeping along the floor and contaminating everything it touched; special caution by keepers was mandatory.

Clumsy racks kept whiskey and Po-T-Rik molasses barrels off the floor at jug-filling height so that their contents could easily flow down into the passing parade of receptacles which came under their spouts. More than mere convenience, however, necessitated keeping the whiskey barrels above the floor. If the barrels were not high enough, or were too near the wall, there was a reasonably good chance that they could be surreptitiously emptied at night by the use of a brace and bit and a short length of pipe. Sometimes these casks were set on iron plates to protect them. Saint Mary's County thieves once bored a series of holes diagonally through the floor of a building hoping to tap a barrel of liquor. At Wynnes Wharf store, a thief once drilled a hole in and permanently fastened a spigot to a barrel from underneath the floor. This efficient device enabled the inventor to enjoy a free-flowing supply of rye whiskey.

There were few Prohibitionists among Bay merchants, but even the most pious were tempted beyond conscience by the easy profits, and they too ordered what affectionately came to be known as "paint remover" by the barrel. From Virginia's stills came the early brands, Wildcat-Family Whiskey, Fairfax County, and Virginia Gentleman bourbon; and from Maryland came Sherwood, Monticello and Maryland Hunt Cup rye. Records show, "that many a pious toper bought bottles of whiskey on a physician's prescription in the name of his wife, or on the flimsey excuse that he was having a special affair and needed a little liquor to help things along."

Wade's Store at Port Tobacco did a general merchandise business, but their liquor trade during Prohibition was of such magnitude that they advertised Charles County Corn Whiskey on their letterhead. Reformers were always upbraiding the country-store liquor trade by citing the charge that "cuttings, fights and rows of all sorts always occurred around the stores because they sold liquor."

Beyond the liquor and molasses barrels, off in one corner, was a long, greasy counter which sat directly in front of one of the grocery shelves. At one end of the counter was the preeminent mechanical cheese cutter, with its sharp knife acting as a sort of guillotine. One stroke of the handle moved the golden yellow disk of cheese around a "nickel's worth." Selling cheese at the lunch counter was never a matter of fractions of pounds, but was governed by rather the "clicking" of a ratchet on the turntable levers. Flanking the cheese cutter were the twenty-four pound boxes of crackers from which clerks grabbed up crackers on the price basis of "one handful, one nickel."

Fishermen of Atlantic coastal waters, Norwegian and Maine canners, and Swift, Armours & Cudahy of the Middle West earned handsome profits from their mackerel, sardines, and link and canned sausages, sold along Bay shores. On Saturdays hungry watermen and farmers consumed literally thousands of cases of tuna, sardines, salmon, Vienna sausages, and tubs of freshly caught herring. Most popular food of all, however, consisted of sardines packed in cottonseed oil, seasoned with pepper sauce, and eaten with salty crackers. This combination was recognized as being the favorite hunger-quencher throughout the entire river store trade.

Both walls of the store were conventionally lined with shelves. On the drygoods side were bolts of cloth and oil cloth. Across the way there was an assortment of schoolbooks, pencil tablets, canned goods, medicine, hardware, spices, castor oil, turpentine, pills, chewing tobacco, snuff, cigars, vanilla extract, laundry soap, baking powder, soda, and Epsom salts.

Dividing the front aisle into two passageways were rows of tables on which were displayed pants, overalls, jumpers, socks, stockings, dishes, caps, hats, sou'westers, pitchers, bowls, and shoes. Back of these were the racks loaded with cheap ready-made clothing, and quality-made oilskins.

A generous circular space was left on the floor surrounding the stove, for this was customers' ground. Kegs of galvanized nails, horsehoes, fish-net weights, rickety chairs, soft-pine boxes, and knife-scarred benches were pulled up to within easy spitting distance of the bulging red-hot stove. This was the scene of gabbling, whittling, yarn-spinning, chewing, snuff-dipping, and sly nipping at the bottle. From the very beginning merchants resigned themselves to the inevitable fact that throughout the winter their stoves were going to be spat upon. Customers looked upon this hit-or-miss practice as one of their inalienable rights and no power short of death could deny it to them. Most merchants attempted to curb this traditional right by providing spacious sandboxes around the bases of the stoves.

When spring arrived and the weather once again permitted the philosophers to move outside, the average pot-bellied stove in a riverside store gave the appearance of having been submerged in the Bay among barnacles for several years.

Down the center aisle, past the public circle, were racks loaded with meal and flour in bags, as well as salt, and feed. Piled up behind these were odd lots of hardware suitable mainly for boat repair. No space was wasted; plows, coils of rope, anchors, duck decoys, oars and oarlocks, plowshares, axes, wedges, sledge hammers, rolls of bagging, and cordage ties were on open display where not too much effort was required to show them to customers. Shopping for a long list of goods became a matter of craning the neck from various portions around the whole store. Hanging down from hooks in the ceiling were many crude but necessary utensils and tools of the everyday life in the rural tidewater country such as horse collars, animal traps, and oaken buckets.

As architecture of river stores was standardized, so was their odor. It seldom varied from one store to the next and it was as impossible to define as any institutional odor could ever be. It was, however, a source of fascination to the sea scouts and me, especially when we tried to identify or compare it. It seemed to be a vital part of the exciting confusion which prevailed everywhere: a casual ad-mixture of hardware, groceries, dry goods and notions, tobacco, onions, salt mackerel, whiskey and soap, the scent was of nothing in particular and everything in general. It was in reality an odoriferous inventory of the entire stock. It was composed of the glaze on the calicoes, the starch in the cheeks (red or blue and white checkered table cloths), rotting cabbages and potatoes, spring onion sets, cheese, neat's-foot oil, leather polish on new shoes, oil and wax on saddles, kerosene, sardines, salmon, the stove, the cat, the customers, asafetida, peppermint and wintergreen candy, and engine oil. It was a blend of salt meat, rats and mice, paint on plow tools, linseed oil, mast grease, bananas, tar, Baltimore copper paint, jute bagging, mixed "sweet" feed, and naptha soap.

Thus it was that the stores on the many points, and in the hamlets of the tidewater country became more than a market for produce and a place in which to buy supplies. Its radiant stove in cold weather and its air-conditioned porch and tree-shaded benches in spring, summer, and fall were places of general assembly. Merchants were busy long hours each day with community affairs. Inside their little latticework doors and beside the tall, breast-high, shelf-like desks, they worked at their books and held whispered conversations with their debtors. Trading followed ritualistic procedure. A boy rushed in with a note and handed it to a clerk and the clerk in turn consulted with the merchant *sotto voce.* The order was either approved or disapproved and the boy was sent on his way. Timid customers led storekeepers from curious ears to talk over their tobacco, fish, or oyster prospects, and credit situations. In this way business went on from day to day in one whispering conference after another.

Storekeeping was one-half orthodox merchandising and the other half sizing up the capabilities and honesty of customers. It was a highly personal sort of enterprise which required a generous amount of giving and taking, a keen sense of humor and an understanding of all the frailities of mankind.

Few river merchants ever bothered themselves with statistics, but they were always well informed as to the crop every customer had planted, and as to its general state of cultivation from week to week. They also know the "going price" for oysters, crabs and fish; and *who* sold *what* and *when*. They knew the approximate size of their customers' shoes, the length of their legs, and their chest measurements and girths. They made mental notes of the prices they quoted on goods which they showed their clientele knowing full well that most customers would go home and debate the matter there before coming back to make the purchase. They were philosophers who weighed out and bagged five pounds of sugar at the time, cut off huge pieces of fat meat, pumped five gallons of kerosene, or dished up buckets of lard, all the while keeping up a steady conversational flow of advice or lamentation. Working hard, living closely, and paying all debts was ever a cardinal rule of economy with them. Their whole philosophy of the credit system was one of strict control. Paying one's debts was ever a virtue, here as elsewhere, which gave a customer high standing at the store.

In words of the editor of *Saint Mary's Beacon* in 1912, merchants often advised their customers to "plant tobacco and turnips this year, make your own meat and bread at home, *but always have an acre of oysters in your nearby creek to bring in clear money at the end of the year."*

Behind the swinging lattice gate of his little office, the storekeeper interminably read illiterate but understandable orders he had received and recorded the charges he would assess against the credit of the customers. He was a puppet-master who made his community go through some peculiar but soundly based economic celebrations. As traffic on the Bay decreased; wharves were abandoned; riverside stores deserted; by 1981 only a few remained... a loss of another colorful tidewater heritage.

Addendum: For over 300 years, watermen considered whiskey as essential to withstand hardships of their trade; and demanded only Maryland rye made of Patapsco limestone-flavored water and German-farm grain. Methodists *cut-it* with rock candy.

UNDERWATER ARCHAEOLOGY

For over 300 years, thousands of rowing and sailing craft were built, worked, and died on the Chesapeake Bay and its estuaries. Some had centurial lives, others lasted for a month or two. Many worked-all-year-round, and some for only short seasons. Many died of old age, abandoned near their owner's home, while others were destroyed by fire, collision, grounding, or warfare.

Nautical underwater archaeology is the scientific study of sunken ships; and of submerged towns, inundated-sites or inserted-sites such as wharves, shipyards, fish weirs, treasured items (coins, guns and the like); and the recovery and evaluation of their artifacts. Successful salvage action often results in profitable sales of recovered items.

The Chesapeake Bay contains over 3000 documented vessels sunk since the English Jamestown establishment in 1607—though Spanish ships (from St. Augustine, 1570-88) ventured here to "find traces of English settlements." Queens Creek, Va is the rumored site of one of their sunken ships (*not* a treasure-ship from Mexico!)

The first known recording of salvage for the sake of history was by Father Joseph Carberry, S.J. who with other Catholic priests found seven cannons in 1824 near the site of the former Fort Saint Inigoes, Md. It is believed that the cannons were salvaged by the English from Spanish ships grounded during the Armada invasion and placed aboard ships bound for colonization in Maryland.

In 1934-5, the first organized effort was made by the Mariner's Museum and the National Park Service to recover artifacts from eight sunken ships of Lord Cornwallis's 24-ship fleet during the siege at Yorktown in September 1781. The French shore batteries set-afire the 44-gun ship *Charon,* and destroyed 3 transports and the fireship *Vulcan.* The 28-gun frigate *Guadaloupe* and 24-gun *Fowey* were scuttled in the York River. Cornwallis sunk numerous less important craft to form a breakwater at the Yorktown Landing. After the conflict, the French captured 4 cutters, 12 transports, and the 14-gun sloop *Bonetta.* Artifacts recovered in 15 to 40 feet of water were: cannon, cannon balls, swivel guns, grape shot, anchors, a bell, grindstone, rum bottles, bar shot, and miscellanea.

In 1976, the Institute for Nautical Archaeology directed by George Bass, aided by state and federal agencies located and surveyed these seven sunken wrecks and engaged in more detailed work upon *HMS Charon*...which is still (1981) going on.

Maryland's first underwater archaeological research project was inaugurated by Donald G. Shomette of Upper Marlboro, Md. who located, surveyed and mapped submerged portions of the colonial port Londontown on the south shore of South River, Md which existed from 1683 to 1747; twelve years of which as the seat of Anne Arundel County. The town included the William Burgess shipyard, 30 to 40 dwellings, harbor facilities, wharves and a ferryboat; much of which is now under water.

The following year, he joined with the Calvert Marine Museum at Solomons in a 3-year effort to locate, inventory, and survey representative sectors of a submerged cultural resource base in the Patuxent River. Within the 40-mile lower stretch of the river (and at the mouth), more than 142 vessels were documented from as early as 1680; submerged in many feet of silt, mostly soil from upstream tobacco farms. The type and number of boats were: row-barge-13, freight barge-5, brig-2, dory-1, dredge-1, galley-1, wooden gunboat-2, log canoe-2, lookout boat-1, pink-1, pungy-3, schooner-50, ram-1, scow-1, freight boat (propeller-gas)-15, freight boat (propeller-oil)-5, sloop-9, flat (sloop)-1, steamboat-3, submarine-1, tugboat-1, unknown-14. To date (1981), exploration work has been in 5′ to 10′ of silt.

A remote-sensing magnetometer survey resulted in location of Commodore Joshua Barney's *Chesapeake Flotilla* sunk in the upper reaches of the river in August 1814; prior to the burning of Washington DC. Nearly one-third of the 18 vessel *Bay Flotilla* was scuttled when confronted with superior British forces at the head of navigation. The defending fleet was: 13 barges, 2 gunboats, 1 row-galley, 1 lookout and a sloop *Scorpion.*

The Karell Institute of Arlington, Va is currently (1981) engaged in underwater research in the Patapsco River, Md, and the Elizabeth River and Hampton Roads, Va.

Man's historic presence in the Bay will be fully appreciated only when extensive archaeological research is produced.

MARITIME VIGNETTES

On 8 July 1901, Robert Barrie wrote: "We sailed on a southeast-wind into Solomons Island on the Patuxent. The harbor is one of the most interesting and picturesque spots on the Bay. The island circles around and incloses an area of perhaps a square mile, which is dotted with little islands covered with longleaf pines, and this gives a Scandinavian look to the place. This resemblance is increased by groups of graceful sailing craft anchored and moored about in the most out-of-the-way places and in the oddest ways.

"As the water is deep close to the shore, canoes and bugeyes are laid up 'in ordinary' (out of commission) and are moored in little coves with their lines made fast to trees on either side. The place is a perfect nest of small shipyards where the bugeye is created in all its glory. These yards are pictures that would drive a painter crazy. Work is done in a leisurely, casual way, with a good deal of resting and gossip under the tall and overhanging pines. It definitely cannot be true, but it does seem as though money were the last consideration here unless we consider that 'time is money,' and that the people here take out their share of the world's goods in that.

"There are about a half dozen little marine railways scattered about the nearby coves and creeks, and all seem to be doing a good business with the large oyster fleet. These oyster boats are fine, big, able bugeyes, rated (or identified) among the natives according to the number of bushels of oysters they can carry. (For example... 'an 80 bushel bugeye.') The sharp rake to their masts, criss-crossed as they lie in the cove, heightens the effect, while an occasional sharp-headed sail set-in-place adds to it all. As we sailed around this snug little world, we expressed the hope that we would be able to bring our little sailer up here in autumn to spend many days at anchor.

"On the island, which is a peninsula at low tide, as the connecting sand bar at the northwest end is bare at low tide at that time, we found a straggling village with a couple of ancient and fish-like general stores, a fine artesian well, and the sole interests of the place is oystering, bugeye building and repairing. On the southwest side there is a suggestion of Holland in the way that one has to climb up a steep dyke-like bank to look out over the water, and this effect is enhanced by the way in which the better class dwellings face along this bank. The houses have little garden fronts, and on summer evenings, the bank is no doubt the promenade, the breeze being generally from the southwest.

"Here, then, we pottered about all morning, made some purchases, principally ice, and started for our boat and lunch aboard. On the way we passed an old Negro with some pickaninnies fishing, and tried to buy some fish; but the old fellow did not care to be bothered, and it was only after desperate appeals that I could get him to consent to let me have a dozen of beautiful rock fish (striped bass). When he was urged to name a price he did not seem to care whether he made a sale or ever got any money or not. Finally, he named a price... the sum of six cents.

"We cleaned, cooked and ate our half-cent fish and rowed ashore to Solomons post office and to get some promised ice. On getting back we had a swim, and watched the antics of a crew of Negroes on an old battered and tattered schooner. Some of them were fine specimens, two of them in particular having magnificent physique. They were all splendid swimmers and divers, and at slack tide loafed about in the water for an hour, as much at home as seals, and, with their black heads, looking very much like them. At the flood (tidal current) they up-anchor and went off up the Patuxent in the most unconcerned way, each man apparently his own officer, doing just what seemed to him best, and doing it when he pleased, yet all doing the right thing.

"While the other two members of my crew went off in the dinghy on some expedition beyond Drum Point, I had a nap, and then gossiped with an oysterman to learn that the British had once been here. A resident in the upper reaches of the river told us there are still visible remains of American ships burned by the owners when chased up-river by our cousins in August, 1814.

On 8 July 1902, George Barrie, Jr., wrote: "We anchored off the pretty village of St. Michael's at half-past three. We did not go into the quaint little harbor, but lay in the river so-called but it is really a salt arm of the Bay, cursed with strong tides (tidal currents). A pleasant old fellow came alongside and remarked that we had selected a pretty bleak harbor; and so we had, but the usual squall that night was not severe, and we did not suffer any unusual discomfort (being wind-and-tide rode). A large Baltimore yacht passed by close-by and advised us to anchor inside...as it can become uncomfortable with a wind against the current.

"Next morning we wandered about the village, which is very attractive. The grass comes down to the water's edge all around the harbor, which is practically landlocked. There is an air of peace and quiet after the turbulent waters of the Bay, and the whole is a strong contrast to the rush of modern life. There is a charm in the haphazard way in which the older part of the village huddles about the harbor; in the grass-covered back lanes, where a broad ribbon of dazzling white oyster shell runs along the centre; in the tarry smell of nets spread about, and the perfume of honeysuckle from old-fashioned gardens, and in the ancient and weather-worn houses. There are some fine large trees in the place. All this, as seen from the harbor, with the church steeple rising up over all, makes a pretty picture.

"There is, however, a brisk air about the place, both in the morning and evening, when the summer boarders, principally beauty and youth, go for the mail; the rest of the day and evening seems to be spent by them in or on the water. It is a great place for canoe (log canoe) sailing, as canoes are everywhere. In the morning the crews, both boys and girls, are in bathing suits; then, if there is a smart breeze, the sailing becomes more than reckless; to capsize means only another bath. They seem to dress for lunch, so that in the afternoon, the sailing becomes more discreet. In the evening, when the girls have on white dresses, and the breeze is generally lighter, things are more placid, and banjos are in evidence. This seems to be the daily round; at Oxford and all the other places on the upper Eastern Shore during the summer."

On 4 June 1905, George Barrie, Jr., wrote: "Up at five-thirty, and while the corn bread was baking we washed down the deck. Never saw such a heavy dew as here in the Annapolis harbor. We were told that some time before noon the side wheeler (steamboat) *Emma Giles* came in from Baltimore. If you are ever in this harbor, when she comes in with her load of freight and excursionists, it is well worth while to pick out a soft piece of the top log of the piled pier and watch the proceeding of getting-off the goods consigned to the merchants of this town. The operation consumes from three-quarters of an hour to two hours, four times a week, and one wonders where are all the people to consume and pay for this enormous quantity of freight. The inhabitants must live like gourmands, and their homes must be filled to the rafters. As there is a 'business coldness' between the storekeepers ashore and the railroads here, most of the food-stuffs, drygoods, and hardware; in fact, everything purchased in Baltimore by the former comes on the steamer *Emma Giles*.

"About half-past ten the vessel will be seen coming from behind Greenbury Point, and as she passes the lighthouse gives a long blast from her whistle. Then the 'tailor (blue fish) fishermen' sitting on the wharf, lift up their rods and gather up their paraphernalia, swing in their legs, and stand among the curious crowd which has gathered, the larger portion being small boys, both white and black; the town loafers, and perhaps a few prospective passengers. In the background are a half dozen run-down hacks, in most of which George Washington rode on the day (23 December 1784) he re-signed his commission on the nearby hillside, and eight or ten wagons awaiting for the freight. In a few minutes the *Giles* is alongside the wharf, the captain being a master hand at this; over the rail leans a crowd of women and children, the latter in such abundance that one is firmly convinced that all the youngsters and babies of Baltimore are out-on-an-outing. Just as the lines are fast, a laggardly hack or wagon will clatter down the vitrified brick street at full gallop, the horses covered with lather and the driver cracking his whip and yelling at the top of his voice to the gaping crowd; suddenly he pulls up, the horses sliding and the pole almost sticking into the barouche (a large four wheel carriage) ahead. When the gang-plank is on the wharf, first off are passengers; a drummer or two, and a few people who have come on a visit, but the majority are 'trippers,' who, while the steamer remains, walk to the US Naval Academy. Then comes another gang-plank and pandemonium breaks loose in the shape of fifteen coal-black Negroes clad in the tatters of shirt, trousers, and shoes. They have been lined up on the main deck, each man with a two-wheel truck in front of him loaded to its utmost; down one plank they tear; up into the freight-house, which is soon filled; dump, and back on board by the other plank.

"They keep this up continuously even on the hottest of sultry August days, singing, shouting, and doing fancy steps, always in a good humor, although they are pestered by small children getting in the way, and there are some narrow escapes, but the stevedore makes a quick turn or a short stop and the stray youngster is hauled off by a chattering parent.

"In the meantime, crates of vegetables, boxes of shoes, pieces of farming implements, sides of beef, even barrels of moulder's sand, window-frames, sofas, bags of flour or meal, which oftentimes leaves a trail along the deck and into the shed, boxes, of canned goods, now and then a barrel of crab-bait, from which a thousand flies have been disturbed, is trundled off, leaving a reeking trail along which persistent flies are buzzing like a pack of hounds on a fox's scent, coils of rope for the ship-chandlers on the city's dock, plumber's supplies; in fact, boxes and bundles of every conceivable size and shape containing all sorts of articles, from the pink shirt to tempt the Negro crabber to a piano for some naval officer's wife, are soon scattered over the wharf.

"When nearly all are off, a few shipments for the landings on West River are taken on, then the trucks are stacked and a carriage or cart followed by a horse is run off; the whistle blows, the last 'tripper' dashes down and jumps on board just as the lines are cast off and the *Emma Giles* backs off into the harbor, leaving a trail of froth dotted here-and-there by a shoe-box which contained some luncheon delicatessen.

"By this time the hacks that were fortunate enough to get a fare have long since swayed off up the street and others are now straggling off; the wagons are loading and soon they will have disappeared; the loafers are gone; the anglers are once more absorbed in catching the toothsome 'tailor' (bluefish); the agent is sitting in the doorway of the freight shed to catch the breeze, his pocket handkerchief in one hand mopping his red face and fanning with his hat in the other. The usual reign of quiet being broken only by the occasional bleat of the small brown veal in the cattle-pen waiting to be taken to Baltimore when the steamer stops on her return trip here in the afternoon."

On 14 October 1912, J. Edwin Lawton wrote: "Over the oyster grounds at the mouth of Coan River, Va, we watched the 'buy-boats' each surrounded by a bunch of canoes like a hen with a flock of young chicks. These buy-boats are bugeyes or schooners, which carry the oysters gathered by the tongers to market. The captain of one of these vessels contracts with a commission merchant in Baltimore to deliver oysters so many times a week (wind or no-wind) and makes from 10 to 15¢ per bushel on all carried. It is interesting to watch the canoes gather around one of these buy-boats, which declare their 'calling' by a basket displayed at the masthead. About three o'clock in the afternoon the tongers begin to leave the oyster beds and sail or row according to the weather, each to his favorite buyer. Along-side they range. The captain stands on the deck of his vessel with a wooden shingle or piece of board on which to keep tally; close by, on a barrel or on the cabin top, is a tin cash-box, well-filled with notes and small change, as all the buying is for cash. Half bushel baskets made of iron are passed to the canoes to be filled, after which are hoisted on board by means of a fall from aloft and lowered into the hold, where a man is stationed to empty them and stow the contents. As each canoe is emptied and the seller has received his money, it moves to allow another of the cluster to take its place; some start right for home, and others like to linger to talk and chaff."

On 21 October 1913, Adrian Sizer of Washington wrote: "The water industries of the Bay and its estuaries kept thousands of rowing and sailing craft busy; oystering, crabbing, fishing, and the transportation of farm food products, firewood and coal. Most men and vessels were employed in oystering during a season when the other three were almost at a stand still...and practically every inhabitant of the surrounding shores was engaged in some way, either tonging, dredging, or in the packing houses called 'factories.' In the early spring, as the oyster season was on the wane, the fish began to run; pound nets were found everywhere, some of them in the lower Bay are veritible forests of piles the size of electric power poles. The toothsome crab next put in his appearance, and it is miraculous that they have not been exterminated by the thousands upon thousands of lines and pots set every day all over the Bay for about six months, plus the hundreds of sailing dredgers working the lower Eastern Shore.

"Between the crab and oyster seasons, a general overhauling of the floating craft and painting is gone through before the farm products are ready to be shipped to the large cities such as Baltimore, Norfolk, Washington, Fredericksburg and Richmond.

"On a cruise there is something very humanizing in the experience of sitting to gossip with the friendly tidewater country people, most of whom are possessed of an astonishing education and dignity of manner. There is a delightful calm independence about the Bay folk in this lotus-land that seems to have given them by nature in poetic justice as compensation for the lack of doubtful joys of money-bought luxuries.

"A simple manifestation of this bred-in-the-bone unconscious dignity is in the way in which the white man, while living in terms of equality and in friendly intercourse with the Negro, exercise a *noblesse oblige* that promotes mutual respect and good-will. This manner is probably the result of atavism, and in it there is no doubt reproduced the manner that it was fashioned during the couple of centuries that slavery existed in this land. This strain continued here largely for the reason that few 'foreigners' of any brand came to this part of the country. The lack of fresh blood has perhaps been a loss to the Bay folk in that they have not gained the commercial and artistic strength that comes from occasional adding of other blood; but nevertheless, they preserved a genuine and unaffected good-will, kindliness, and courtesy that adds greatly to the pleasure of cruising in the waters of the Chesapeake Bay. The scenery is varied, and always picturesque, whether in the pleasant sheltered bays of the Eastern Shore, the bold Calvert Cliffs above the Patuxent, or that of the tropic-like pine-fringed Piankatank and the cypress-flavored brown waters of the Pocomoke. Fish, crabs, and oysters are plentiful in season and cheap. Ice is cheap, but not always available, and a cruising-man's necessities: milk (raw), fresh butter, eggs and chickens are found at every farm. Strange to relate, fresh vegetables are the hardest things to get; and when found, require more persuasion to induce owners to part with them than any other of desirable things in which the country abounds.

"My favorite harbor is Rhode River where I can always get a fine bath from the clean sand-spit that gives protection on the southeast and the thrill of being totally-alone. There is no village here; only two houses in sight, and one of them that of a gentleman of the old school. You can anchor behind the low spit in deep water with good holding ground and lie unmovable as though on shore. On a busy day there is visible a constant process of craft of all sorts up to the largest steam-ships passing up-or-down the Bay; the sailing craft generally all bound one way, as the wind may favor. All this gives the feeling of being in touch with the world, while still being alone and unseen."

On 7 June 1915, James Tull wrote: "One of the most amusing episodes of our cruise while in Crisfield as occurred aboard a small bugeye of about forty feet on which were 10 or 12 Negroes. We never could get the exact number, as several looked alike and they never all were on deck at the same time; even at meal time you would think they must all be there when suddenly a head would appear out of the hatch then disappear and in a few moments another appear. Some slept in the cabin, some in the hold, and some wrapped in a sail on deck; one fearfully wet night I expected to see the latter pretty well bedraggled in the morning, but they unfolded themselves apparently as dry as toast and all in good humore. We never heard them quarrel the whole four days they were there; although the arguments were pretty lively at times and words were flying from all directions, their principal theme appeared to be the 'cotchin' of oysters,' one evening there was a heavy discussion on the proper pattern of tongs, another the exact location where to find so and so had 'cotched' eighteen bushels in one day last winter."

On 21 October 1919, Dan Fowler wrote: "How pleasant and peaceful to anchor in one of these out-of-the way creeks in the lower Bay where the air is flavored with the odor of pines and wildgrape.

Listen to that faint ringing of cow bells coming from the little nearby marsh. Cow bells, No! Thousands of small singing 'turkles' (turtles) at 'evensong.' Hear the whippoorwills on starboard, then to port, now very faint on the other side of the creek. Now a boat of tired, light-hearted Negroes row slowly past, returning from their day's berry-picking, some singing, others talking in a low tone and again a loud peal of laughter. Happy-go-lucky outfit. Our larder is filled with food, and crabs and fish for the catching. Over yonder is a bugeye slowly drifting down the river with her crates of berries, boxes of canned tomatoes, or barrels of crabs for the Baltimore market. Soon the moon rises and the soft night breeze rustles the foliage on the neighboring bank...and we crawl into bed."

On 5 September 1930, Frederick Tilp wrote: "Even in the Chesapeake Bay country where the food is abundant, its preservation is difficult or impossible especially aboard sailing boats. Before 1850 home canning was unknown. Without refrigeration, food spoils rapidly during the scorching summers. The climatic conditions favor dry, salty foods that did not spoil readily, foods such as parched corn, smoked hams or salt pork, dried fruits as apples and peaches.

"Seafood aboard sailing vessels is usually smoked or fresh fish, oysters, and crabs. Breakfast is fried eggs, fried bacon or sausage meat, Indian fry-bread and black coffee. Maybe twice a week, hot porridge (of Quaker oats, wheat, rye, or corn) is served drenched in Gail Borden's (diluted) Condensed Milk and flavored with Po-T-Rik molasses. Dry cold cereals such as Post Toasties, Grape Nuts, or Shredded Wheat are forbidden. Dried fruits as apples, peaches and prunes are tolerated, but never a thought is given to fresh fruit or even canned fruit juices. Apple cider is an acceptable purgative.

"Dinner (noonday lunch) is cold or cooked hot dogs or cold canned salmon or Vienna sausage with cold canned beans and floods of ketchup; cow crackers and longhorn cheese with hot fry-bread dunked in Po-T-Rik molasses. Supper being the *big meal;* variations of Campbell's Condensed Soup, boiled chip-beef, smoked or fresh fish, fried fish, oysters, crab-meat, fried potatoes, fried onions, fried tomatoes, salt pork, fried ham, fried roe, fried chicken, fried mush or Indian fry-bread. Often we have hot hominy from Mrs. Mannings Cannery in Baltimore, sprinkled with Potomac caviar. Desserts are Hershey chocolate bars, canned fruits, ginger snaps or Indian fry-bread soaked in cheap whiskey. A large bowl of hot samp (fried coarse-ground yellow hominy) with oleo and Po-T-Rik molasses is religiously served at Sunday supper. Hardly are there fresh vegetables except wilted cabbage, onions and carrots.

"Thus, fried foods became the watermen's specialty; all meals are floating in 'extraordinary rivers of grease.' To a city-bred passenger aboard a Bay sailing ship... they face breakfast only to find the food 'afloat in a menstruum of oleaginous matter'... it seems that grease enters 'largely into the compositon of every dish.' If fish or anything else is boiled, it is only half-done; overcooking is a cardinal sin. Eggs are kept on racks and in darkness below deck; turned over 180 degrees every day, usually at night in order to keep them fresh for weeks-at-a-time. Soft boiled eggs are a favorite change from fried-eggs, as the plates, knives and forks are easily cleaned.

"These men seldom drink water which is generally wretched, except when freshly obtained from nearby artesian drilled wells usually located at a fish-factory, oyster-shucking plant or tomato cannery. Rain water is not always available because of droughts, while water from shallow wells is usually cloudy. Then too, many watermen think water to be lowly and common; after all, it is the drink of pigs, cows, and horses.

"Cooking techniques were primitive during the 19th-century and are still (1930) unsophisticated; open wood fires in an open brick-hearth on deck. Then about 35 years ago, came the famous 'Shipmate stove' made in Souderton, Pennsylvania and the cooking action on some vessels descended below deck into the galley; equipped with a metal smoke stack called 'Charlie Noble.'

"This well-designed iron stove burns pea-coal and wood; has an oven which was hardly ever used, as cooks prefer the easier method—frying. As freshly baked bread quickly becomes mouldy because of the high humidity, Indian fry-bread is the staple item of food. It is eaten hot or cold, breakfast, dinner, or supper. In 1929, when I sailed out of Coan River aboard the pungy *Amanda F. Lewis;*

the cook Russel Rice gave me his recipe for 12 pieces of Indian fry-bread:

1½ cups unsifted unbleached white flour
1½ cups corn flour
1 tsp salt
1 cup water, body temperature
Peanut oil

In a medium-size bowl combine the two flours and salt. Mix in the water. Knead dough until smooth (about 5 minutes). Separate dough into 12 equal size pieces. Cover these pieces with a towel and let them stand for 20 minutes. No baking powder. Russel Rice used only flour as ground at Charlie Rice's Mill near Heathsville.

On a lightly-floured board, roll each piece out not to exceed ½ inch in thickness. Heat 1 inch of peanut oil in a deep frying pan and test for its readiness by dropping in a tiny piece of dough. If it comes to surface quickly, oil is ready.

Fry each piece in oil until golden brown on both sides. Pieces should puff-up well when placed in oil. Drain them on brown paper. Serve warm or cold.

Fay Tilp, the author's wife (1981), who is a Pennsylvania Dutch culinary genius says: "Indian fry-bread is great." Cover the fry-bread lightly with King Syrup or Po-T-Rik Molasses made by Mangels, Herold Company located on Baltimore's waterfront. Po-T-Rik is a *must* on every commercial Bay boat I visited.

"With all this stuffing-the-stomach with fried foods, there is a demand for a complimentary beverage... which turns out to be whiskey distilled by local tidewater moonshiners. The strength of the whiskey flavoring overcomes the blandness of the fried-stuffs, while the sweetness neutralizes the unpleasant puckering effects of salt pork and other pig-products. Its high proportion of alcohol warms the throat and cleanses the teeth of layers of clammy grease. One of my preferred Chesapeake-gems is rye-flavored oyster stew... it is simple... just slowly float a half jigger of hot Maryland rye whiskey into a bowl of rich, hot oyster stew made from your favorite formula. Please, do not dump cold rye into the stew as it will curdle, resulting in a mess.

"Tradition taught that hard liquor aided a waterman's digestion, and Bay watermen who indulge in starchy fried foods need all the aids they can find. During the warmer seasons, locally distilled whiskey is their choice (rye, bourbon, corn, in that order) and rum in the winter. Tradition again came-into-effect, as their favorite is a dark rum (like their ancestors swilled) from Jamaica, and Demerara of British Guiana. Oddly, sugarcane (from which rum is made) was first brought to Jamaica in 1493 by Christopher Columbus on his second voyage.

"Their pet 'weatherizer' to meet nature-in-the-raw is a mixture in equal portions of hot black coffee and hot 151 proof dark rum with a bit of brown sugar, cloves, and butter in a hot mug for standing-watch-during-a-snow storm, being careful not to go below into the warm cabin or else they'd pass-out... so if the watch was eight hours on deck, the warm body *glowed* and became perspired with hot coffee-flavored rum. Why, the freezing rain and snow melted instantly when in contact with the warmed oil-skins. Surely, no place for a pusillanimous person."

On 14 September 1938, Robert Hedges wrote: "Foodstuffs eaten by the many friendly Negro families visited by my sea scouts were strange and of various sorts, such as: muskrat pie flavored with chestnuts, onions and red peppers at Taylor's Island, Md; caviar *au natural* on Nolde's white bread at Mallow's Bay, Md; cold smoked menhaden at Whitestone Point, Va; baked oppossum with sweet potatoes at Sherwood, Md; black mulberry pie at Solomons, Md; and overcooked-terrapin stew at Onancock, Va."

During World War II, Hulbert Footner wrote: "... the gentle southwest wind pushed us slowly through the devious and narrow channel of *The Muds* which join the Pocomoke Sound with Pocomoke River. Our native pilot, Bill Bradshaw commented on how the swamps were scented with magnolia blossoms in the spring; of the fun of gathering fox grapes in a log canoe and the delicious wine and jelly made from them; and of the many rope-ferries crossing the river.

"Between Shelltown and Rehobeth, the salt marshes gradually disappear, and above the big bend, the river assumes its own unique character. Cypress trees grow larger here than any other place on the Bay; the narrow river, lined with dark trees standing in the water, has a tropical quality. It is said to be the deepest river in the world for its width. It has a sinister, yet awesome and beautiful look.

"And it changes with the seasons. In the spring the dark cypresses are mantled with a fairylike green. In October, I discovered that the trees are not all cypressses; the black river had burst into georgeous color, the purple and crimson of the gums; orange and yellow ocher of the poplars, scarlet and vermilion of maple and dogwood, the whole picked-out with rich green cedar. There are no cut-banks along the Pocomoke to scar its beauty; at high tide no earth at all is visible; the leafage springs directly from the water. When the tide is out, only a foot of sooty earth is revealed with grotesque cypress knees poking out of the water.

"Above Pocomoke City, the river immediately becomes even wilder and more deserted. Where the land back of the bank is cultivated (the farmers count 210 growing days a year) a thick screen of trees hides it. In the whole 12 mile stretch to Snow Hill, not more than three or four openings are to be seen. The old steamboat landings are rotting into the water and the roads leading to them have been taken by the jungle. There is no river traffic except an occasional three masted ram being pushed by her yawl-boat carrying fertilizer to Snow Hill.

"The virgin timber was cleaned out a long time ago, but here and there a magnificent specimen has been left standing among the second growth. An aged cypress is the most individual and beautiful decorative of trees. Bird life is plentiful; reed birds and summer duck along the lower reaches; kingfishers, blue heron and ospreys above, and even a bald eagle, hanging about for a chance to steal an osprey's fish. It is a unique experience thus to be ascending an unbroken tropical-seeming river under a cool northern sky.

"The land surrounding Nassawango Creek is underlaid with bog ore; nearby is an ancient iron furnace which was surrounded with a village, stores and a hotel until about 1847. All is gone except the ancient chimney; there a green forest has covered it.

"Above Nassawango, the Pocomoke is hemmed in on both sides with cypress swamps and the tortuous channel is broken by swampy islands... the most beautiful part of the river. Then civilization intrudes again (26 miles above the river's mouth) in the town of Snow Hill, though the river meanders down through 20 or more miles of swamps from Delaware.

"Snow Hill may be called 'slow' or 'backward,' but it provides a welcome refuge from a too-violent world! What a charming place to have been raised in! It is noted for good food; terrapin stew, steamed oysters, and deviled crabs! Their specialty is Sunday pone, called 'sweatpone,' a damp but delicious delicacy... it is cooked all night in an iron pot. Our country will be poorer when the last old-time village like this is spurred into modernity.."

On 20 July 1957, Frank Wade wrote: "A Pacific Paradise on the Potomac opened today at Freestone Point, Va, and at a nearby wharf is the only legal gambling ship in North America, the 200′ *S.S. Freestone* (former excursion steamer *Tolchester*). Her first deck accommodates 200 slot machines, her second deck seats several hundred persons in a smartly furnished and expensive restaurant, and her third deck in Hawaiian decor is for dancing and drinking to pulsatory music of the South Seas; open 363 days a year.

"All piers and ships in the river are immune from Virginia prosecution because the Potomac is completely in Maryland where gambling is allowed... the boundary being the high-water mark on Virginia shore. Machines, repair parts, and beverages will be transported from Maryland by boat. Property taxes are paid to Maryland; water, sewer and power charges to Virginia. Police service 50/50.

"Virginia's Potomac shores oblige over 2000 gambling machines on wharves at Coles Point, Muses Beach, Fairview Beach, Belvedere Beach and Freestone Point; Colonial Beach boasts four wharves, viz. *Jackpot, Little Reno, Monte Carlo, Little Steel Pier.* Other casino spots are planned at Craney Island, Jones Point, a barge off Mt. Vernon and in a private boat clubhouse at Alexandria."

Requiem: Slot machines were first brought by boat from South River to Southern Maryland on 25 March 1934 for the Tercentenary Celebration and were "kept active" until midnight, 1 July 1968.

FOLKLORE etceteras

Folklore can be a very loose word, used to cover a lack of knowledge of the very thing that folklore means; many things are passed off as folklore that are plain mistakes or inventions. When there is nothing else to attribute a hearsay belief to, it is often branded as genuine folklore. Weather folklore is generally true. Traditional rowing and sailing craft of the Bay were doomed to disappearance along with our slowly vanishing landscape and waterscape; notwithstanding, folklore will live forever.

Bad luck to a vessel was assured if any of the following were brought aboard: an umbrella, freshly-cut flowers, black luggage, black-eyed peas, walnuts, a cat, or a cross-eyed man.

Bad luck was assured aboard a vessel if: clothes were sewed during stormy weather; a water bucket or swab was lost; a crewman sneezed while on the port side; a looking-glass was broken; nails were driven, wood painted or kindling chopped on Sunday; bread was baked on Good Friday; an owl, hawk or crow lighted on the vessel; a water bucket was left half-full on deck; a knife was left sticking in a bread loaf; a crewman walked on top of a pile of freshly dredged oysters; salt was spilt on the table; drinking water was tossed overboard; a pig was brought aboard during the vessel's first trip; a crewman whistled before breakfast, or shot a gull, or pointed at a star, or stepped aboard the vessel with his right foot, or forgot to wash-down the decks between sun-rise and sun-set, or turned a hatch cover upside-down on deck; a priest in black clothing was allowed aboard; pancakes were not eaten on Good Friday; sassafras wood was used for kindling wood.

Good luck is assured if; a honey bee came aboard; if the vessel passed through a flock of gulls sitting on the water without disturbing them; if a person sneezed while on the starboard side of the vessel; an egg, when opened contained a double yolk; a vessel docked on the eastern side of a wharf; if a horseshoe was nailed (with the horns up) on the after face of the main samson post on the vessel's bow.

Black bags were usually carried by lawyers . . . persons who were intensely hated by watermen who called them "land sharks."

Women were disliked aboard a vessel by crew members; as the captain's wife (so they said) countermanded orders and found fault with the personal appearance of the crew.

The thirteenth day of any month was "not a good day;" tradition had it that Sodom and Gomorrah were "destroyed on the 13th." The best day of a week is Wednesday; Friday is the worst.

Friday's bad character was attributed to early Catholicism, it was the day on which Christ was crucified...thus priests advised watermen to "await tomorrow's sun." Criminals were usually hung near the county court house on Fridays, especially in Southern Maryland; wherein it oddly became a day of celebration. Superstition about Friday did not seem to bother Bay watermen.

Cats were breeders of foul weather . . . as they carried "a gale in her tail." The malevolent character of the cat in maritime is universal...as it was connected with the *number one job* that a sailor hates—that of raising anchor; thus we had a *cathead*, *catfall* and *cat blocks*. A *catboat* is considered to be the meanest type of vessel to handle under sail. Weak drinks aboard are called *cat-laps,* and an unsatisfactory sleep is a *cat-nap*.

Walnut as a shipbuilding wood was hardly ever used...as it was considered bad luck—probably was too expensive. The same applied to copper sheathing on a vessel's hull for protection from ice—probably was too expensive.

During a flat calm, a favorable wind may be purchased by tossing a penny off into the compass direction of the "wanted-wind." The greater the denomination of the coin, the stronger the wind—a dime may stir up a gale.

A live oyster will wince when a drop of lemon juice is placed upon the oyster while in the open shell. If the oyster fails to wince... then it is dead.

Oysters will live longer out of water with the hinge upward and the central edge downward—this being the favorite position for the retention of water within the gill cavity.[1]

Blue color paint was never used aboard a Bay boat (except as accents on shipcarvings) because it was the favorite color of Spaniards, archenemies of the English for four centuries.

A female crab has two genital pores; a male crab has two small pleopods (appendages) side-by-side, and their love-making act takes from five to twelve hours... in one position.

Folklore about the appetites of Eastern Shore mosquitoes would have covered three printed pages in this book; such as *they ate canvas sails right out-of-the-bolt ropes, leaving only spars.*

If two crows fly close-together across the bow of an oyster tonger before noon—the boat will be "full-to-the-gunnel" by sundown.

Silver dollars were the only form of money used aboard Bay vessels, as paper money tends to be blown overboard.

The ninth or sometimes the tenth wave was called the "mother wave" and was usually a bit larger than the others.

A yellow sail or a yellow painted boat has the longest visibility range, but attracts the most mosquitoes.

If the winds blow favorable on Good Friday—there will be favorable winds for the remainder of the year.

Prepare for a disaster—if the ginger-snap jar on the cabin is left totally empty.

To ward-off rheumatism, Capt' Gus Rice of the pungy *Amanda F. Lewis* wore flannel underware inside-out during all seasons.

Dark colored paint generates heat on a boat hull; heat dries out the wood, causing leaks.

During Christmas holidays, a freshly cut pine tree was hoisted to a mast top of a sailing vessel when in port.

The preferable time to catch soft shell crabs is at the full moon or at high tide during the early morning.

Eggs aboard an oyster-tongers boat predicts wind and tongers do *not* want wind.

Fisherman always throw their first fish overboard, and they never count their fish until they are finished fishing.

If one of the crew died aboard a vessel, he was quickly buried ashore and his clothes destroyed.

A fog on the water during summer, makes for good weather, A fog on the water during winter, makes for bad weather.

Deck dry at night—rain you will get, Deck wet at night (from dew), sunny sky you will get.

A vessel with a *humble name* is likely to pass unnoticed by the elements; one with a *haughty name* is bound to land in trouble.

Oysters are fatter on a full moon.

Sing if you would catch oysters; be quiet if you would catch fish.

Wrap an eel skin around your wrist for a sprain.

Dogs are forbidden aboard an oyster boat at all times.

MARINE POLICE

Policing waterways has always been a difficult problem. Early settlers fled the English "police state" to gain freedom from taxes and oppression. However, it was found that certain types of policing were necessary even in a rebellious society.

The plundering of English ships at London docks, the pillaging of warehouses, the conspiracies between receivers of stolen goods and ship's officers, and even the raiding of vessels at anchor during daytime reached crisis proportions which called for drastic action. Parliament in 1789, to protect the 3000 or more ships on the Thames each year, established the Marine Police Institution with 80 men and a small fleet of "armed rowing barges."

On the Chesapeake, during the early 1800s, big towns such as Baltimore and Norfolk formed their own harbor police with a compliment of market masters and port wardens. Waters of the Bay would have never needed police except for the treasure of marine and wildlife existing there... which spawned animosity between Marylanders and Virginians, Eastern Shoremen vs Western Shoremen, oyster tongers vs dredgers, fish seiners vs pound netters... and all this developed an open-air theater for maritime warfare by watermen out to make a quick-dollar.

For over 200 years, all was quiet on the Chesapeake, until Yankees showed up to exploit the rich oyster rocks (beds). America's first packing house at Fair Haven, Ct sent down their fleet of sailing dredge boats in 1811, returning with glowing reports which brought the "Great Oyster Rush" by New Englanders. Eventually, Bay watermen awoke, watched and learned the secrets of dredging. They then screamed so loudly about "plundering by foreigners" that in 1830 both States enacted laws banning "oyster raking by outsiders." This was followed by more stringent laws prohibiting Virginians from dredging in Maryland waters (and vice versa), and allowing tongers to work *only* in their home county waters. However, without effective enforcement the laws were just something-on-the-books displayed in the county court houses.

In 1868, Maryland established the Oyster Police Force with one steamer (a side-wheel tug) and two sloops to patrol their 324,000 acres of natural oyster rocks plus 32,000 acres on the Potomac. The banner year for Maryland oysters was 1880 with 26,000 persons employed, 1450 dredge boats, and 2825 tonging boats. The same year, the Oyster Commission said, "Every vessel engaged in dredging requires a police vessel to watch it. The police fleet has to be as large as the oyster fleet (which is a warlike flotilla of water Arabs.")

Maryland's waterways were divided into eight oyster police districts: 1) Kent and Queen Anne counties, 2) Queen Anne and Talbot, 3) Talbot and Dorchester, 4) Wicomico, 5) Somerset, 6) Anne Arundel, 7) Calvert, Charles and St. Marys with one vessel for the Patuxent and two for the Potomac, 8) waters off the Atlantic Ocean. Headquarters were located at Chestertown, St. Michaels, Cambridge, Whitehaven, Crisfield, Annapolis, Solomons and Girdletree. By 1894, the police fleet had grown to 9 schooners, 3 sloops, 1 bugeye and 3 steamers.

Between 1870 and 1930, they had schooners *Folly, Helen M. Baughman, Bessie Jones, Julia Hamilton, Nelly Jackson, Frolic, Regulator, Anna B. Smith, Daisy Archer,* and *May Brown;* sloops *Avalon, Bessie Wolford, Nannie Merryman, Mary Compton, Carrie Franklin, E.B. Groome, Eliza Hayward, Katie Hines,* and *Louisa White:* bugeyes *Brown, Smith & Jones* and *Coronet*; steamers *Leila, Governor R.M. McLane, Gov P.F. Thomas, Gov W.T. Hamilton* and *Tech.* supplemented by many smaller power boats.

In 1870, Virginia established the "Oyster Navy" to patrol their 240,000 acres of natural rocks. Their waters were divided into 3 geographical districts to be policed by 3 steamers; in 1873 a sailing vessel was added to guard the Maryland-Virginia boundary line. Because of difficulties by large vessels in shallow waters and cogent complaints by Hampton Roads oystermen; state waters were divided anew by the 1900s into 48 oyster districts, each with its own inspector and a launch when required. Between years 1873 and 1930, the fleet consisted of steamers *Nannah, Accomac, James River, Rappahannock, Phillips, Commodore Maury* and the schooner *Pocomoke*; reinforced by small launches.

Enforcement of whiskey-running during Prohibition years (1918-33) was ignored. Duties of present day (1981) police are different in comparison to "guarding oyster rocks," such as checking: sewer outlets, plane crashes, theft, drugs, waterfowl and animals, oil spills, trash dumping, boat registration, ad infinitum.

MOLASSES and RUM

Molasses and its by-product, rum is a story of the other English colonists who came to America in the 17th-century, the ones who chose the Caribbean rather than New England or the Chesapeake Bay... they were members of the same migration, and settling the islands for many the same reasons. They employed similar colonizing techniques and shared similar colonizing experiences. Tobacco was initially their staple crop in Barbados and the Leeward Islands as in Virginia and Maryland.

Each colony was administered by a governor,council, and representative assembly, with parish churches, vestrymen, and justices of the peace at the local level, and a militia for protection. And yet—inexorably and very rapidly, the islands (British West Indies) and mainland (Chesapeake) plantations evolved into two separate communities.

Once the English colonists in the Caribbean learned how to grow and process sugarcane in the 1640s, they developed a life-style all their own. They turned their small islands into amazingly effective sugar-production machines activated by windmills and armies of black slaves. They became far richer than their cousins in the Chesapeake wilderness. They lived fast, spent recklessly, played desperately, and died young.

Although they persuaded the politicians in Parliament that the sugar-colonies were more valuable than the tobacco-colonies, they could not persuade themselves to live in the Indies any longer than necessary. By the close of the century, when Englishmen in the Chesapeake were "turning into" Americans, the Englishmen in the islands had one consuming ambition—to return home to England as fast as possible.

These sugar planters became shadowy and half-forgotten men. They never wrote much about themselves—not caring to advertise their newly found wealth to the inquisitive authorities of the Crown—and they have left few tangible remains in the islands.

Economically interdependent, these two sections of English America developed cognate trades lasting through the twentieth century. Grain became the islands' largest import from the Bay augmented with lumber (barrel headings and staves, shingles, trunnels), naval stores, foodstuffs (pork, biscuit, beans, butter, peas, hams and beef) tobacco, geese, candles, cattle and beeswax. Their principal exports to the Bay were sugar, molasses, rum, salt, ginger, cocoa, cotton, lime juice, citrus fruit, and coconuts; pineapple faded out about 1900. The century-old trade in campeche or logwood (used for drugs, dye tanning) ended about 1940, while sugar and molasses continued to be shipped by Bay sailers until their total demise.

For 300 years, molasses as a sugar substitute has been in the larder of all Bay boats... used in coffee, and on porridge, pancakes, bread, soup, pork and beans, sausage; brushed on meats, poultry, fish and cooked vegetables and even "Eskimo Pies" in 1930. King Po-T-Rik as processed on Baltimore's waterfront by Mangels, Herold Company was originally delivered in a one-horse wagon to nearby harbored vessels for shipment down the Bay. The thin true-molasses known as "wet sugar" was imported from Antiqua, Barbados, and Jamaica (each island had its particular flavor) aboard 3-masted schooners taking about 10 days. It was shipped in 84 gallon puncheons made of oak trapped with hickory. These were stored below decks in ventilated holds for protection from the hot sun. Decks were "wetted-down" hourly to keep the explosive molasses cool.*

Ashore at the Mangels' Granby Street plant, a bit of western corn syrup was added and the blended product was funneled into 31½ gallon wooden barrels (with steel straps), thence by water-carriage to the hundreds of wharves on the tidewater Chesapeake. Here, sitting in a favored corner of every country store, equipped with a hand-operated pump for self-service . . . Po-T-Rik became the best known "West Indian food" on the Bay.

Now, about rum... all Englishmen tended to drink heavily in the 17th-century, and those of the Caribbean drank very heavily. Rum made from molasses became a Chesapeake status symbol which eventually "sailed up" the Bay, for in 1774 Daniel Roberdeau built

*N.B. Several Bay vessels carrying molasses *did* explode because of heat expansion. Boston's inner-harbor was deluged with molasses when a 2,360,000 gallon tank (50′ high and filled to the brim) blew-up and flooded Charles River on 15 January 1919; death toll of 21 persons and 35 horses... and hundreds of "sticky boats."

the first distillery (2500 gallons capacity) at Alexandria with adjoining molasses storage. The favorite of Bay watermen was dark rum imported from the West Indies as it was better aged in their oak casks originally used for "wet sugar," and subsequently "burnt" inside forming a sugar-charcoal; a bit of caramel was dumped-in for deeper coloring. Aging was accelerated and the flavor improved by the rolling motion of sailing vessels transporting the rum bound for the Bay.

To understand the significance of rum to the Chesapeake Bay country, its economic status must be made clear. The colonists were dependent on England for their manufactured goods and in return they exported forestry products and agricultural staples. The value of their exports did not equal their imports—the balance of trade was always in favor of England. The colonists therefore, needed money. In place of money, they had a large surplus exportable merchandise for which they found a market in the friendly West Indies...British, French, Danish and Dutch islands, which not only had money, but sugar, molasses and rum.

Parliament passed a prohibitive tax in 1733 on the importation of sugar, molasses and rum from non-British islands to the colonies, greatly effecting trade to the Bay. George Washington during his trip in 1751 to the Barbados noted the economical importance of rum to his homeland on the Potomac River. Pitkin's Statistical View of 1817 showed "three times the trade from the Bay to the Indies as was sent to England." The moving power of rum was stupendous, and laws made by Parliament in 1733 and 1763 imposing a heavy duty on rum, and later laws by Congress in 1808 and 1820 forbidding slave trading were ineffectively enforced. Just so long as there was a big demand for West Indian rum and for slaves, the trade from the Bay continued despite all laws.

Pig meat reinforced rum as a catalyst to the great West Indian trade, Salt pork nourished crews of Bay trading vessels which regularly transported cargoes of salt fish and meats to planters on the Sugar Islands. Pork also fortified the hardy colonial appetite to a degree that required rum...a thirst that built a new industry, pivotal in commerce of the Bay for over a century. Next to specie...rum was the most widespread medium of exchange.

The name "rum" is definitely related to the Chesapeake, as George Washington's home Mount Vernon was so named out of respect for his British naval idol...Admiral Edward Vernon, who in 1745 discovered that his men were suffering from scurvy while in the Caribbean. Not knowing what to do about it, he cut the daily ration of beer and replaced it with the strange, new West Indian beverage, which conquered the scurvy problem and won him the lasting regard of his men, who referred to him affectionately as "Old Rummy" and in his honor called the new drink "rum," because in 18th-century England the word *rum* was a slang expression used to describe "people, things or events that were very good, the very best." Even Protestant clergymen preached that rum was "a good creature of God" and that "Man should partake of God's gift..."

The dark rum guzzled by seamen of yesteryear was nothing more than caramel-flavored concentrated sugar-cane spirits...and this is the way it was made: The sugar-cane (Saccharum officinarum) was harvested in the fields and immediately passed through heavy crushing rollers that expressed the juice. The juice was boiled causing the sugar in the syrup to crystalize and was then separated. What remained was molasses, which was sometimes still 5% sugar. The molasses was placed into huge wooden barrels (imported from the colonies or states) called hogsheads, each holding 1800 pounds or nearly one ton of molasses. They were then rolled to the nearby distillery or rolled to the beach into a molasses lighter; rowed to and lifted by slave labor aboard seagoing ships anchored offshore.

Rum distilleries during the late 1700s at Baltimore, Norfolk and Alexandria found it cheaper to import molasses and distill rum at home. However, a reversal of this occurred in 1825, when an English wheelwright named John Wray in Kingston, Jamaica began to blend and ship dark rum to the new country called United States. Today (1981) this is the oldest rum distillery in continuous operation, which produces 16 different types of rum.

Author's warning: Most distilled rums are about 86 proof which are for pantiwaist Bay sailors. For those who like to meet *nature-in-the-raw* off Point Lookout...try the Demerara rum from British Guiana...as it comes to 181 proof...great for stomach cauterizing.

And so, if Chesapeake Bay sailors of the present day have an urge to discover new and different horizons, the author suggests cruising the West Indies, formerly called the "Sugar Islands." But first... a bit of history: when Columbus landed, he claimed everything for his sponsor, the Spanish Queen who promptly ordered the Carib Indians decimated. Other countries challenged the Spaniards and moved-in to establish their claims.

A list of major West Indian island names; land area expressed in square miles; and the European country which permanently settled the island. Reference: US Defense Mapping Center.

SPAIN

Island	Sq. miles
Cuba	44,200
Puerto Rico	3,455
Santo Domingo	18,500
Trinidad	1,864

GERMANY

Island	Sq. miles
St. Peter	2

ENGLAND

Island	Sq. miles
Anguilla	35
Antigua	108
Bahamas	5,380
Barbados	166
Barbuda	62
Cayman Isles	100
Jamaica	4,410
Montserrat	40
Nevis	36
St. Kitts	65
Tortola	21
Turk's Isle	193

SWEDEN

Island	Sq. miles
St. Barthelemy	10

DENMARK

Island	Sq. miles
St. John	20
St. Thomas	28

HOLLAND

Island	Sq. miles
Aruba	70
Bonaire	112
Curacao	178
Saba	5
Sint Maarten	16
Sint Eustatius	12
Tobago	116

FRANCE

Island	Sq. miles
Dominica	290
Grenada	133
Guadeloupe	687
Haiti	10,714
La Desirade	10
Marie-Galante	58
Martinique	220
St. Croix	84
St. Lucia	238
St. Martin	17
St. Vincent	113

CHESAPEAKE BAY MARITIME MUSEUMS and SMALL CRAFT EXHIBITS 1981

Baltimore Inner Harbor
Baltimore, Maryland
Exhibit: skipjack

Calvert Marine Museum
Solomons, Maryland
Exhibits: doryboat, rail skiff, crabbing skiff, yawl-boat, log canoe, bateau, brogan, oyster buy-boat, dugout

Chesapeake Bay Maritime Museum
St. Michaels, Maryland
Exhibit: log canoe, bugeye, rail skiff, Delaware ducker, sinkbox, bushwack boat, sneak box, gunning skiff, ice box, garvey box, pound net boat, crabbing skiff, skipjack bateau, gilling skiff, striker boat, dugout canoe

Chesapeake & Delaware Canal Museum
Chesapeake City, Maryland

Chesapeake Bay Watermen's Museum
Yorktown, Virginia

Crisfield Historical Museum
Crisfield, Maryland
Exhibit: gill net skiff

Indian Queen Tavern Museum
Bladensburg, Maryland

Jamestown Festival Park
Jamestown, Virginia
Exhibit: pinnace, galleon

Mariners Museum
Newport News, Virginia
Exhibit: dugout canoe, bateau, striker boat

Neild Maritime Museum
Cambridge, Maryland

New Point Comfort Lighthouse
Mathews, Virginia

Outdoor History Museum
St. Mary's City, Maryland
Exhibit: pinnace, longboat (tender)

Oxford Museum
Oxford, Maryland

Patuxent River Park
Croom, Maryland
Exhibit: log canoe, rail skiff

Portsmouth Naval Museum
Portsmouth, Virginia

Potomac Museum
Coltons Point, Maryland
Exhibit: doryboat

Radcliffe Maritime Museum
Baltimore, Maryland

Salisbury State College
Ward Foundation
Salisbury, Maryland
Exhibit: bushwack boat, sinkbox, ice box, sneak skiff

Smithsonian Institution National Museum of American History
Washington, DC
Exhibit: dugout canoe

Truxton-Decatur Naval Museum
Washington, DC

US Frigate Constellation
Baltimore, Maryland

US Naval Academy Museum
Annapolis, Maryland

U.S. Navy Memorial Museum
Washington, DC

THE HENRY HALL REPORT

Shipbuilding in the United States increased rapidly following the Civil War and by 1880 it had become one of the largest industries along the shorelines of the East and West Coasts, Great Lakes, Gulf of Mexico, and the Mississippi River. Congress instructed Charles W. Seaton, Superintendent of Census to have a thorough investigation made and prepare a printed report.

Henry Hall, business manager of the *New York Tribune* was assigned the task and his work started in November 1880. It was completed in November 1882 with the 276 paged meticulous and informative *Report on the Shipbuilding Industry* which was printed in small type face by the Government Printing Office in 1884. His personal manuscript (which is much longer than the Government report) is at the Penobscot Marine Museum, Searsport, Maine and the printed report is at the Library of Congress. A partial report of shipbuilding on the Chesapeake Bay follows.

MARYLAND

"Chesapeake Bay has been known from the earliest times for the speed and beauty of its vessels. The rakish air of the fishing boats has also been shared by the larger vessels of the Bay. The schooner rig was popularized at an early day, and schooners and brigs were the principal trading vessels engaged in the trade to the West Indies, were also built largely for the slave trade, both employments calling for speed and a handy rig. In its origin the slave trade was regarded as a proper mode of obtaining workmen for the West Indies and the continent of America, and was carried on mainly by the British, French, and Portuguese. In 1761 the British had 28 vessels (3475 tons) in the trade, and in 1776 they had 192, measuring 22,296 tons. By a return to parliament in 1789 it appears that 38,000 slaves were carried annually in British vessels to America and its islands, 20,000 in French, 10,000 in Portuguese, 4000 in Dutch, and 2000 in Danish vessels, about 74,000 in all. Slaves cost from $22 to $60 in Africa, and sold for from $78 to $98 in the West Indies.

"It was a profitable business, and appears to have been engaged in to a large extent by American vessels built on the Chesapeake. They were generally built especially for the trade, and were sold in the West Indies and elsewhere to those who carried on the business. The between-deck space of 5 or 6 feet was divided by bulkheads into rooms for the men, women, and boys, respectively, and in a large brig there was room for 600 people. The hold was about 10 feet deep, and carried from 30,000 to 40,000 gallons of water, stores for a cruise of about 100 days, and the ballast. The schooners and brigs, both merchantmen and slavers, were broad of beam before the center and above the waterline and sharp on the floor, often having about 20 degree of dead rise. The bow was sharp and flaring above the water, the front of the forecastle deck being often as round as the section of an apple. The hulls were lean aft, and thus sailed with considerable drag. They were long in proportion to breadth, had low bulwarks, looked low in the water, and carried raking masts, in order to bring the effort of the sails farther aft, where the lateral resistance of the vessel in the water was located. The topmasts were so slender that they sometimes bent to the wind like whips; a circumstance thought favorable to speed.

"These vessels were able to carry a heavy press of canvas, would go into the wind remarkably fast, were smart and handy, and had a world-wide fame. Cheap, good, and abundant timber made Chesapeake Bay an active ship-building region even before the Revolutionary War, and after the independence the shipwrights of Baltimore were among the first to petition Congress for legislation in behalf of the maritime interests of the country. The legislation that followed was a great benefit to Baltimore, and made her one of the principal shipyard centers of the continent.

"The history of the industry in Baltimore is about the same as that of the other large commercial ports, except that her tonnage was chiefly in fore-and-aft-rigged vessels and she would build 125 schooners in a year to 20 ships and brigs. The fisheries and local trading of the Bay called for the production of large numbers of small schooners; and the same style of vessel was employed in coasting and in the large trade to the West Indies which sprang up in course of time. In the busy years after 1840 there were as many as 15 shipyards in south Baltimore and elsewhere in the harbor actively engaged in building schooners, brigs, clipper ships, and steamboats. Some of the old builders, still living, remember the time when from 20 to 25 vessels were on the stocks at once and everybody was making money, and the industry was growing so fast that in the large yards there were anywhere from 15 to 20 apprentices at a time learning the trade.

"The clipper ships of Baltimore had many of the peculiarities of the schooners. They were as sharp on the floor, sailed with a drag, had flaring bows and raking masts, and were noted for their quick voyages, but carried high bulwarks to keep the ship dry. The extreme vessels ceased to be built after the California excitement (the Gold-rush) was over, as their tendency to sag at the ends and get out of shape operated against them; but improvements were made in the model, and some of the best vessels in America were then launched from the Baltimore yards. The *Cyane,* a clipper bark built in Baltimore 35 years ago, is to-day a strong and good vessel. She is 132 feet long over all, 24 feet beam, and 12 feet, 6 inches hold, having one deck, but with a second and open tier of beams to strengthen her. The bulwarks are 5 feet, 9 inches high. She requires ballast when empty, being so sharp as to be top heavy; but when loaded to her draught of 13 or 14 feet she is a good carrier, easy at sea, and a fast sailer. The war of 1861, with the changes which took place in that period in favor of steam vessels and the strikes and high wages, put a virtual end to ship-building in Baltimore, few merchant vessels, other than side-wheel steamboats and propeller tugs, having been built since that time.

"The principal business of Baltimore now is the repairing and outfitting of vessels. Sails and outfits are supplied by a few large firms, which operate on an extensive scale and are able to buy cheap and to undersell all their competitors on the Bay. There are 17 ship-yards in the city, with 19 railways and 3 floating dry docks. One yard, near Fort McHenry, is devoted to the building and repair of iron vessels, and has a full outfit of machine, boiler, and other shops, besides a large fixed dry dock built of masonry. The length from the groove of the outer gate to the head of the dock is 470 feet; from the inner gate, 450 feet; greatest width on top, 113 feet; width on bottom, 45 feet; depth, 26 feet, leaving, with the blocks, 23 feet for a vessel. The dock is elliptical in plan, the sides descending in steps. Over 8000 piles were driven to support the sides, in which about 2,000,000 feet of lumber were used. The width at the entrance is 123 feet; at the gate 83 feet. The gate is a caisson built like the hull of a vessel, to displace water enough to sustain its weight. It has two decks, the lower one for the machinery. The pumps are operated by steam on shore, and can empty the dock in two hours.

"Congress ceded the land for this structure on condition that government vessels should be docked free of charge. The other docks and railways of the city are large enough to accommodate wooden ships of the largest class. A large number of the smaller vessels of the Chesapeake are owned by colored men, and in order to secure prompt and inexpensive repairs of their vessels they organized a stock company a few years ago with a capital of $40,000 and established a yard with two marine railways. Originally there were 300 stockholders in this enterprise, but the number has been reduced to about 150. The yard employs 70 men, nearly all of them Negroes, and pays them the current rate of wages in the city. They haul out about 460 vessels a year. The shipwrights of the port have formed an association, with rules, which bring a great deal of work on foreign vessels to them. The Italian, Norwegian, and British grain ships avoid expense where they can, and used to go upon the railways, paying hauling fees only, and doing as much as possible of the calking, painting, etc., themselves; but the association requires that the repair work shall be done by the yard hauling out the vessel, so that the system in vogue in New York of running a dry-dock merely for the hauling fees does not prevail here. These rules have, however, driven a great deal of the work on the Bay vessels from this port to country railways scattered along the Bay.

"The fees for hauling in Baltimore were as follows: Side-wheel steamers, 15 cents per register ton, or 7½ cents a ton a day for 5 days, and 5 cents a ton a day thereafter; propeller steamers, of 800 tons and over, the same; of from 600 to 800 tons, 12 cents a ton, or 6 cents a ton a day for 5 days, and 5 cents a ton a day thereafter; tugs under 100 tons, $10, or $6 a day for 5 days, and $5 a day thereafter; from 100 to 150 tons, $15, or $8 a day; sailing vessels of 800 tons and over, 15 cents a ton, or 7½ cents a ton for 5 days, and 5 cents a ton a day thereafter; from 600 to 800 tons, 12 cents, or 6 cents a ton a day for 5 days, and 5 cents a ton a day thereafter; from 100 to 600 tons, 10 cents a ton, or 5 cents a ton a day; from 50 to 100 tons, $10, or $6 a day; from 25 to 50 tons, $8, or $5 a day; under 25 tons, $6, or $4 a day; scows of over 100 tons, 10 cents a ton, or 5 cents a ton a day; under 100 tons, $10, or $6 a day.

"Builders also charge a regular commission on the labor bills and materials used. There are no spar-yards here, each yard making its own spars, nor is there any machine for punching nail holes in sheathing metal, the work being all done by hand. A punching machine was once tried, but the workmen objected to its use. Wages were $2.50 and $2.75 a day. The timber used has always been Maryland and Virginia oak and pitch-pine, and Pennsylvania white pine until late years, when Georgia pine has been imported, on account of having more heart and less sap-wood. Spruce spars come from West Virginia. Oak has always been cheap; but it used to range from $15 to $20 per thousand feet, though by watching for chances the yards at times have got it as low as $5. Oak in the flitch now costs $25, and planking and heavy pieces, for keelsons, $45. Georgia pine is $35 per thousand feet. One firm in Baltimore ceils ships for grain and fits them for cattle transportation, using about 4500,000 feet of white and yellow pine yearly.

"Havre de Grace has a marine railway and ship-yard. Scow schooners for duck shooting and coal barges are the principal new work, but the repairing of coal-boats and schooners is the main support of the yard. There was on the stocks in the census year a barge 170 feet long, 21 feet beam, and 13 feet deep, with 4 feet sheer. The floor was flat, the bilge square, the sides slightly flaring, the bow and stern sharp, stem straight, and the stern broad on deck and overhanging. The whole boat was built of oak, 140,000 feet being required. The framers were 98 in number; the top timbers 6 by 8 inches; side planking, 3 inches; ceiling of sides, 5 inches; bottom plank, 4 inches; ceiling of floor, 2 inches, and about 400 bushels of salt were used above light-water mark. Carpenters were hard to get.

"At Annapolis, on the Bay below Baltimore, there is a small marine railway, and a small fishing boat is occasionally built.

"At Cambridge, on the eastern shore of the Bay, there are 3 yards, including 2 railways, and a little community of sailmakers, riggers, and blacksmiths. The moving spirit of this town is one of William H. Webb's apprentices, a builder of long and varied experience, who has plied his art both on the Atlantic and Pacific coasts and in China. Several coal barges for the Lehigh Valley Company were built here of the same model as those at Perth Amboy. The building at Cambridge has been confined to sloops and schooners for the Bay and tugs and barges; but the place is favorably situated for an extensive business, as it is in Dorchester county which is clothed with fine oak and pine timber down to the coast and on the islands of the coast. Although this region has furnished frames for the New England ship-yards for fifty years, and although large quantities of planking and oak of all sizes for the construction of wharves, houses, etc., are exported annually, yet many tracts of first-growth oak and pine remain untouched. When Cambridge was visited a track was passed at Airey's station, a few miles from the town, through which were strewn the frame timbers for a large vessel, hewn to the proper shapes and lying on the ground, ready for shipment to some New England yard. Probably building can be carried on to the best advantage here when the builder is also the owner of his own timber. His oak frames would not cost him over $15 per thousand feet; when bought from the saw-mills in the flitch the cost was only $25 per thousand, or $10 less than in New England. Three small schooners and a tug were built in the census year. Wages were from $1.25 to $2 a day, a few men getting $2.50.

"At Pocomoke City there are 2 yards, which produce a few Bay and river vessels of small size every year. In the census year these yards built 4 schooners, registering 162 tons, and costing $16,500. Much repair work is done. Wages range from $1 to $2 per day, the average being less than $2. There were no labor-saving appliances in the yards, but one yard was run in conjunction with a saw-mill. Worcester county is heavily wooded with oak and pine, and the saw-mill was paying not to exceed $10 per thousand for large oak trees in the round, delivered in the yard, the cost for sawing being about $2.50 per thousand. A great deal of the heavy timber around here has been cut off and exported from the Bay. South of Pocomoke there have been camps for several years employed in cutting timber for the ship-builders of Maine, their operations being now carried on nearer Accomack, Virginia, and some of the forests have been culled for everything above 12 inches in diameter; still, much heavy timber remains in other places, and there is an abundance for a local ship-building industry. In the flitch oak is sold at Pocomoke for $22 and less per thousand.

"At Crisfield, in Somerset county, a little fishing town built on a solid bank of oyster shells about 50 rods (825 feet) wide and 150 rods (2475 feet) long; there are more than 1400 fishing vessels owned here, 700 of them being log canoes not large enough to register at the custom house...all coming from rivers of the lower Bay. Here is the center of the Bay's fishing industry, employing large numbers of people on shore and a great deal of small capital in both new and old work. About 175 oyster boats are produced on the lower Eastern shore yearly, and there are 20 marine railways, costing from $3000 to $4000 each, for hauling the vessels out of the water for painting and repair, each doing from $2000 to $5000 worth of work yearly. Many of the boats, and indeed all the framed ones, are made in the yards of professional builders; but it is surprising to notice that, after all, about one-half of the whole number annually produced are to be credited to private builders, fishermen mostly, who make their own boats, either in the woods or in their own back yards. Give a fisherman a boat, and let him spend three or four years sailing it on the Bay, gathering oysters and fish, loading his boat until its capacity is tested, going with his catch to market, hauling his boat out on the bank two or three times a year, painting it, calking the cracks, repairing it when injured, seeing it, in fact, in all possible lights, and comparing notes with his neighbors, and when the time comes for him to get a new boat the chances are that he will make the boat himself, knowing by that time all there is to know about how to do it; but if he should have it built for him, it will generally be because he is prosperous, and would prefer to spend his time in some other way than in boat-building.

"The islands on the Maryland and Virginia's Eastern Shore became densely populated early in the history of settlement, especially Smith's, Deal's, and Tangier's islands. From the necessity of their position the people were obliged to have the means of crossing the water, and from the earliest times they bought or made for themselves wooden canoes, each hewn from the trunk of one tree. Almost every family owned one, two, and even three boats, and the men were out in them the greater part of the time, taking the daily meal of fish for the family, traveling to and fro, or sailing off to market somewhere with a canoe loaded down with oysters and fish. A great deal of general trading took place in these boats. The inhabitants of the islands went to church in them on Sundays, and in fact the whole population, white and black, were used to owning and handling canoes, and knew how to make them.

"Pitch-pine timber has always been abundant on the Bay, particularly on the southern part, and it is from this tree that boats have been made. The supply has lasted for 250 years now, and there are still enough large trees to make all the canoes that are needed. The durability of a pitch-pine canoe is great, one well made from a sound tree lasting from 30 to 50 years if care for and painted every year. Canoes played a part in the Revolutionary War, and from that day to this there has never been any other kind of boat used on the Chesapeake for small fishing and oystering.

"The ordinary canoe is 20 feet in length, 4 feet wide across the gunwales, and 18 inches deep inside. It is made from a single log, is straight in the bow, but is pointed at both ends. Formerly 30-foot boats, 5 and 6 feet wide, were also made in one piece. The famous 'Methodist canoe,' which carried 'the parson of the islands' for so many years while visiting the members of his congregation, was one of these boats. The tree from which this canoe was hewn was too large to be useful at a saw-mill, and an Annamessex man finally bought it for $10 and felled it himself, the job occupying nearly three hours. Two logs were cut from the tree and hauled to King's creek, and then towed around to Annamessex, each log making a canoe, the larger one being the boat above referred to. Few of these big trees now exist, and therefore the larger canoes have to be made of more than one stick. When three logs are put into the boat, one is carved to make the keel, floor, stem, and stern, the other two forming the sides to the gunwale. Many are made of 5 and even 7 logs each, and others are carried up on the sides by adding two or three streaks of narrow and heavy plank, which are bolted through into the sides of the canoe.

"The 35- and 40-foot boats, which have from 6 to 11 feet beam, are generally carved from 5 or 7 logs, with top streaks as above described, the different logs being joined to each other by wooden keys and dowels and by treenails and iron bolts driven in edgewise. None of the smaller boats are decked, but all have an 8- or 12-inch wash-board, with a narrow coaming the whole length of the boat along each gunwale. This top work is supported by light knees spaced from 4 to 6 feet apart; and sometimes short crooked pieces, cut to fit the curvatures of the surface, are nailed along the bilge inside, to strengthen that part of the boat. A 35- or 40-foot boat generally has a short length of decking in the bow, and sometimes a small house. The thickness of the walls of a canoe is as follows: In a 30-foot boat, about 3 inches on the bottom, 2¼ or 2½ inches on the bilge, and 1 inch at the gunwale, gradually thickening towards the ends; in the bow, 3½ or 4 inches on the bottom, 2½ to 3 inches on the bilge, and 2 at the gunwale. In a canoe of smaller size the thicknesses would be in proportion. In a large 7-log canoe building at Point Lookout, Maryland, in the 1880 census year, 40 feet long, 11 feet wide at the main beam, and 3½ feet deep amidships, the wood was 5 inches thick near the keel, 4 inches in the bilge, and 2½ and 2 inches at the gunwale, being a little heavier toward the bow. In a large boat there is often, but not always, a center-board, but there is seldom a center-board in a boat of less than 30 feet in length.

"In rig these canoes are the most unique and interesting in the United States. A 20-foot boat carries one pole mast, with triangular sail forward of amidships; all others two masts, with triangular sails, the foremast being the tallest and raking 1-1/4 inches to the foot, the mizzen, which is two-thirds the length of the other, raking 1-3/4 inches to the foot. A 20-foot boat has no jib, but in a longer one there is often a 12-foot pole bowsprit, stuck up in the bow at an angle of 40 degrees, with a horizontal line, carrying an odd-looking triangular jib, which is spread by a halliard tied to the mast about three-fourths of the way up from the gunwales. When the bow is decked over there is a short horizontal bowsprit with a long and narrow jib. The main and mizzen sails are spred by a sprit, and are furled by taking out the sprit and wrapping the sail around the mast. The rig is a safe and handy one. The center of effort is very low, and a canoe is consequently seldom capsized.

"The model given both speed and capacity. These canoes are very nearly flat on the floor amidships, and a 30-foot boat, weighing 2000 pounds, will skim over shallows in safety, drawing, with keel, only 12 inches of water. The water-lines are hollow forward and aft, the after body being lean enough to give a drag of 6 or 8 inches. The keel is deepest at the bow, tapering from 5 to 8 inches at the forefoot to 2 inches at the stern. The broadest beam is usually a trifle forward of amidships/ but many place it in the middle of the length, and a few a trifle aft of the middle.

"Canoe builders hew out their boats with no other guides than the eye, sometimes aided by a rough draft on a piece of paper, and use no other tools than the ax, adze, square, callipers, two-foot rule, plane, auger, and hammer. A 20-foot boat costs from $50 to $60; but the price increases rapidly with the size, 40-foot boats costing $500 and $600 each.

"A great many canoes are now made by farmers and their boys for other purposes than fishing. Near the cities of Baltimore, Annapolis, and Norfolk, and near many Bay towns reached by steamboats, there are numerous farms devoted to the raising of melons and vegetables. Boats must be had to carry the produce to market, and rather than buy one the proprietors of these farms will often build; and it often happens that some smart farmer's boy, having thus become initiated into the art of canoe building, will continue the industry as a regular calling. It is usual for the builder of a canoe, professional or amateur, to go into the woods, select his trees, and buy them standing, paying a fixed sum per log, per cord, or per thousand board feet. Logs cost from $3 to $5 each, and the sum of $35 will buy all the trees needed for a 40-foot boat, worth, when finished, from $400 to $500. All the value over $35 is given to the boat by felling the trees, hauling them to a convenient stream, towing them down to the boatyard, and then expending upon the materials the time and labor of the builder and his men. Sometimes the canoe is carved out of the felled trees in the woods and is hauled down to the water's edge when finished. The outside of the boat is first roughly formed with the ax; the inside is then carved out, the pieces are joined with keys, bolts, spikes, and treenails, and the thwarts, etc., fitted to their places.

"Solomon's Island, on the Patuxent River, has two yards and two railways. The fishing industry supports this place. Bug-eyes and pungies are the vessels built.

"At several places on the Bay, notably at Oxford, Saint Michael's, Broad Creek, Sharptown, Whitehaven, and Salisbury, there is a good deal of repairing of vessels at small railways. There are at least two hundred or more small shipyards on the Eastern Shore of Maryland and Virginia, seemingly tucked away in every creek.

"What makes a ship is principally wood, iron, and men's labor. Large schooners, barks, and ships each consume from 280,000 feet of lumber, 18 tons of iron, and 4300 days of labor, to 960,000 feet of lumber, 120 tons of iron, and 9000 to 14,000 days of labor, according as steam saws, derricks, and other labor-saving appliances are used in the yard or not. If Maryland were to become an active ship-building state, it is probable that the cost of labor would rise to the scale paid in Maine; but in the purchase of oak and pitch-pine her builders would enjoy an advantage of from $10 to $15 a thousand feet for oak and about $3 to $5 a thousand for pine. With labor-saving machinery they could build the cheapest wooden vessels on the Atlantic coast.

VIRGINIA

(Author's note: M. V. Brewington states: "Sir Thomas Gates was sent out by the Virginia Company in 1610 to the Bay with 2 shipwrights, 20 shipcarpenters, 10 caulkers, 2 sparmakers, 4 smiths, and 2 rope-makers...")

"The ship-building of this state began in 1622 when the Virginia company, at great trouble and expense, sent out Captain Thomas Barwick with 25 carpenters in order to build the pinnaces, shallops, and large vessels needed for trade and transportation in the new province, and on their arrival they began to build small sail-boats for the river and Bay trade. The magnificent extent and the excellence of the timber were noted in all reports on the colony's shipbuilding, as there were other occupations that paid them better, the best industry being agriculture, to which they devoted their whole attention, leaving to the inhabitants of the rugged and poor soils of New England the construction and management of ships. A number of small vessels and boats were made, but seldom in the whole history of the colony and state down to the present has more than 2000 tons of shipping been built in any one year. The town in which the industry has principally flourished is Norfolk, and from 1840 to 1855 barks and ships were occasionally built there for the West India and the Brazilian trade for local shareholders. In 1853-54, at the Norfolk yards, 10 vessels were launched, registering a total of 3600 tons; but since 1855 there has been no building of large vessels, except a few steamboats.

"At Alexandria, there are two ship-yards, with a marine railway. The principal concern, started in 1874, had built two large three-masted schooners and one tug and repaired a large number of Potomac River vessels when the yard was visited in the census year. Schooners cost $50 per ton. Vessels have been built here occasionally from the earliest days, and there was a public ship-yard during the Revolution for the construction of government vessels. Alexandria enjoys some advantages with reference to timber, and is a convenient point for the repairing of steamboats and sailing craft plying to and from Washington. A new yard has started within two years, and is now building its second vessel. Squared oak costs from $20 to $22 a thousand at the yard, pitch-pine $23 and $25; but in the log oak can be delivered for about $15 a thousand for what can be squared out of it. The yard has a complete outfit of steam saws, and does its own squaring of the timber. A boat of a style peculiar to Chesapeake Bay and the Potomac River was building here in 1881. It was a 'longboat' an undecked center-board schooner with two fore-and-aft sails and a large jib-many of these vessels being employed in carrying cord-wood to Washington. (See "longboat" chapter in this book). Preparations are making in Alexandria for the cheap manufacture of rolled iron by a new process, with a view to iron-ship building; but so far the company has only been making blooms, not having put in the necessary machinery for rolling iron. Confidence is felt in the experiment, and an iron-ship yard is the ultimate object in view. Few places have better advantages than Alexandria for the manufacture of iron ships in materials, climate, labor, and cheap transportation.

"Going down the Potomac and into the Chesapeake one passes headlands, rivers, and bays in profusion which seem to have been qualified by nature for ship-building. The water is deep, and the shore is covered with oak and pine, and in spite of more than half a century of cutting there is a great deal of large timber left. Tracts can be bought where the stumpage, as it is called, does not exceed $1 a thousand feet; that is, the trees standing in the woods will sell for what can be squared out of them at the rate of $1 a thousand. There is no building in these beautiful bays of the Virginia coast, however, other than canoes and small fishing and trading schooners, the work being on canoes principally. There are few regular builders, except at Pocoson (Poquoson), Back Bay (Back River), and Hampton.

"At Norfolk there are four yards, and, in addition, two or three in which something is occasionally built. In all, the yards have five marine railways for repairing, one of them sectional. The latter will hold two vessels at once, one of which can be launched without disturbing the other. Ship work here was originally on small vessels, but in the years of general maritime excitement the city ventured into full-rigged ships, four ships of a total of 2900 tons register being built in 1853-54, as well as a number of brigs and schooners. The yellow fever broke out in 1855, destroying this prosperity completely. There has been some small building since in different years, but the vessels have not exceeded 300 tons register, except the *Rockaway*, a steamboat of 1950 tons, 275 feet long on the keel 293 feet on the deck, 38 feet wide in the hull, 66 feet over all, 11-1/2 feet deep, drawing 6 feet of water, which was built in 1876, and was calculated to make 20 miles an hour. The empty hull was sent off to New York in the spring of 1877 to receive her machinery, but she broke adrift in a storm, went ashore, and was dashed to pieces. The work of the city is now chiefly on tugs, barges, canal-boats, river steamers, and the large fleet of small produce schooners employed in this locality, and consists principally of repair work.

"The builders say that the presence of the navy-yard has the effect to keep up prices and wages, which is detrimental to the private yards. Wages were from $2 to $3 a day in the census year; laborers got $1.50; the average was about 50 cents a day higher than in Maryland and Delaware. Oak was $22.50 a thousand in the flitch, $30 for short plank, $40 for long plank; pitch-pine about $28, the price varying from $20 for short stuff to $40 for the finest, the fair average of a cargo being $28 a thousand. Black gum wood has been much used here for keels, on account of the great lengths obtainable, its tenacity, and strength. The worms are thought to bit it quicker than oak, but by coppering this can be prevented. In 70- and 80-foot lengths gum costs $25 a thousand; in short lengths from $15 to $18. Vessels have been planked with gum at Norfolk, and the wood was found to be serviceable. A marine railway was built with gum in 1838, and when the ways were repaired two or three years ago the wood was sound and bright and the iron bolts in it were scarcely corroded.

"The grading vessels peculiar to Norfolk were the little farming sloops and schooners, which flock into the harbor in large fleets in the summer time, bringing vegetables for the New York and Baltimore steamers. Often 150 of these little vessels enter the harbor about two hours before the departure of a steamer, racing at full speed, with everything set, and loaded high above the deck with a profusion of boxes and barrels packed with melons, cabbages, tomatoes, and vegetables of nearly every description. They dash straight in to get the best positions near the wharves, and often crowd in so thick that the steamer cannot make its berth. In consequence, a number of them are obliged to cast off and go swarming out into the Bay, and cruise back and forth like a swarm of butterflies until they are allowed to return, when in they come again with a rush, jostling and crowding, the air being torn with the good-natured jabbering and arguing of the crews. There are a good many bugeyes and canoes in this 'trucking' fleet. These boats, large and small, are owned largely by Negroes, and their crews are principally Negroes. They are built on the vegetable farms all around Norfolk and across the James River on the peninsulas above.

"There are a few regular builders on the Nansemond, Chuckatuck, and Back rivers. A sloop 26 feet long, 11 feet broad, and 3 feet deep will cost around $300; a large sloop 45 feet long, $2000. An average size, 9 tons, would be 35 feet in length, 13-1/2 feet beam, and 3-1/2 feet hold. Owners follow their own fancy in rig, some preferring the sloop rig, others the schooner. The majority of the boats are schooners, but they seldom have topmasts or topsails, and the space amidships is open. The boxes and barrels are stowed in this hatchway until the hold is full, and are then piled clear across the deck and as high as the sails will allow. Aft there is a little house. These boats have no bulwarks, but only a chock or low rail around the planksheer. They are full and flat, partaking of the canoe model. Some of the sloops are of a flat-iron shape. The smart boats each make from $8 to $12 a day in the summer time. The charge for freighting vegetables is 3 cents for a box and 6 cents for a barrel, or from 4 to 10 cents according to the distance. Oysters are carried for from 3 to 5 cents a bushel, and sometimes the boats can make two trips in one day. The colored men make money with them, and when of a frugal disposition save money, and are often able to buy schooners of larger size."

REQUIEM

The annual Federal Report *Merchant Vessels of the US* list nearly 2400 sailing (non-self-propelled) vessels working in 1910 on the Chesapeake Bay. The survivors during the year 1981 are noted below by name, owner and Maryland address, size, where and when built.

Rebecca T. Ruark. Emerson Todd, Cambridge. 47x16x4. Taylors Isle Md. 1886

Ruby G. Ford. Bartlett Murphy, Cambridge. 45x16x3. Fairmont Md. 1891

Susan May. Clifton Benton, Crisfield. 46x15x3. Pocomoke City Md. 1901

Elsworth. Norris Lewis, Wingate. 40x14x3. Hudson Md. 1901

Sigsbee. Wade Murphy, Cambridge. 47x16x4. Deal Isle Md. 1901

Kathryn. Malcolm Wheatley, Wingate. 50x17x4. CrisfieldMd. 1901

Stanley Norman. Edward Farley, St. Michaels. 47x15x4. Salisbury Md. 1902

Maggie Lee. Webster Clifton, Crisfield. 51x16x4. Pocomoke City Md. 1903

S.J. Bennett. Gerald Cohen, Cambridge. 43x15x3. Inverness Md. 1903

Fannie L. Daugherty. Norman Benton, Wenona. 41x15x4. Crisfield Md. 1904

Virginia W. Harry Salmon, Cambridge. 38x14x4. Guilford Va. 1904

Ralph T. Webster. William Bradshaw, Tilghman. 48x16x4. Oriole Md. 1905

Hilda M. Willing. Robert Sweitzer, Tilghman. 40x14x3. Hallwood Va. 1905

Ida May. Elbert Gladden, Deal Isle. 42x14x3. Deep Creek Va. 1906

Minnie V. City of Baltimore, Baltimore. 45x16x3. Wenona Md. 1906

F.C. Lewis Jr. Stanford White, Wenona. 39x15x3. Hopkins Va. 1907

Clarence Crockett. Loudy Horner, Wenona. 45x15x3. Deep Creek Va. 1908

Geneva May. Roland Pianka, Wenona. 50x17x4. Wenona Md. 1908

Howard. Stanley Daniels, Wenona. 45x15x3. Deep Creek Va. 1909

E.C. Collier. John Larrimore, Tilghman. 52x18x4. Deal Isle Md. 1910

Thomas Clyde. Charles Abbott, Wenona. 54x18x5. Oriole Md. 1911

Nellie L. Byrd. William Todd, Cambridge. 54x17x5. Oriole Md. 1911

Sea Gull. Jesse Thomas, Deal Isle. 47x16x4. Crisfield Md. 1924

Wilma Lee. Ralph Ruark, Wingate. 47x16x5. Wingate Md. 1940

Helen Virginia. Carroll Bozman, Upper Fairmont. 43x16x2. Crisfield. 1948

City of Crisfield. Arthur Daniels, Wenona. 45x16x2. Reedville, Va. 1949

Somerset. Walton Benton, Wenona. 45x16x2. Reedville Va. 1949

Lorraine Rose. Clyde Evans, Ewell. 44x15x2. Reedville Va. 1949

Caleb W. Jones. Clifton Webster, Wenona. 44x16x2. Reedville Va. 1953

Rosie Parks. Orville Parks, Cambridge. 46x17x2. Wingate Md. 1955

Martha Lewis. Daniel Dize, Tilghman. 46x17x2. Wingate Md. 1955

H.M. Krentz. Walter Webster, Wenona. 45x16x5. Harryhogan Va. 1955

Lady Katie. Stanley Larrimore, Tilghman. 46x17x2. Wingate Md. 1956

In 1981, the Maryland Natural Resources Police list *Dee of St. Marys* (Francis Russell, Piney Point); *Lady Agnes* (James McGlinty, Oxford): *Anna McGarvey* (Michael Ashford, Annapolis).

SHIPYARD SITES and HOME PORTS

Since 1866, the US Departments of Commerce, Treasury, Labor, or Transportation have published a yearly register titled *Merchant (Sailing) Vessels of the United States*. A time consuming inspection by the author found that 1910 was the peak-year for the number of sailing craft "working" on the Chesapeake Bay, with a total of 2393; Crisfield claimed the largest registry of sailing vessels of any port in the nation. A vessel to be registered and documented at a "home port" was of 5 net tons or over; thus there was no federal record of thousands of small workboats in the fishing, crabbing, and oystering business.

This federal publication noted for each vessel the: official registration number; rig; name of the vessel; gross and net tonnage; length, breadth and depth; when built; where built; service (such as freight, oyster, fish, passenger, tank or miscellaneous); number of crew; name of owner; address of owner; and the home port (where registration papers were issued). In 1910, the number of Bay vessels and places listed as "home port" were:

Crisfield Md	- 625	Cape Charles Va	- 161
Baltimore Md	- 504	Chincoteague Va	- 138
Annapolis Md	- 179	Alexandria Va	- 74
Tappahannock Va	- 178	Richmond Va	- 45
Newport News Va	- 176	Washington DC	- 26
Norfolk Va	- 175	Seaford De	- 12

Registration of vessels on the Bay was originally imposed by Parliament in 1673 with specific intentions: 1) to ensure that colonial competitors did not enjoy tax-free benefits unavailable to Englishmen at home; 2) to restrict colonial commerce, particularly in commodities needed in England; 3) to limit colonial trade, with consequent reduction of shipments to foreigners; 4) to augment home revenues by increasing supplies of taxable imports as tobacco; 5) to tighten English control over colonial markets. As early as 1630, Virginians had smuggled over 500,000 pounds of tobacco to France, Portugal, Spain (via Cuba), Holland and the West Indies.

In 1710, Ports of Registry called *customs houses* were established in Maryland at Williamstad (Oxford), Patuxent, Wicomico, North Potomac, Pocomoke, South Potomac, Annapolis, Chester, Patapsco, and Sassafras River areas: in Virginia, at Accomack, Lower James, Upper James, York, Rappahannock, South Potomac, Cape Charles and Elizabeth River areas.

Registration was required by King's agents; name and port-of-hail painted on the transom. Confusion resulted when many Southern Maryland ships were named *Mary* (for the Catholic queen) and Virginia ships named *Virginia* (for the Protestant virgin Queen Elizabeth). The First US Congress (1789) required the name and net tonnage carved in 3'' letters (3/8'' deep) on the after face of the main deck beam in addition to transom lettering.

Ship owners were required to give bond, and note on their shipping papers, restrictions of the cargo and destination. Violators such as William Byrd (1738) and Robert Carter (1754) made large shipments of Virginia-grown gingseng to China instead of England because it sold for higher prices. Lloyds of London pressured Parliament for stricter registration and mainly for an exact and detailed written descriptions of all vessels—this became almost impossible with Bay shippers who excelled in short-changing customs and insurance agents, especially in their profitable and nefarious Caribbean trade.

Ports of Registry were places where ship's captains mingled with their fellow skippers, learned the latest maritime news (especially about pirates and convoy assignments), current tobacco and rum prices, cleared their cargos, registered their goods, attended to their marine insurance, paid the appointed Crown-tax, obtained their sailing papers, and in general conducted the usual shore business of their profession. However, a British naval captain whose ship was stationed in the Bay reported that "noe officer of the Customs in Maryland or Virginia can live without a good guard." General laxity of enforcement was reflected in a Maryland surveyor's report: "Ports here scarcely Serve to any other purpose than to Screen a Clandestine Trade and to Furnish permits for Goods illegally imported."

"Shipyard sites" noted in the MSVUS as "where built" were those places as written by the original owner on the official application for registration. Many Eastern Shore (Va) vessels sailing exclusively on the Bay registered in Chincoteague because the owner's home was near that town. Many sites were geographic place-names such as a county or a creek, having no relationship with a federal post office.

Some shipyard sites have sunk below the water since 1910 because of erosion; others were place-names in existence for only several years. Some shipyards were on farm sites far from the water—requiring the hull to be hauled to a waterway by ox-carts.

The "where built" site and the number of vessels as noted in the 1910 MSVUS register documented for the Chesapeake Bay area were:

Somerset County Md	- 328	Tilghman Island Md	- 30
Crisfield Md	- 137	Sharptown Md	- 30
Pocomoke City Md	- 133	Talbot County Md	- 26
Oriole Md	- 113	Taylors Island Md	- 24
Cambridge Md	- 100	Oxford Md	- 23
Baltimore Md	- 98	Norfolk Va	- 23
Dorchester County Md	- 91	Deal Island Md	- 23
Solomons Md	- 73	Bethel De	- 22
St. Michaels Md	- 61	Fishing Creek Md	- 22
St. Peters Md	- 58	Wicomico County Md	- 21
Madison Md	- 52	Monie Md	- 20
Fairmont Md	- 50	Mathews County Va	- 20

Other "where built" sites in **Virginia** were:—Alexandria-13, Accomac County-19, Accotink-4, Bakers Creek-1, Bridgetown-1, Bushy-1, Big Mills-1, Berkley-3, Bayford-1, Brick House-1, Battery Park-1, Chesconnessex-10, Chisemans-1, Cape Charles-8, Cobbs Creek-2, Coke-1, Cappahosic-4, Cobbs Island-1, Chincoteague-12, Cashville-2, Crittenden-1, Chuckatuck-3, Deep Creek-19, Dreka-5, Exemore-1, Essex County-2, Eastville-1, Enoch-1, Finneys Wharf-2, Fairport-2, Fishneck-1, Fitchetts-1, Greenback-8, Gloucester County-5, Guilford-6, Grafton-2, Greenpoint-1, Girdletree-1, Hunting Creek-8, Hangars Creek-1, Harborton-1, Hunts Point-1, Hills Landing-1, Hopeside-1, Hampton-1, Isle of Wight County-1, Justiceville-7, Jamesville-1, Jamestown-1, Lancaster-11, Laban-1, Leemont-1, Millford Haven-2, Messongo-7, Marsh Market-3, Metomkin-1, Mearsville-2, Millenbeck-1, Montague-1, Muddy Creek-1, Middlesex County-1, Norfolk County-14, Newpoint-3, Northumberland County-5, Nansemond County-5, Nashville-4, Newport News-1, Onancock-12, Occoquan-8, Oyster-2, Parkers Creek-1, Portsmouth-19, Poquoson-14, Port Royal-1, Pungoteague-3, Port Haywood-4, Piankatank-1, Queens Creek-1, Reedville-1, Sandy Bottom-1, Stratford-1, Severn River-1, Smithfield-1, Sarah Creek-3, Sinnickson-1, Swansgut-1, Sanford-1, Seldon-1, Tolley Creek-1, Tangier-1, Tappahannock-4, Timberneck Creek-1, Urbanna-4, Westmoreland County-2, West Point-2, Willis Wharf-1, Whealton-1, Whitestone-1, Ware Creek-1, Wormleys Creek-1, Yorktown-10, York County-13.

Other "where built" sites in **Maryland** were: Annapolis-7, Annamessex-3, Almondsville-1, Applegarth-4, Allen-1, Bishops Head-11, Barren Creek Springs-4, Broomes Island-4, Boxcar-1, Belleview-2, Berlin-2, Big Monie Creek-2, Bishopville-1, Bedsworth-2, Champ-3, Crapo-4, Chance-5, Churchton-3, Calvert County-7, Church Creek-9, Chestertown-2, Cabin Creek-1, Cecil County-1, Caroline County-1, Crocheron-2, Capitola-1, Cedar Bush Creek-1, Compton-1, Crabb Island-1, Dames Quarters-4, East Creek-1, Easton-2, Ewell-6, Elkton-13, Elliot-4, Federalsburg-1, Fairhaven-1, Fishing Island-5, Fairbank-4, Fox Creek-1, Fruitland-1, Green Run-2, Golden Hill-6, Greensboro-1, Grays Creek-1, Havre de Grace-14, Hooper Island-8, Hopewell-10, Hellens Creek (Patuxent R)-1, Holland Point-2, Hallwood-1, Herring Bay-1, Hills Point-1, Harrison-3, Hoopersville-3, Inverness-15, Jones Creek-3, James-1, James Island-2, James Point-1, Kent County-1, Kent Island-1, Lawsonia-3, Leonardtown-1, Landonville-1, Mount Vernon-1, Mill Creek (Patuxent)-2, Marion-4, Mardella-2, Milton-1, Morumsco Creek-1, Magothy River-1, Newark-3, Nanticoke-4, Newton-9, Ophelia-1, Prince George County-1, Poplar Island-1, Parsonville-1, Palmers-1, Point Breeze-1, Queen Anne County-5, Rhode River-1, Rock Hall-6, Royal Oak-3, Rehobeth-1, River Springs-2, Russom-1, Sparrows Point-1, Southpoint-1, Saint Georges-1, Sandy Hill-1, Saint Catherines Bay-1, Smith Island-9, Shelltown-1, Salisbury-10, Stockton-4, Secretary-1, Shad Point-1, Saint Marys-4, Snow Hill-5, Sherwood-3, Timonoke-1, Tobacco Stick-3, Tyaskin-2, Toddsville-1, Town Creek-1, Thomas-1, Upper Fairmont-3, Upper Trappe-1, Wingate-4, Wallville-1, Wayside-1, Whites Landing-1.

Additional "where built" sites were Washington DC-8; and in Delaware: Jones Creek-1, Laurel-4, Lebanon-1, and Seaford-1.

Addendum: Ports of Entry were of such importance that the Fifth Act of the First Congress, First Session, 31 July 1789 established Customs ports in **Maryland** at Baltimore, Chester (Kent I), Oxford, Vienna (Nanticoke R), Snow Hill (Pocomoke R), Annapolis, Nottingham (Patuxent R), Nanjemoy (Potomac R), Georgetown; in **Virginia** at Hampton, Norfolk, Richmond, Yorktown, Tappahannock, Kinsale, Dumfries, Alexandria, Folly Landing (6m north of Wachapreague), Cherry-Stone (1m north of Cape Charles town), South-Quay (Southern Branch, Elizabeth R) and an office for control of non-tidal waters.

SHIPBUILDING WOODS

WHITE OAK (*Quercus alba*) was especially suited for frames and vertebral pieces of vessels in spite of its weight 48 pounds/cubic foot, when dry. It is very hard, extremely strong, very tough, close-grained, durable and of a light brown color.

The best growths were located near the Atlantic Coast and near the slow moving streams of the Eastern Shore, being remarkably free of defects of every kind, and so abundant that early builders used nothing else except the heart of oak in their vessels, sawing off the outer or sap-wood, and selecting nothing except the durable inner portion. The fastidiousness of the builders led to unnecessary destruction of the tree, for the timber thus handled became one-half waste. So cheap was oak that vessels built on the Bay for the first hundred years cost one-half the price of oak vessels in Europe. Regardless of cost; smugglers, privateers, and the US Navy demanded oak planking for protection from cannon fire.

Originally, no timber was put into a boat's frame except that which had a natural curvature; when the crooked timber had been culled from the forests, there was some doubt whether replacement could be supplied. However, the practice of "hewing frames" out of straight timber became acceptable. This led to another great destruction of trees, as frames cut from the log wasted at least one-half of the original log.

The Bay, containing the largest oak forest on the East Coast, supplied shipbuilders of Maine, New England and New York for more than a hundred years. Oaks grew on rich, moist lands exposed to salt breezes to 100′ in height with diameters to 4′; yielding logs 2½′ square and 60′ long without a spot or defect. The mere possession of this abundant supply of cheap oak led to prosperous development of the shipbuilding industry in the two states, even though ninetenths of the oak felled was cut for exportation to other North American or European markets.

Oak was first sold at $1 a 1000 feet standing in the tree; by 1880 it was seldom lower than $3 standing. By the time it was felled, hewed into frame timber, and transported by water to Maine, the value had risen to $35 a 1000 feet. The finest pieces intended for keels, stems, sternposts, and rudderposts were cut expressly for Canadian markets which gradually increased to hasten the disappearance of the once enormous forest. Serious inroads had already been made into the supply at the time of the Civil War; and an immense quantity was cut to supply demands of the Union Army and Navy, on lands owned by mostly southern sympathizers. At one time during that War, there was serious apprehension relative to the supply of large oak timbers, and large quantities were cut and shipped north for storage in Navy Yards, so that at least the Union would have suitable material in reserve for their fleet.

Worcester County of Maryland had more virgin oak than any other locality before the railroads penetrated the interior of the peninsula in 1860. By 1880, over half of the Bay's greatest forest of oaks had been stripped and *all* first-growth trees near navigable water had been removed.

For centuries, lumber shysters on the Bay have "pawned-off" inferior red oak as being comparable to white oak for marine use, so please dear reader "beware."

Because of the demand for white oak in cooperage, it is sometimes called "stave oak." It was and still (1981) is the leading wood for boat construction, thus becoming the state tree of Maryland.

LONGLEAF PINE (*Pinus palustris*) was and still (1981) is second to white oak in importance, growing in the warmer climates of the lower Bay; northward to the shores of the Patuxent on the Western Shore, Choptank on the Eastern Shore, and Indian River in Delaware; to heights of 120′ with diameters of 3′. The wood weighs 43 lb/cu ft; is exceedingly hard, strong, tough, coarse-grained, durable, and of a light red to orange color. Known as "longstraw pine" on the Eastern Shore; it is full of turpentine and would hold iron tenaciously, being free of acids which tend to destroy metal bolts and nails. Used principally in planking, ceiling, keelsons, water-ways, rails and beams of vessels, and occasionally for decking and spars. Lower masts of larger vessels such as clippers were fabricated with a core of oak and an outside coat of longleaf pine, bolted and hooped together. In a typical 2000-ton clipper ship such as Donald McKay's *Lightning,* there would be 200,000 board feet of oak and 800,000 of longleaf pine—all from the Chesapeake Bay. This species of pine was the leading producer of naval stores (pine tar, pine oil, resin oil, and turpentine), the gum being cooked down to a thick tar and used in colonial days to preserve cordage and caulking oakum.

PITCH PINE (*Pinus rigida*), being called "bull pine," was third in popularity, growing all-over-tidewater lands, and used as an "illicit substitute" for longleaf pine. Growing to heights of 100′ with diameters of 3′. The wood weighs 35 lb/cu ft; is soft, moderately strong, brittle, coarse-grained, very durable, a light brown or red color. It is difficult to work and holding power of bolts is very poor. Loaded with resin it was popular as a fuel in ship's stoves.

BALDCYPRESS (*Taxodium distichum*) is held in the highest esteem because of its high resistance to decay, even though it absorbs considerable water, which makes it heavy. It was found in slow-moving streams and swamps in the lower Bay, northward to the shores of the Patuxent and Sassafras Rivers in Maryland, and Smyrna River in Delaware. Inland species on drier soil were of no marine value. Heights range to 150′ with diameters to 5′. The wood weighs 35 lb/cu ft (when dry), soft, moderately strong, close-grained, very durable, easily worked (especially for carving), having a rancid odor and a color of light to dark brown. It is the preferred choice for planking where weight is not a factor. The lowlands on the site of Washington City was once mostly swamp containing cypress and swamp white oak. A few cypress swamps still remain in the Bay area, protected by federal or state control.

LIVE OAK (*Quercus virginiana*) grew in a dense forest of thousands of acres along the shores of Mobjack Bay and sparsely in areas south of the Potomac, Patuxent, and the Choptank. The tree matured at a height of 50′, with trunk diameter of 4′. The heaviest of all Chesapeake species at 59 lb/cu ft, the wood has characteristics similar to white oak. It is difficult to saw and work, used mainly for blocks (pullies), deadeyes, and knees on sailing vessels. It is locally called "Virginia oak."

SWAMP WHITE OAK (*Quercus bicolor*) grew in moist fertile soils and cold swamps of the upper Bay, north of the Potomac and the Choptank Rivers. Swamp white oak and cypress covered most of the original swamplands of the Washington City. The mature tree reached to a height of 100′ with trunk diameters up to 8′. The wood weighs 50 lb/cu ft; very hard, strong, tough, close-grained, durable, and light brown in color. Uses are similar to white oak.

EASTERN WHITE PINE (*Pinus strobus*) locally called "soft pine" was and still (1981) is one of the most valued trees on the Bay, but found only in deep sandy loams of the upper Bay on the Western Shore above the Patapsco River and along the Potomac above Great Falls. Strangely, the upper reaches of the James River yielded 100,000 board feet per acre in the early 1800s. Record heights were observed by early lumbermen at 250′ with diameters of 5′. The wood weighs 25 lb/cu ft; is soft, clear, free from knots, extremely buoyant, but not strong enough for structural timbers; straight-grained, easily worked, and of light brown color. It is most suitable for decking, cabin construction, carving, masts and spars.

So great a value was white pine, that in the early patents of land granted to colonists the trunks suitable for masts were reserved for the English Navy. Before the Revolution the best was marked by the famous "King's Broad Arrow." A Royal Surveyor was appointed by the King; given license to go into the Bay forests and mark such trees having a minimum diameter of 24″ measured just above the butt. Persons who felled one of these marked trees without permission were liable to a fine of 180 pounds ($500). Records indicate white pine timbers delivered to English shipyards during the 1770s were uniformly sized at 108′ long by 38″ in diameter.

Trees were brought by oxen using several carts, and by rafts floating down from the headwaters of the Susquehanna, Potomac, and the James Rivers to loading wharves at the fall line.

SHORTLEAF PINE (*Pinus echinata*) locally called "North Carolina Pine" grew all-over-the Bay to heights of 120′ with diameters of 4′. Frequently sold as longleaf pine, but is lighter (38 lb/cu ft) and less strong (in fact, it is variable in strength), coarse-grained, moderately durable, color from an orange to yellow-brown. Used mainly for interior finish, and for cheap marine construction work.

VIRGINIA PINE (*Pinus virigianna*), frequently called "scrub pine" because of its shortness in height, (40′ with diameters of 18″); and its open straggly crown. It is found throughout the Bay where hardly little else will grow. Wood weighs 33 lb/cu ft, structurally weak and brittle, coarse-grained though durable; a light orange color. It is used in marine work only when nothing else is available.

LOBLOLLY PINE (*Pinus taeda*) locally called "Oldfield pine," grew in the same warm area as longleaf pine to heights of over 170′ with diameters of 6′. Wood weighs 38 lb/cu ft, soft, variable from weak to tough, brittle, coarse-grained, not durable, and of a light-brown color. Originally used only for interior marine work and cheap construction.

TAMARACK (*Larix laricina*) known on the Bay as "hackmatack" and "eastern larch," and obtained only from headwaters of the Potomac, James and the Susquehanna Rivers. This wood was not used by early builders because of the distance of its growing grounds to the Bay, but became popular after the Civil War. The wood weighs 38 lb/cu ft, light-brown in color, very tough, coarse-grained and durable. A vessel completely built of this wood could carry 25% more freight than an oak-built ship. It was not strong enough, however, to be used in parts of ships exposed to variable stresses, and was found eventually valuable only for use as knees, stanchions, and top timbers. Tamarack has the important peculiarity of being free from acids which corroded iron bolts; it holds a tenacious grip, even better than oak. It grew to heights of 80′ with diameters up to 2′ in well drained, colder uplands far from the tidewater Bay. It is favored especially for the strength of its natural bends for use as knees.

RED SPRUCE (*Picea rubens*) known locally as "West Virginia spruce," like tamarack was brought-down in rafts or by a series of oxcarts from the upper and colder areas of the Susquehanna and Potomac Rivers. The mature tree reached heights of 40′ with diameters up to 12″. Imports of this wood from New England augmented the local supply for use as booms, gaffs, and yards. Isolated and dwarfed stands along the Bay shores were originally used for distillation of the popular spruce-beer or as floor boards in cabins. The wood weighs 28 lb/cu ft, soft, close-grained, not strong, and of a pale yellow color tinged with red. When used as spars or light oars it should be well-protected by paint or oil such as "mast slush," as it has low resistance to decay. Black spruce was used in making beer and chewing gum.

AMERICAN CHESTNUT (*Castanea dentata*) known locally as "chestnut," was found throughout the Bay area except the southern parts of Virginia's Eastern Shore and the lower James River. Heights ranged to 100′ with diameters of 4′ and when not crowded by other trees it grew to heights of 120 feet. The wood weighs 31 lb/cu ft, is soft, moderately strong, liable to check and warp when dry, easily split, and of a light reddish-brown color. Used frequently as a substitute for white oak wherever a straight timber was required. Healthy trees are very rare in the year 1981.

WHITE ASH (*Fraxinus americana*) grew all-over-the-Bay on well drained sites near/alongside estuaries, and especially on slopes facing north and east. Because of its extreme stiffness, the wood is primarily used for cleats, tillers, long oars, and spars. The phrase "white-ash breeze" was coined by oarsmen who rowed a large ship with sweeps (long oars) when becalmed. The wood weighs 41 lb/cu ft, is hard, strong, close-grained, elastic, tough and of a light-brown color. Because of its low resistance to decay, it requires numerous "oilings."

CAROLINA ASH (*Fraxinus caroliniana*) grew in dense-swamp forests of the upper tidewater Potomac River; was sparsely distributed over the entire Bay and called "water ash." As the wood is easily split and bent, it is mainly used for mast hoops, and barrel hoops. Rarely did it grow over 50′ in height with diameters of 12″, weighs 40 lb/cu ft, soft yet tough, elastic, durable, close-grained and of a white color tinged with yellow.

BLACK ASH (*Fraxinus nigra*) grew in only the cold deep swamps of the Western Shore on the upper Bay, north of Herring Bay. It grew to heights of 90′ with diameters of 20″. The wood weighs 34 lb/cu ft, rather soft, moderately strong, durable, coarse-grained and light-brown in color. Locally known as "swamp ash, hoop ash or basket ash," and used for hoops and short oars.

BLACK LOCUST (*Robinia pseudoacacia*). Historian Parke Rouse, Jr., wrote: "when in 1607, the first Englishmen landed upon a little island in the James River, and tied their ships to some great-trees leaning over the bank..." Professional forest historians say that "those great trees were 'black locust.' " The tree was impressive, growing all-over-the-Bay to a soldierly height 80′ with a trunk 3′ to 4′ thick. The wood weighs 50 lb/cu ft, and is the strongest of all woods on the Bay, with flexural strength exceeding that of hickory by 40%; yet shrinking the least of all woods; it is 2½ times more durable than white oak. Very hard, very close-grained, tough, extremely so on tools, and of a rich bright-brown color tinged with red. A native ruinous locust borer-beetle usually destroys the young tree before it could become the "most-wanted" of all trees. Traditionally used for cleats, bitts, deadeyes, treenails, capstan-bars, tackle-blocks (especially sheaves), thole pins; it was called "ship-mast locust."

BLACK WALNUT (*Juglans nigra*) flourished in the deep, rich soils of river bottom-lands adjoining the Bay, heights of 150′ and diameters of 6′ reached in maturity. There were dense great forests along the James River and Virginia's Eastern Shore. The finest of all cabinet woods, the trees were cut-down and used locally and for world export during "The craze age for Victorian elegance," (1830-1860). By the Civil War, the few remaining trees in tidewater lands of the Bay were comparatively rare. Used in shipyards only for interior cabinet work on luxury type ships. The wood weighs 39 lb/cu ft; it was hard, strong, coarse-grained, easily worked, very durable; a rich, dark-brown color.

RED MULBERRY (*Morus rubra*) was mentioned in many colonial records as a "convenient" boatbuilding timber and "good for planking," growing to heights of 70′ with diameters of 4′. The wood weighs 37 lb/cu ft, is soft, structurally weak, rather tough, coarse-grained, very durable and of a light orange color.

SASSAFRAS (*Sassafras albidum*), locally known as "white sassafras," was the most sought-after tree or plant prior to tobacco, as a "drug plant" during the early days of settlement. The *Susan Constant* returned to England in 1608 with a hold of sassafras roots, because of their supposed aphrodisical qualities. It grew to heights of 90′ with diameters of 6′. The wood weighs 32 lb/cu ft, soft, weak, rather tough, brittle, coarse-grained, extremely low shrinkage, very durable and of a light-yellor color. It was the preferred wood prior to the Civil War for building of small craft and short oars.

AMERICAN ELM (*Ulmus americana*), locally known as "water elm," grew along streams and open shores all-over-the-Bay to heights of 140′ with diameters of 10′. The wood weighs 45 lb/cu ft, hard, strong, tough, coarse-grained, and of a light-brown color. It was used extensively as a substitute for white oak, especially in the keel, keelson, and garboard strake having great holding-power of bolts, nails and screws. Elm was superior to oak, especially in places where air was excluded. Carriages supporting the cannons on American frigates were always of elm. It was the preferred wood for tackle-blocks and pump logs. The bark was used to make canoes.

ATLANTIC WHITECEDAR (*Chamaecyparis thyoides*) was called "juniper or swamp cedar" by those who lived in the tidewater swamp lands all-over-the-Bay. It grew to heights of 100′ with diameters of 4′. The wood weighs 20 lb/cu ft, soft, weak, coarse-grained, slightly fragrant, and of a light brown color tinged with red. Used for planking of small boats and for interior finish in cabins; in great demand because of high resistance to decay and lightness of weight; the choice of ship carvers. The cold tidewater cedar swamps attracted sailing skippers to fill their casks with the slow moving and ale-colored waters which had lasting purity qualities.

EASTERN HOPHORNBEAM (*Ostrya virginiana*), locally called "ironwood" which grew scatteredly and singly all-over-the-Bay on well-drained ridges. Heights up to 60′ with diameters of 2′ with a tremendous spread. The strong, hard wood is light brown color tinged with red; tough, close-grained and weighing 52 lb/cu ft. Being very durable it was used for cleats, rails, sheer poles; shipping boxes and crates.

TULIPTREE (*Liriodendron tulipfera*) called "yellow poplar"; grew all-over-the-Bay and was used when nothing else was available; growing to heights of 150′ with diameters up to 8′. The wood is light yellow to brown, soft, close-grained and easily worked; when dry it is 26 lb/cu ft and is used solely for painted interior finish and cabin work.

OSAGE ORANGE (*Maclura pomifera*), though not native to the Bay; it was introduced during the early 1800s because of its growth form—a short, stout and divided trunk with large curving branches which proved suitable for knees and curved frames. Heights to 60′ with diameters up to 3′. The wood is a bright yellow, turning brown when exposed; weight of 48 lb/cu ft when dry; stronger, harder and more durable than oaks, and having a clear straight grain. Used for blocks (pulleys), belaying pins and rails.

PERSIMMON (*Diospyros virginiana*). Captain John Smith (1608) speaks of three sorts of plums, the red and white, like the English hedge plums, "but the other, which they [the Indians] call Putchamins, grow as high as Palmata. The fruit is like a medlar (small apple); it is first green, then yellow, and red when it is ripe. If it is not ripe it will draw a man's mouth awrie with much torment, but when it is ripe it is delicious as an Apricock." Growing to heights of 130′ with a diameter of 3′; the wood is dark brown or black, close-grained, hard, strong and tough, weighing 53 lb/cu ft when air-dry; used for blocks, rails, belaying pins and cleats.

Lamentation. Because of forest fires, arson, insects, diseases, grazing and destructive lumbering practices, the Bay's shipbuilding woods for commercial use have been totally "cleaned-out."

WHARVES

Numerous wharves were built on Bay shores to serve rowing, sailing and power vessels. In addition to public wharves, private wharves were built for sawmills, canneries, seafood factories, grain storage, farm produce, shipyards, etc; usually named for the owner such as Browns Wharf, Jones Landing, Smiths Point. Listed below are those during the sail-steamboat era (1870-1930), and read from the estuaries' mouth to upstream. Bracketed numbers note the number of miles of navigable water in 1981.

EASTERN SHORE

Cape Charles

1. **Cherrystone Inlet** (2); Cherrystone.
2. **Hungar Creek** (2); Taylors, Hungars.
3. **Nassawaddox Creek** (2); Bayford, James, Stewart.
4. **Occohannock Creek** (4); Concord, Reads, Morley, Davis, Miles, Shields, Rues.
5. **Nandua Creek** (3); Hacksneck, Cedar View, Nandua.
6. **Pungoteague Creek** (3); Hoffmans, Harborton, Evans, Boggs.
7. **Onancock Creek** (5); Mears, Finneys, Poplar Grove, Onancock.
8. **Chesconessex Creek** (2); Chesconessex.
9. **Hunting Creek** (2); Hopkins.
10. **Messongo Creek** (5); Marsh Market.
11. **Pocomoke Sound** and **River** (26); Hopkins, Marsh Market, Guilford, Saxis, Shelltown, Pitts, Cedar Hall, Rehobeth, Powell, Puncheon Landing, Newton (Pocomoke City), Stevens, Winter Quarter, Pusey, McMasters, Cottingham, Cellar House, Wills, Mattaponi, Milbourne, Calahan, Adams, Deep, Drexel, Weeks, Shad, Red, Stimson, Dyghtons (Snow Hill), Hayward, Blue House.
12. **Tangier Sound;** Tangier, Ewell, Rhodes, Crisfield, Deal Island, Dames Quarters, Wenona, Chance.
13. **Big Annemessex River** (6); Ford, Coulbourn.
14. **Manokin River** (15); Inverness, Champ, Dashiells, Princess Anne.
15. **Wicomico River** (20); Mount Vernon, Whitehaven, Widgeon, Wagner, Polk, Allen, Collins, Parrott, Sims, Keroo, Cox, Truitts, Quantico, Upper Ferry, Patrick, Shad Point, Salisbury.
16. **Nanticoke River** (35); Roaring Point, Nanticoke, Bivalve, Waltersville, Tyaskin, Sandy Hill, Lewis, Athaloo, Vienna, Riverton, Walnut, Wheatley, Brookview, Eldorado, Hart, Ellis, Sharptown, Truitts, Hurtts, Phillip, Ellis, Bailey, Bethel, Cannon, Laurel, Woodland, Seaford.
17. **Marshyhope Creek** (9); Walnut, Brookview, Ennall, Harrison, Brown, Federalsburg.
18. **Fishing Bay** (17); Elliot.
19. **Transquaking Creek** (6); Best Pitch, North Cedar, Brick House.
20. **Honga River** to **Little Choptank;** Wingate, Applegarth, Hoopersville, Fishing Creek, Honga, Golden Hill.
21. **Little Choptank River** (8); Taylor Island, Speddens, Hudson, Ross, Madison, Milton, Church Creek.
22. **Choptank River** and estuaries (57); Sharps Isle, Tilghman, Avalon, Fairbank, Wittman, Neavitt, Corners, Oxford, Bellevue, Johnston, Double Mills, Easton Point, Castle Haven, Clora, Travers, Trappe, Wallach, Kirby, Cambridge, Chancellor, Oyster Shell, Jamaica, East New Market (Secretary), Ellwood, Cabin Creek, Clark, Wright, Choptank, Windyhill, Medford, Lloyd, Orange, Hog Island, Dover, North Wales, Kingston, Turkey Creek, McCarty, Wings, (Tuckahoe Creek), Ganeys, Todd, Downes, Towels, Two Johns, Potters, Williston, Pealiquor, Lyford, Denton, Smith, Passapae, Brick Wall, Greensboro, Clora, Wallaces.
23. **Tuckahoe Creek** (11); New Bridge, Cowards, Coveys, Waymans, Hillsboro.
24. **Poplar Island;** Valiant.
25. **Poplar Island Narrows;** Lowes, Sherwood.
26. **Eastern Bay** and **Miles River** (12); Claiborne, Romancoke, St. Michaels, Tunis Mills, Easton Landing, Wye River (10): Brown, Wye, Powell, Probasco, Skipton.
27. **Chester River** and estuaries (37); Love Point, Jackson Creek, Queenstown, Bogles, Overton, Spring Point, Grays Inn, Long Cove, Becks, (*Corsica Cr.,* Earles, Emory, Posey, Centreville), Spaniard Point, Cliffs, Indian town, Ashland, Quaker Neck, Bookers, Wilmers, Riverside, Neuman, Southeast, Windmill, Kennersley, Rolph, Piney Grove, Chestertown, Roundtop, Buckingham, Travilla, Spry, Deep, Ford, Kirby, Jones, Crumpton, Millington, Churacre.
28. **Swan Cr, Rock Hall Creek;** Gratitude, Rock Hall, Deep Pt.
29. **Wortons Creek** (2); Gales, Green Point, Vannort, Buck Neck.
30. **Still Pond Creek** (2); Harris.
31. **Sassafras River** (10); Betterton, Wilson, Turner, Cassidy, Shellcross, Raison, Fredericktown, Georgetown, Grove, Wilson, Budd, Fox Hole, Fuyer.
32. **Elk River** (19); Reybold, Ford, Town, Hack Point (in Bohemia Creek), Old Frenchtown, Elkton.
33. **Northeast River** (5); Charlestown, Northeast.

Norfolk

1. **James River** (78); Pig Point, (Nansemond River), Crittenden, Rock, Fergusson, MacKimmie, Battery Park, Smithfield on Pagan Creek, Menchville, Rushmere, Kings Mill, Homewood, Cobham, Scotland, Jamestown, Dillard, (Chickahominy River), Sandy Point, Reynolds, Claremont, Brandon. Oldfield, Sturgeon Point, Milton, Ruffins, Upper Brandon, Pope, Wilcox, Stanley, Blair, Harrison, Kimage, Westover, Hopewell, Shirley, Hardens, Pickett, Curls, Meadowville, Richmond.
2. **Nansemond River** (15); Wilson, Lee, Ferry Point, Godwins, Trotman, Gilroy, Wilson, Suffolk.
3. **Chickahominy River** (20); Nightingale Point, Shipyard, Fish Hole, Lanexa, Craves, Cypress Bank, Osborn, Wynn, Old House, Holly.
4. **Back River** (2); Amory, Messick Point.
5. **Poquoson River** (3); Yorkville, Hunt.
6. **York River** (29); Perrin, Yorktown, Gloucester Point, Carmine, Clements, Bigler, Clay Bank, Capahosic, Almondsville, Richardson, Miller, West Point.
7. **Mattaponi River** (32); Clifton, Courthouse, Mattaponi, Locus Grove, Scotland, White Oak, Walkertown, Pointet, Jones, Aylett.
8. **Pamunkey River** (37); Sweet, Hall, Morgan, Cook, Lester Manor, Brickhouse, Cumberland, White House, Northbury, Carters, Retreat.
9. **Mobjack Bay;** Bayside. **Severn River;** Lady, Cod. **Ware River;** Hockley, Smith, Bailey, Roanes. **North River;** Auburn, Dixondale. **East River;** Philpotts, Diggs, Williams, Hicks.
10. **Piankatank River** (14); Jacksons, Deltaville, Cherry, Ruark, Grenells, Warehouse, Hundleys, Conrad, Green Point, Dixie, Heeleys, Stampers, Bland, Freeport, Segars.
11. **Milford Haven;** Cricket Hill, Callis, Point Breeze, Fitchetts.
12. **Rappahannock River** and estuaries (93); Westland, North End, Mill Creek, Adams, Clark, Whitestone, Riverview, Irvington, Weems, Millenbeck, Merry Point, Moran, Ottoman, Burhan, Burtons, Urbanna, Remlik, Waterview, Whealtons, Bay Port, Monaskon, Boer, Butylo, Morattico, Oakley, Sharps, Bowlers, Woodhouse, (Totusky Creek), Wares, Wellfords, Tappahancock, (Mt. Landing Creek), Naylors Hole, Lewis, Jenkins, Blandfield, Carter, Smith Mount, Layton, Leedstown, Saunders, Port Micou, Wilmont, Greenlaw, Woodlawn, Oaken Brow, Camden, Waverly, Port Royal, Port Conway, Moons, Haymount, Parks, Hop Yard, Ratcliff, Maryton, Arnold, Hayfield, Fredericksburg.
13. **Totuskey Creek** (4); Deep, Shipyard, Phillips, School, Cedar Point, North Bend, Yellow Bank.
14. **Mount Landing Creek** (3); Salt Bank, Baker, Mose, Persimmon Tree, Gram, Hickory.
15. **Dymer Creek** (2); Foxwell, Ocran, Chases.
16. **Indian Creek** (3); Grace Point, Byrdton, Eubanks (Kilmarnock).
17. **Dividing Creek** (3); Ditchely, Harvey, Harding, Highland.
18. **Great Wicomico River** (6); Fleeton, Timbs, Fairport, Reedville, Sidney, Harcums, Mila, Blackwell, Tipers, Sampson.
19. **Little Wicomico River** (5); Sunnybank.
20. **Potomac River.**
21. **Saint Jerome's Creek** (2); Airedale, Deep Point.
22. **Patuxent River** (38); Drum Point, Pearson, Millstone, Solomons, Spencer, Hickory, Clark, St. Cuthbert, MacKall, Sollers, Planter, Sotterly, Cashner (Jones), Broomes Island, Parker, Forrest, Queen Tree, Williams, Horse Landing, Duke, Cremona, Trent Hall, Holland, Benedict, Leitch, Trueman, Deep, Holland Cliffs, Milltown, Naylor, Magruder, Lower Marlboro, White, Bowling, Ferry, Nottingham, Lyons Creek, Selby, Jackson, (Railway bridge), Mt. Calvert, Iron Pot, Bristol (Leon), Hill, Mt. Pleasant, Wooton, Clagett, Taylor, Queen Anne.
23. **Drum Point to Herring Bay;** Cove Point, Governors Run, Dares Beach, Plum Point, Chesapeake Beach, North Beach.
24. **Herring Bay** (2); Fairhaven, Deale.
25. **West River** (3); Shadyside, Galesville, Cumberstone, Chalk Point.
26. **Rhode River** (4); Carr, Murray, Contee.
27. **South River** (7); Edgewater, Burchs, Riverview, Taylorsville, Lee, Hodges.
28. **Severn River** (10); Annapolis, Dreams, Whitney, Round Bay.
29. **Magothy River** (5); Wilson.
30. **Patapsco River** (8); USC&G Survey records show 210 public and private wharves on this river and estuaries. Those popular during the steamboat era were: Browns Pavillion (later Pavillion Retreat), Holly Grove and Tivoli. **Rock Creek;** Ft. Smallwood, Colonial Beach, Fairview, Browns Grove, Gray's, Heintzmans, Patapsco Club, Fox Point, Jenkins. **Stoney Creek;** Stony Beach, Krebs (later Rivera Beach), Simmons, Summit Grove, Holtzs, Altoona Beach, Beauty Beach, Old Glory Beach, Outing Park (later Green Haven), Thomas, Weedons.
31. **Susquehanna River** (4); Havre de Grace, Port Deposit . . . flowing nontidal 500 miles to Lake Otsego, NY.

POTOMAC RIVER — VIRGINIA SHORE (104)

1. **Coan River;** Walnut Pt, Lewisetta, Point Pleasant, Reeders, Cowart, Lake Bundick, Coan, Nokomis, Bond, Rowe.
2. **Yeocomico River**; Cintra, Mundy, Harry Hogan, Lodge, Bell, Kinsale.
3. **Lower Machodoc Creek**; Cole, Allen, Edgewater, Tidwell.
4. **Nomini Bay** and **Creek**; Beale, MacGuire, Mt.Holly, Deep, Nomini, Peach Pt, Wood, Davis, White, Beale Mills.
5. **Currioman Bay**; Mt. Airey, Currioman, Poor Jack.
6. ...on the river; Stratford, Popes Creek, Bridges Creek.
7. **Mattox Creek**; Massey, Wirts.
8. **Monroe Creek**; Colonial Beach, Stave Landing.
9. ...on the river: Hollister's at White Point.
10. **Rosiers Creek**; Wilkerson, Watt, Monroe, Weedon, Millville.
11. **Upper Machodoc Creek**; Dido, Redmond, Berry, Hoge, Brickhouse, Ashton, Frank, Little Ferry, Rollins, Belle Isle, Millford, Waveland.
12. ...on the river: Mathias Pt, Watkins, Stewart, Widow Martin, Somerset Beach, Chatterton, Stiff, Fairview Beach, Belvedere.
13. **Potomac Creek**; Belle Plain.
14. **Aquia Creek** (north shore); Simms, Schackley, Bennett, Fox, Paine, Harper, Raymond, Towson, Norman, Dent, Wharton. (south shore)-Youdedamn, Thorney, Watson, Gourd, Davis, Hope, Doctor, McGregor, Coal, Hart, Knight.
15. ...on the river; Widewater, Clifton.
16. **Chopawamsic Creek**; Missouri Mills, Griffin, Cedar.
17. ...on the river; Evansport, Carrborough, Newport.
18. **Quantico Creek**; Bulletts, Dodge, Dumfries.
19. **Neabsco Creek**, Neabsco Mills, Willis, Atkinson.
20. **Occoquan Creek**; Colchester, Occoquan.
21. **Gunston Cove**; Iona, Coates, Accotink.
22. **Hunting Creek**; Broomilaw, Brickyard.
23. ...on the river; Alexandria, Jackson City.

POTOMAC RIVER — MARYLAND SHORE (104)

1. **Point Lookout;** Cornfield Harbor.
2. **Smith Creek;** Wynne, Miller.
3. **St. George's Creek;** Adams, Hobbs.
4. **St. Marys River;** Bacons (Portobello), Bromes (St. Marys City), Jones (Grayson Landing) in St. Inigoes Creek.
5. ...on the river; Piney Point.
6. **Flood Creek;** Moore.
7. **Breton Bay;** Abell, Pabst, Blakiston, Leonardtown.
8. **St. Clements Bay;** Blakiston Island, Coltons Pt, Palmers, Morris, Cobrum, Guest, Howard, Stone (Bayside).
9. **Wicomico River;** Rock, Lancaster, River Springs, Plowden, Bushwood, Chaptico, Budd, Newport, Allens Fresh.
10. ...on the river: Morgantown, Popes Creek.
11. **Port Tobacco Creek;** Chapel, Brent, Henson, Warehouse.
12. **Nanjemoy Creek;** Taylor, Blossom Point, Friendship.
13. ...on the river; Riverside, Tolson, Smith, Liverpool, Main Wood, Sandy Point, Budd.
14. **Chickamuxen Creek;** Posey, Linton, Point.
15. **Mattawoman Creek;** Kudd, Grinder, Mattingly, Nelson, Dent, Sweetman, Rum.
16. ...on the river; Jenkins, Philpot, Indian Head, Marbury, Glymont, McGhiesport, Hollis, Marshall Hall, Bryan, Farmington in Piscataway, Riverview, Brick, Tent, Fort Foote, Fox Ferry, Shepherd, Mann, Grimes, Giesboro.
17. **Anacostia River;** Poplar Barry, Navy Yard, Bladensburg.
18. **Washington. Georgetown.**

Compilation from charts and maps at the Library of Congress and the National Archives . . . with help from the steamboat historian H. Graham Wood of Baltimore.

MORE ROWING & SAILING CRAFT

"Watermen and boatbuilders on the Chesapeake Bay developed rigs and hulls to suit their pocketbooks . . . probably more sub-types were developed here than any other body of water in the United States."

Howard I. Chapelle

LOG CANOE

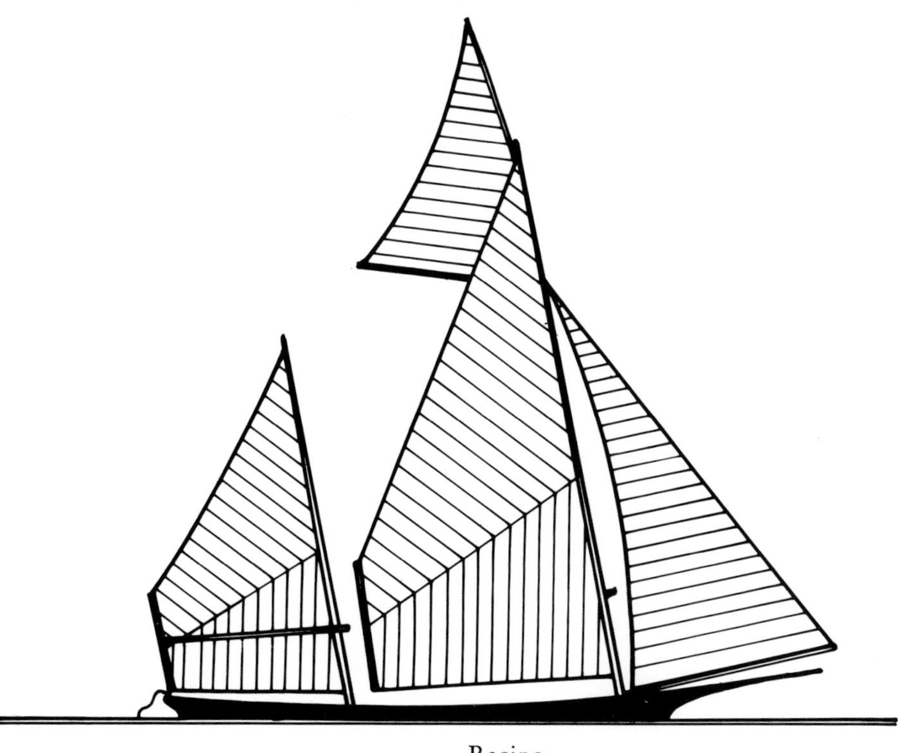

Racing

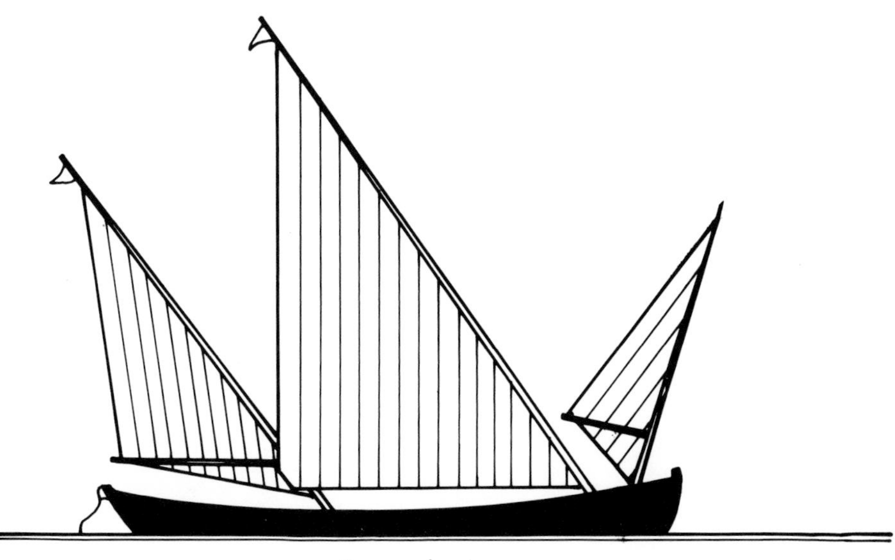

Pocomoke

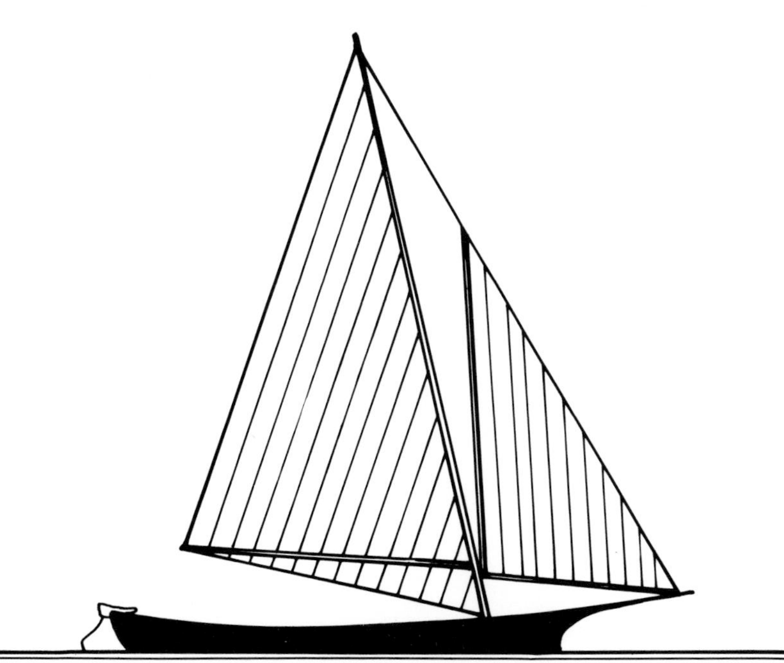

Poquoson

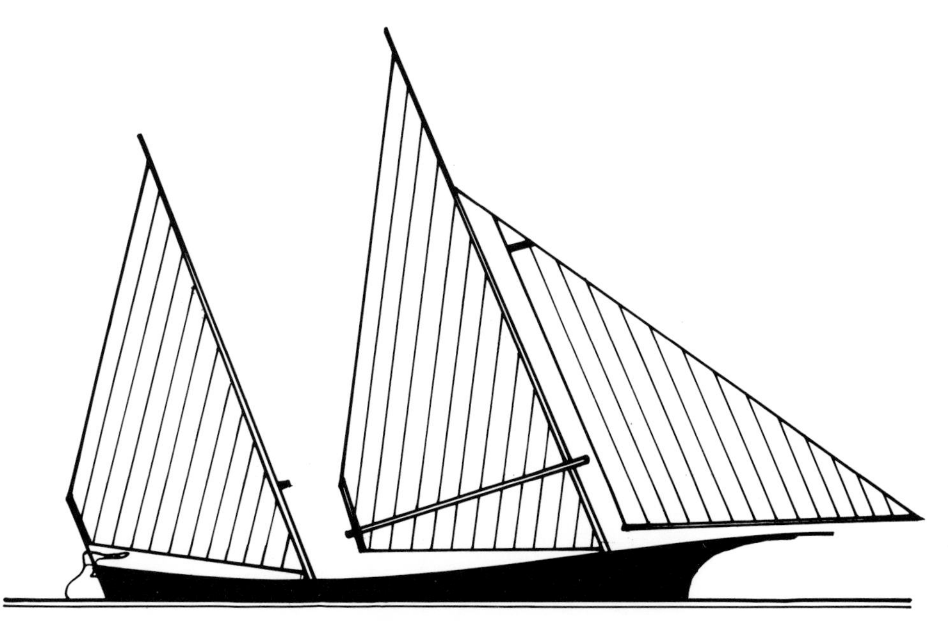

Tilghman Isle

SLOOP

Dhiru Thadani '81

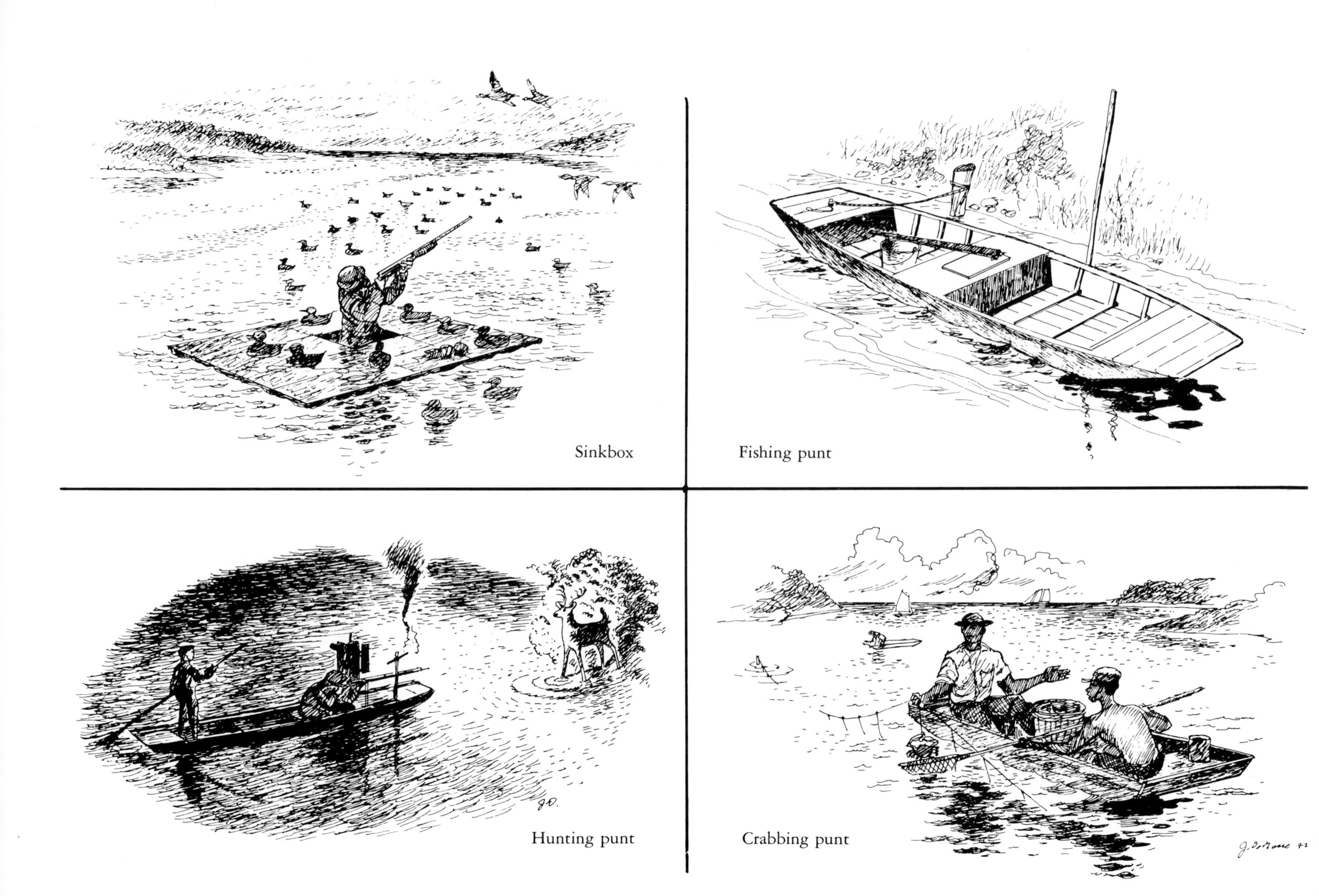
Sinkbox
Fishing punt
Hunting punt
Crabbing punt

STURGEON SKIFF

SCHOONER

BARBER

BARBER

GLOSSARY

A complete glossary of Chesapeake maritime and marine terms would be voluminous. Listed below are a few word definitions which may be considered as vague, obscure or antiquated.

abaft, after, towards the stern.
anti-fouling paint, a paint for a vessel's bottom containing poisonous ingredients for destruction of marine growth and worms.
baggywrinkle, chaffing gear made of short rope yarns giving a bushy appearance, wrapped around a stay or lift, thus saving wear and tear on a sail.
bar, a shoal, usually at the mouth of a river.
bilge, the turn of the hull below the waterline; where bilge water collects.
block, a mechanical contrivance consisting of a frame or shell which supports a sheave ("shiv") or roller over which ropes are run. A typical Bay schooner may have over 50 blocks, each for specific purposes such as: a *bee-block, cat-, cheek-, clew-, dasher-, down haul-, euphroe-, fish-, girt line-, halyard-, sheet-, sister-, secret-, snatch-, top block.*
boom, a spar of many uses; the foot of a fore-and-aft sail is laced to a *boom.*
boxes, dead oysters.
capefull, a few bushels of oysters tonged by an unskilled tonger during a full work-day.
ceiling, the inside planking of a vessel.
chafing gear, a winding (or wrapping) or canvas or rope around rigging and spars to prevent wear.
club, a spar serving as a boom on a headsail or topsail; the vertical spar at the after end of a quadrilateral sail, or at the top of a triangular sail leech.
draft, the depth of water necessary to freely float a vessel.
drift net, a net buoyed to float and drift in a vertical position where the fish are caught in the meshes by their gills.
ducktail, a platform extending over the stern of a double-ended vessel, such as a *bugeye.*
ebb, the return of tidewater towards the sea.
eskimo pie, a 1½ oz chocolate-covered vanilla ice cream bar, stickless; wrapped in gleaming foil; patented 1921.
flat, a level area of mud or sand which is bare at low water.
flitch-sawn, the lengthwise cutting of a log perpendicular to the radial rings, yet clear of the pitch; also called *rift-sawm.*
flood, the inflow of tidewater as opposed to *ebb.*
fore-and-aft rig, a method of setting sail from a vertical mast or stay, instead of from a horizontal yard as on a square-rig.
foremast, the first mast abaft the bow.
foresail, on a schooner, that sail set from the foremast.
gaff, a spar for extending the head of a fore-and-aft quadrilateral sail.
galvanize, application of a zinc coating on metal to provide resistance to corrosion.
grating, a wooden lattice hatch cover admitting light and air; or a platform arranged for water drainage; both forming flush walking and working surfaces.
halyard, a rope for hoisting sails or spars.
horse, a round iron rod, running athwartship, secured to the deck or rail, supporting a sheet block.
jag, a large catch of oysters by a skilled tonger.
jib, a triangular sail set forward of the foremost mast.
jigger, a light luff tackle for various types of work, such as a *main throat-halyard jigger*; also called a *jig.*
kicker, the engine in a yawl boat.
lick, the act of pulling a dredge over an oyster bed.
luff tackle, comprises the rope, a double and a single block; a tackle not destined for any particular part of the vessel, but used wherever needed.
mainmast, the second mast from the bow of a vessel.
mainsail, the large fore-and-aft sail set from the mainmast.
mast coat, a piece of canvas around the mast, where it passes through the deck, to prevent water from getting below.
mess, an adequate catch or serving, as a *mess of crabs.*
naval stores, manufactured products of gum extracted from pine trees, as crude tar, turpentine and rosin oil.
neck, a narrow peninsula of land, such as *Northern Neck.*
oakum, a caulking material made of tarred rope fibers used in preventing leakage through seams between planks or strakes.
oarlock, a swivel crutch for holding an oar when pulling or steering.
oilskins, waterproof coat, trousers and headgear of treated cotton, linen or silk worn as protection against heavy weather.
painted ports, alternate black and white rectangulars painted in a band along a ship's side in imitation of *gun ports.*
parral, a band with revolving wooden balls, that connect the gaff jaws forward of the mast.
patch, a favorite area for an oysterman who has traditionally a good *sight* in viewing *his* oysters on *his* bottom.
port, the left side of a vessel looking forward; also a place for loading and unloading a ship's cargo.
rake, the angle that a vessel's mast takes with the vertical; also oyster tongs, such as a *pair of rakes.*
reef, to reduce sail area by folding-up part of it and securing it by tying-in *reef-points.*
rig, a vessel's particular character as to sail and mast arrangments.
rope, a general term for cordage over one inch in circumference, anything less was called *small stuff.* Aboard a Bay sailing vessel, the common name for cordage was *line*; exacting names for each line was given according to its specific purpose such as: *halyard, brace, lift,* etc. Surprisingly, there were many *ropes* on a typical Bay schooner such as the *back rope, bell rope, bolt-, breast-, bucket-, buoy-, bull-, clew-, crown-, crotch-, crab-, drag-, draw-, entering-, foot-, gab-, gob-, grab-, guess-, guy-, head-, hook-, heel-, jaw-, leach-, leach-, limber-, man-, mast-, parral-, ring-, rudder-, ridge-, rolling-, slew-, slip-, train-, tiller-, top-, tow-, wheel-, yard-,* and *yoke rope.* A Bay schooner required over 2000′ of line for running rigging only, such as halyards, sheets, downhauls, jigs and lifts.
run, the part of a vessel where her designed hull lines converge towards the sternpost.
running free, sailing with the sheets eased and the wind coming over the stern.
sailing, to move along over the water by suction of wind on the sails. To yachtsmen, it may mean *the fine art and fun of getting wet and becoming ill while slowly going nowhere at great expense.*
samson post, a single (bitt) wooden head placed forward of the mast and set vertically to which mooring, towing and anchoring lines are made fast.
scull, to work an oar over the stern at such an angle to drive the boat ahead.
scuttle butt, a wooden barrel used for storing drinking water. Slang for *rumors.*
seaworthy, said of a vessel properly designed, constructed, equipped, manned and in good condition for the purpose in which it is employed.
sheer, the longitudinal curvature of the deck at each side between the stem and sternpost.
sheet, a rope fastened to the after lower corner of a sail, used to extend it or change its direction.
shoal, an area of relatively shallow water.
shrouds, pieces of wire or rope fitted over the masthead, supporting the mast to the sides of the vessel.
small stuff, generally small lines (or ropes) less than one inch in circumference for special use on a vessel as: *marline, spunyard, roundline, houseline, hambroline, ratline,* and *seizing line.*
spars, a term applied to all masts, gaffs, booms, bowsprit, sprit, club, etc.
spritsail, a quadrilateral sail extended by a sprit reaching diagonally from the mast to the upper after corner of the sail.
southwester, *sou'wester,* an oilskin hat whose brim projected considerably more to the rear than to the front.
square sail, a sail hung from a horizontal yard and ractangular in shape. After mid-1800s, on the Bay, a *square sail* was a name given to a fore-and-aft sail hung from a gaff.
starboard, the right side of a vessel looking forward.
stay, a piece of rope, usually of wire forming part of the standing rigging, used to support spars.
step, a cavity into which the heel of a mast is set; a silver dollar "heads up" was set here as a survival of a Roman custom

whereby if the ship met with a mishap while sailing . . . the crew had ample money to pay the ferryman Charon for transportation over the River Styx to Hades.

sweep, a long and heavy oar used on large rowing and sailing craft for rowing and steering.

swill bucket, a can used in the galley (kitchen) for table scraps.

tar, the residue of pine gum after distillation, used for protection of standing rigging such as shrouds.

tackle, a combination of ropes and blocks working together affording a mechanical advantage for lifting or pulling weights.

teredo, a shipworm, *Teredo navilis*, found in warm salt or brackish tidal waters; very destructive to unprotected wooden hulls; growing 8″ to 9″ long.

thole pin, a wooden pin which fits vertically in the gunwale of a boat to keep the oars in-place while rowing.

thwart, a seat in a small boat.

tidal current, horizontal movement of tidewater, occuring periodically as the result of moon and sun attraction, measured in knots. The strongest (1.7 knots, ebb) is at the Indian Reservation on Mattaponi R, Va.

tide, the inflow and outflow of tidewater, a vertical measurement in feet and inches. The greatest (4.5 feet, spring range) is at Walkerton, near headwaters of Mattaponi R, Va.

tiller, a bar of iron or wood connected with the rudder head and leading usually forward; serving to move the rudder for steering purposes.

topsail, the sail above the gaff, called the *fore-* or *main-gaff topsail.*

trap stake, a pile driven vertically to support nets.

treenail ("trunnel") a cylindrical wooden pin used for securing planks or timbers together.

turtle deck, one of very pronounced camber or crown (like a turtle's back), in order to shed water rapidly in heavy weather.

vang, a line leading from the peak of a gaff in order to steady it in a desired position.

waterline, the line indicated along the side of a boat hull by the plane of the surface of the water. The line separating the bottom (antifouling) paint from topside paint.

way, a vessel's movement through the water.

well, a fishing boat is generally provided with a *well* in which sea water circulates to keep the fish alive from the time they are caught until the vessel makes port.

wind vane, usually called *telltale*. A pivoting device on the foremost mast top to indicate wind direction; shaped like an arrow, galloping horse, hunting dog pointing, a centaur with drawn bow or a chanticleer (a crowing rooster).

yard, a spar crossing a mast horizontally from which a square sail is hung; a tract of land on the waterfront used for construction and repair of vessels.

Addendum: Leading maritime dictionaries for further reference are: *International Maritime Dictionary* by Rene de Kerchove, 1948; *A Glossary of Sea Terms* by Gershom Bradford, 1943; *The Oxford Companion to Ships and the Sea,* edited by Peter Kemp, 1976. *The Sea-Man's Dictionary* by Henry Mainwaring, 1644.

TOPONOMY

Toponomy is the study of geographical place names; their meaning and derivation. Indians lived on the Bay, travelled by water, depended on fishing, and named the many waterways. On account of this, their immemorial language lives on! Acceptable translations of estuaries are:

Accokeek, 'where the edge of the hill is'
Accomac, 'place on the other side of the water'
Accotink, 'at the house of chief Assaomeck'
Anacostia, 'at the place of traders'
Annemessex, 'creek abounding with logs'
Appomattox, 'sinuous tidal estuary'
Aquia, 'tall or high lands'
Chaptico, 'big broad river'
Chesapeake, 'great salt water river'
Chesconessex, 'at the house of chief Chesconessex'
Chickacomico, 'dwelling places by the big water'
Chickahominy, 'land of much grain'
Chickomuxen, 'high land nearby'
Chopawamsic, 'at the separation of the inlet'
Choptank, 'place of the big current'
Chuckatuck, 'closed-up place, refuge'
Coan (Chicacone), 'smelly waters'
Corrotoman, 'meeting of the waters'
Currioman, 'good fishing place'
Dogue, 'little creek'
Honga (Hungers), 'bay of many geese'
Jotank (Chotank), 'it flows in the opposite direction'
Machodoc, 'at the big tidal river'
Magothy, 'land of the maggoty bean, a pretty flowering pea'
Manokin, 'where the earth is dug out'
Marshyhope, 'a blind valley'
Mattaponi, 'a sand spit at the meeting of waters'
Mattawoman, 'where one goes pleasantly'
Mattox, 'shortening of *Appomatox*'
Messongo, 'bare earth'
Mobjack, 'worthless earth'
Monie, 'deep water'
Morrattico, 'at the house of chief Morrattico'
Nandua (Andua), 'good Indians'
Nanjemoy, 'one goes on donward'
Nansemond, 'a the house of chief Nansemond'
Nanticoke, 'land of tidewater people'
Nassawaddox, 'between two streams'
Nassawango, 'between two streams'
Neabsco, 'where there is a dangerous rock'
Nomini (Onawmanient), 'deep stream with current'
Occohannock, 'place of many bends in the river'
Occoquan, 'at the end of the water falls'
Occupacia, 'site of the hot-house (steam bath)'
Onancock, 'foggy place'
Ottoman, 'shortening of *Corrottoman*'
Pamunkey, 'a flowing muddy stream'
Patapsco, 'penetrating into rocky lands'
Patuxent, 'at the little falls in a stream'
Piankatank, 'at the house of chief Piankatank'
Piccowaxen, 'nearly torn shoes'
Pasquahanna, 'forked or dividing stream'
Piscataway, 'a high passable bank at the bend of river'
Pocomoke, 'pierced or broken ground'
Pohick, 'land of hickory trees'
Pomonkey, 'a river twisting into the land'
Poquoson, 'low wooded swamp'
Potomac, 'a river of traders'
Port Tobacco (Potobaco), 'jutting of water inland'
Poropotank, 'at the house of chief Poropotank'
Pungoteague, 'a place of dust and sand flies'
Quantico, 'place of dancing people'
Rappahannock, 'quick-rising water'
Susquehannah, 'smooth flowing stream'
Tomokokin, 'beaver lands'
Transquaking, 'white cedar swamp lands'
Tuckahoe, 'land of roots used as food'
Tyaskin, 'land of animal trap-builders'
Wetipquin, 'place of many skulls'
Wicomico, 'land of pleasant dwelling (living)'
Yeocomico, 'tossed to and fro on water'
Zekiah, 'dense swamp'

Reference: Hamill Kenny
Mary R. Miller
Steven Potter

BIBLIOGRAPHY

ALBION, ROBERT. *Forests and Sea Power.* Cambridge, 1926.
ARBER, EDWARD, ed. *Travels & Works of Capt' John Smith.* Edinburgh: 1910.
BAKER, WILLIAM. *Colonial Vessels; Sloops & Shallops.* Boston: 1962.
BARRIE, ROBERT AND GEORGE. *Cruises, mainly in the Bay of the Chesapeake.* Philadelphia: 1909
BARROW, THOMAS. *Trade & Empire.* Cambridge, Ma: 1967.
BATTERSON, MARK, editor. *Salt, the mysterious necessity.* Washington DC: 1972.
BEITZELL, EDWIN. *Life on the Potomac River.* Washington: 1968.
BRADY, WILLIAM. *The Kedge Anchor.* New York: 1852.
BRAY, MAYNARD. *Watercraft.* Mystic Ct: 1979.
BRAY, MAYNARD. *Taking Care of Wooden Ships.* Brooklin Me: 1979.
BREWINGTON, MARION. *Chesapeake Bay.* Cambridge: 1953.
BREWINGTON, MARION. *Chesapeake Bay log canoes and bugeyes.* Richmond: 1941
BREWINGTON, MARION. *Chesapeake Sailmaking.* Baltimore: 1954.
BRIDENBAUGH, CARL. *Jamestown, 1544-1699.* New York: 1980.
BURGESS, ROBERT. *This Was Chesapeake Bay.* Cambridge: 1963.
BURGESS, ROBERT. *Chesapeake Circle.* Cambridge: 1965.
BURGESS, ROBERT. *Chesapeake Sailing Craft.* Cambridge: 1975.
CHAPELLE, HOWARD. *The History of American Sailing Ships.* New York: 1935.
CHAPELLE, HOWARD. *Migrations of an American Boat Type.* National Museum Bulletin 219, GPO. Washington: 1960
CHAPELLE, HOWARD. *American Small Sailing Craft.* New York: 1951.
CHAPELLE, HOWARD. *Boat Building.* New York: 1941.
CHAPELLE, HOWARD. *The History of the American Sailing Navy.* New York: 1949.
CHAPELLE, HOWARD and E.T. ADNEY. *Bark canoes and Skin boats of North America.* Smithsonian Institution Bulletin 230. GPO. Washington: 1964.
CHATTERTON, KEBLE. *Fore and Aft.* London: 1920.
COKER, W.C. and H.R. TOTTEN. *Trees of the Southern States.* Chapel Hill NC: 1972.
COLLINGWOOD, G.H.. *Knowing Your Trees.* Washington: 1978.
CONSTANTINE, ALBERT. *Know your woods.* New York: 1959.
CULLER, R.D. *Skiffs and Schooners.* Camden Me: 1974.
CURTIS, W.J. *The Elements of Wood Ship Construction.* New York: 1919.
DAVIS, CHARLES. *Silhouettes of Sailing Craft.* Portland Me: 1929.
de KERCHOVE, RENE. *International Maritime Dictionary.* New York: 1948.
DOW, GEORGE. *Slave Ships and Slaving.* Brattleboro Vt: 1927.
DUNN, RICHARD. *Sugar and Slaves.* Chapel Hill NC: 1972
EARLE, SWEPSON. *Maryland's Eastern Shore.* Baltimore: 1924.
EARLE, SWEPSON. *Chesapeake Bay Country.* Baltimore: 1923.
ELLER, ERNEST, editor. *Chesapeake Bay in the American Revolution.* Centreville: 1981.
EVANS, CERINDA. *Some Notes on Shipbuilding and Shipping in Colonial Virginia.* Newport News: 1957.
FRYE, JOHN. *The men all singing.* Norfolk: 1978.
GARDNER, JOHN. *Building Small Boats for Oar and Sail.* National Fisherman: Camden Me: 1971.
GARITEE, KEROME. *The Republic's Private Navy.* Middletown, Ct: 1977.
GOODE, GEORGE BROWN. *The Fisheries and Fishery Industries of the US.* GPO. Washington: 1884.
GOLDENBERG, JOSEPH. *Shipbuilders in Colonial America.* Charlottesville: 1976.
GRIFFITHS, JOHN. *The Shipbuilders Manual.* New York: 1853.
GRIMM, W.C.. *The Book of Trees.* Harrisburg Pa: 1962.
HALL, HENRY. *Report of the Shipbuilding Industry of the US.* GPO. Washington: 1884.
HAMSHERE, CYRIL. *The British in the Caribbean.* Cambridge, Ma: 1972
HERNDON, MELVIN. *Tobacco in Colonial Virginia.* Williamsburg: 1957.
HORSLEY, JOHN. *Tools of the Maritime Trade.* Camden Me: 1978.
JACKSON, MELVIN and HELEN MILLER. *Tobacco and the "Brilliant." Smithsonian Institution.* Washington: 1976.
JAMESON, FRANKLIN. *Privateering and Piracy in the Colonial Period.* New York: 1923.
JOHNSON, WILLIAM. *Bahamian Sailing Craft.* Nassau: 1973.
JUDGE, EDWARD. *The Past, Present and Future of the Canned Food Industry.* Baltimore: 1914.
KEMP, PETER, editor. *Oxford Companion to Ships & the Sea.* New York: 1976.
KNIGHT, EDWARD. *American Mechanical Dictionary.* New York: 1876.
KUNHARDT, C.P. *Small Yachts.* New York: 1853.
LEAVITT, JOHN. *Wake of the Coasters.* Middletown Ct: 1970.
LILLARD, RICHARD. *The Great Forest.* New York: 1947.
LITTLE, E.L. *Check List of Native Trees in the US.* GPO. Washington: 1953.
LIVINGOOD, JAMES. *The Philadelphia-Baltimore Trade Rivalry.* Harrisburg, Pa: 1947.
LUNN, IVER. *Antifouling* (paint). Thame, England: 1974.
LYMAN, JOHN. *Log Chips.* Chapel Hill NC: 1948-59
MARVIL, JAMES. *Sailing Rams.* Laurel De: 1961.
MIDDLETON, ARTHUR. *Tobacco Coast.* Richmond: 1953.
MILLARD, JOHN. *American Ships of the Colonial & Revolutionary Periods.* New York: 1978.
MORRIS, EDWARD. *The Fore-and-Aft Rig in America.* New Haven: 1927.
OSBORNE, MICHAEL. *The State Barge of the Stationer's Company (1680-1850).* London: 1972.
PERCY, ALFRED. *Piedmont Apocalypse.* Lynchburg Va: 1949.
PERCY, ALFRED. *Tobacco Rolling Roads to Waterways.* Lynchburg Va: 1949.
PETRIDES, ANNE. *State Barges on the Thames.* London: 1959.

RADOFF, MORRIS. editor of *The Old Line State.* Annapolis: 1971
REYNOLDS, HEZEKIAH. *Directions for Ship Painting.* Worcester, Ma: 1978.
ROBINSON, JOHN and GEORGE F. DOW. *The Sailing Ships of New England.* Westminister Md: 1953.
SALAMAN, R.A. *Dictionary of Tools.* New York: 1977.
SCHUBEL, J. *The Living Chesapeake.* Baltimore: 1981.
SEMMES, RAPHAEL. *Captains & Mariners of Early Maryland.* Baltimore: 1937.
SHOMETTE, DONALD. *Battle of Saint Leonard's Creek.* Solomons: 1979.
STEINLINE, ERIC. *Historic American Marine Survey.* Smithsonian Institution, GPO. Washington: 1937.
STOREY, D.A. and J.N. CLAYTON. *The Building of a Wooden Ship.* Barre Me: 1971.
TATHAM, WILLIAM. *Essay and the Culture & Commerce of Tobacco.* London: 1800.
TILP, FREDERICK. *This was Potomac River.* Alexandria Va.: 1978.
TUNIS, EDWIN. *Colonial Craftsmen.* New York: 1967.
US LIBRARY OF CONGRESS. *Maritime Folklore Resources.* DC.: 1980.
US NAVY BU-SHIPS. *Marine fouling & its prevention.*
VAN HORN, LEE. *Out of the Past.* Baltimore: 1976.
WALSH, HARRY. *The Outlaw Gunner.* Cambridge: 1971.
WARNER, WILLIAM. *Beautiful Swimmers.* Boston: 1976.
WOODS HOLE OCEANIC INSTITUTE. *Marine Fouling & Its Prevention for the USNBuShips.* DC: 1952.

MANUSCRIPT SOURCES

COLONIAL WILLIAMSBURG INC. Williamsburg Va: Norton Papers (1750-95).
HALL OF RECORDS, Annapolis: Port Books, Ports of Annapolis and Oxford.
LIBRARY OF CONGRESS. British transcripts. Colonial Office Papers, Public Record Office.
MARYLAND HISTORICAL SOCIETY. Baltimore: Annapolis Port Records; Oxford Port Records; Basil Sollers. *Number of Ships built in Maryland 1746-75.*

NEWSPAPERS

District of Columbia: *Washington Post, Evening Star, Washington Federalist, Intelligencer, Washington Times.*

Maryland: *Baltimore Sunpapers, Maryland Gazette, St. Marys Beacon, Times-Crescent, Calvert Journal Gazette, The Talbot Banner, Bay Times, Kent County News, Dorchester News, Salisbury Advertiser, Marylander & Herald.*

Virginia: *Virginia Gazette, Alexandria Gazette, Daily Press, Richmond-Times Dispatch, Northern Neck News, Rappahannock Times, Northumberland Echo, Herald Progress, Eastern Shore News.*

MAGAZINES

American Neptune, Maryland Historical Magazine, Virginia Magazine of History & Biography, William & Mary Quarterly, Journal of Forest History, Nautical Research Journal, Wooden Boat, Rudder, Yachting, Fore & Aft, Forest & Stream, Commercial Fisheries Review.

RECORDS

Bureau of Fisheries, US Fisheries Commission, Bureau of Marine Inspection & Navigation in the Industrial & Social Branch of the National Archives in Washington, US Geological Survey, US Board of Geographic Place Names, Virginia Institute of Marine Science, Potomac River Fisheries Commission, Maryland Natural Resources Institute, Wye Institute, Maryland.

A NOTE ABOUT THE TYPE

The type chosen for this book is called *Garamond.* It is named for Claude Garamond, a Paris native who designed the "fonts," as the sets of letters or printing types are called, in about 1530. It is a face that captures the vivacity that was France when Marie de Medici ruled with her son, Louis XIII. Most Parisienne of all its characters are Garamond italics. Garamond is a "Tiffany" type face.

The designer perfected the shape of roman type faces, and was one of the first punch cutters to work independently of printers. His fonts were superior to the best existing romans and influenced European punch cutters for over 150 years.

With encouragement of King Francis I of France in the 1540s, he cut the famous *gracs du roi* ("royal Greeks") which had larger and more emphatic capitals than were common. Cut for the scholar-printer Robert Estienne, they were later confiscated by Cardinal Richelieu and used for his personal book under the name of *Caracteres de l'Universite.*

At the age of 65 Garamond began to publish books, but apparently was not successful in business for he died poverty-stricken in 1561 at the age of 81.

The grace and clarity of *Garamond* coupled with an appearance characteristic of the luxury and refinement in the French Renaissance, continues to set it apart from all other kinds of composition used in printing. It is suggestive of quality, dignity, and in a restrained manner, novelty.

Because it is completely incompatible with price appeal or advertising purposes, it is never seen in commercial broadsides. The Garamond italics are especially outstanding, eccentric and fragile, they add a lively touch and subtle attraction to the composition. Changeover from regular to italic type is so smooth and unnoticeable that the reader's train of thought is never interrupted or jolted.

The members of Scott Photographics Incorporated of Bladensburg, Maryland (the author's birthplace) enthusiastically contributed their skill and hand, mind and eye to the composition and design of this volume. Text and titles were set on the Mergenthaler VIP using the Advanced Typography Program.

INDEX

MARYLAND

On 22 November 1633, the 61′ pinnace *Dove* and the 125′ ship *Ark* sailed from Cowes (a village on The Isle of Wight in the southern central English Channel) with 130 or more women and men to settle permanently in a new colony—Maryland (named after Queen Henrietta Maria;) and chartered by King Charles I. Their leader was Cecilius Calvert (Lord Baltimore II); the purpose was to have "freedom of conscience, extension of the Christian religion, and expansion of the Empire."

They sailed in "northeasterly trade winds" with stops at the Spanish-held Canary Islands (150 miles west of Africa), and West Indian Islands of Barbados, Martinique, Nevis, and Saint Kitts. Anchor was dropped off North America's mainland at Point Comfort, Virginia on 27 February 1634. The first landing made in Maryland was on Saint Clements Island in the Potomac River, 25 March 1634. The 6820 mile ocean voyage took 121 days which includes 37 days at anchor.

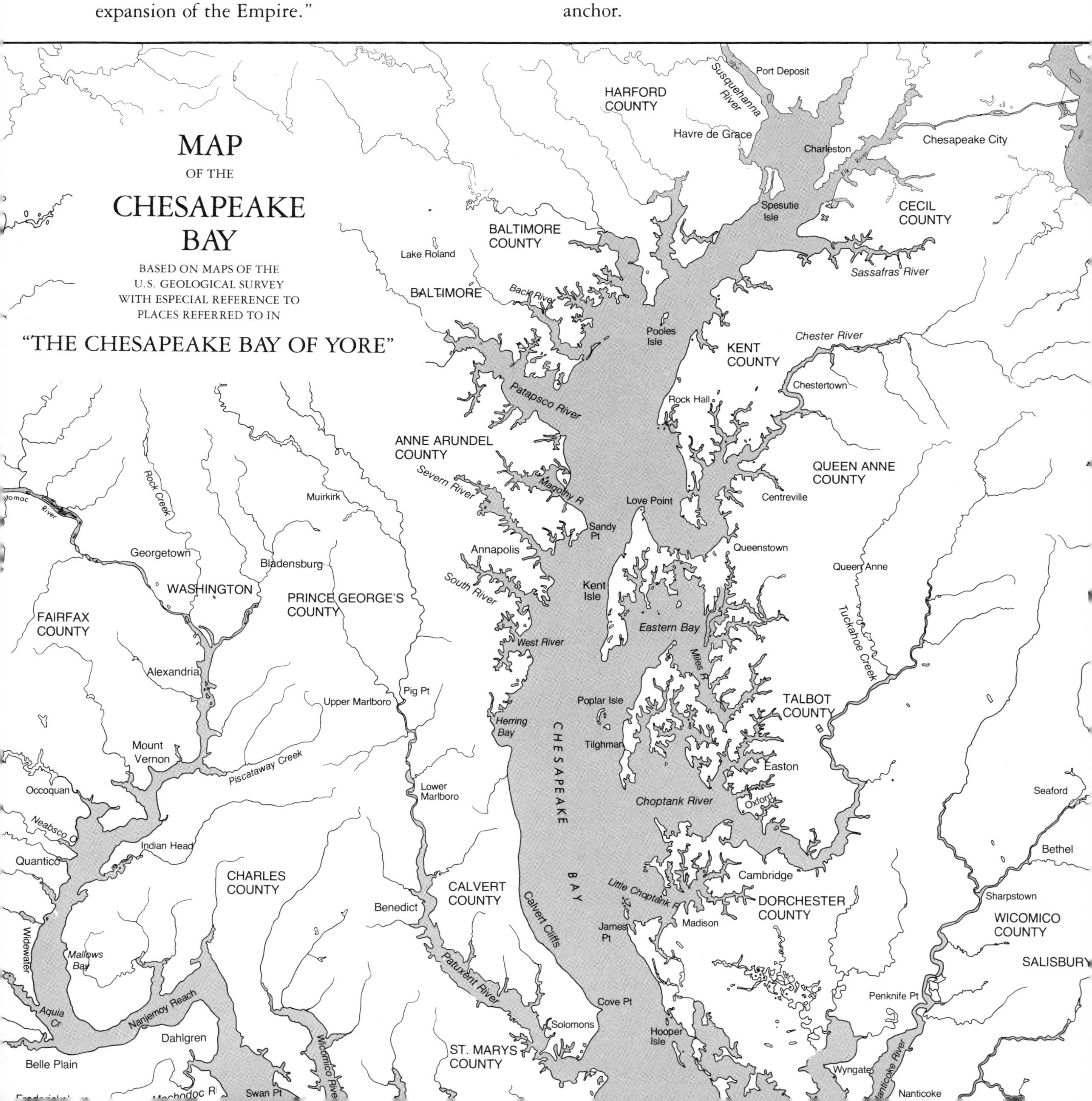